Faster Isn't Smarter

Messages About Math, Teaching,
and Learning in the 21st Century

A resource for teachers, leaders, policy makers, and families

CATHY L. SEELEY

Foreword by Marilyn Burns

Math Solutions
Sausalito, California, USA

Math Solutions
One Harbor Drive, Suite 101
Sausalito, CA 94965
www.mathsolutions.com

Library of Congress Cataloging-in-Publication Data
Seeley, Cathy L.
    Faster isn't smarter: messages about math, teaching, and learning in the 21st century:
    a resource for teachers, leaders, policy makers, and families / Cathy L. Seeley;
    foreword by Marilyn Burns.
        p. cm.
    Includes bibliographical references and index.
    ISBN 978-1-935099-03-1 (alk. paper)
    1. Mathematics—Study and teaching (Elementary)—United States. 2. Mathematics—
    Study and teaching (Secondary)—United States. I. Title.
    QA135.6.S446 2009
    372.7—dc22
                                                            2009038875

Editor: Jamie Ann Cross
Production: Melissa L. Inglis-Elliott
Cover and interior design: Wanda Espana/Wee Design
Cover photos of the author, from top to
    bottom: Brant Bender; Armando Solares; Mary Butkus
Cover image: "Family on Beach" by Image100 Photography.
    © Veer Incorporated. All rights reserved.
Composition: MPS Limited

Printed in the United States of America on acid-free paper
16 15 14 13 12   ML   6 7 8 9 10

This book is dedicated to teachers and others who see the potential in every student, who believe with all their hearts that each of them can accomplish great things, and who commit to doing whatever it takes for every student to reach that potential.

This book is also dedicated to students, who have so much ahead of them, especially six students close to my heart—Hanna, Andrew, Christian, Blake, Maisey, and Hailey. May you all become the productive, creative, fulfilled adults I see reflected in the eyes of the beautiful, loving, accepting children you are today.

Contents

I · School Mathematics for the 21st Century

II   Great Ideas Whose Time Has Come (and Gone?)

MATHEMATICS ISSUES FACING SCHOOLS AND DISTRICTS   69

III Real Students and Real Teachers

MATHEMATICS IN TODAY'S CLASSROOMS   147

Foreword

I met Cathy Seeley more than twenty-five years ago when I was in Texas providing math professional development for school districts. At that time, I was impressed by Cathy's commitment to math education, the energy she devoted to it, and her signature booming Texan voice with which she delivered her messages. Since that time, I've been a loyal fan of Cathy's, appreciative of her leadership at the Texas Education Agency, deeply admiring of her choice to enter the Peace Corps and teach math for two years in Burkina Faso in West Africa, and delighted by her influence when she served as president of the National Council of Teachers of Mathematics (NCTM). The list of the many other ways Cathy has served mathematics education during the time I've known her is long and varied, and it is testimony to her extraordinary commitment.

When Cathy was president of NCTM, I always looked forward to reading the columns she regularly wrote to address the membership. Her commitment, energy, and voice rang through all of her messages. Even when Cathy addressed a topic that wasn't of immediate concern to me, her message still pulled me in and provoked me to think.

I was especially pleased when Cathy agreed to write a Math Solutions book based on her messages, and I'm even more pleased now that I've had the opportunity to read the final version. It's wonderful to have Cathy's ideas available in one place rather than scattered in different file folders, and revisiting her ideas has sparked and renewed my own thinking. In the introduction to *Faster Isn't Smarter*, Cathy mentions that it's not necessary to read the book from front to back. I've followed her advice, dipping in and out of the book, taking short bursts of time to read one message or longer periods of time to read several. I appreciate Cathy's links to related messages, which have allowed me to easily follow a thread of a message that has especially interested me. This feature not only makes the book accessible and enjoyable but also customizes the book so that I've been able to follow what has particularly engaged me while also gaining additional entry into Cathy's thinking as I have read how she sees particular ideas connecting with others.

In her messages, Cathy offers support and confirmation for teachers working to improve their classroom practices. She helps explain the rationale for effective instructional choices. She provides references that offer further support and expand our thinking. And her messages are ideal for reflecting on alone or with colleagues.

Cathy's hope for the book is that it sparks, enhances, and reinvigorates our thinking. I've found that her messages do just that. They are important and thought provoking, and they make a needed and valuable contribution to all who are interested in math education. Keep the book close at hand—it's a perfect vehicle for stimulating your thinking in new and surprising ways.

MARILYN BURNS

FOUNDER, MATH SOLUTIONS

Introduction

When I began my college education at Virginia Tech, I dreamed of a future in the exciting world of computers. In those days, a computer was the size of a building and less powerful than my current laptop, but I was entranced by the capabilities of these amazing machines. My parents had raised me to believe that I could be whatever I wanted to be. So they supported their daughter in making what was an unusual choice for a young woman at that time—to pursue a career in mathematics and technology at an engineering school. My mother also offered fallback advice, specifically that I should take enough education courses so that "if all else fails, you can be a teacher."

After moving to Colorado to start my career, I was dismayed to find that, if left in the hands of corporate America, my future would consist of wearing short skirts and demonstrating computers at trade shows. As the 1960s turned into the 1970s, I found myself trying to break a barrier I hadn't realized existed. It turns out that my mother was right, but perhaps for the wrong reasons. Following her advice led me to a profession that I've loved for more than thirty-five years. I've found it both more challenging and far more rewarding than I ever imagined.

From 1999 to 2001, thirty years into my career as a mathematics teacher, supervisor, and educator, I chose to follow a dream I'd had for many years. I knew I needed to return to the classroom again to confirm for myself that I could put into practice what I was asking teachers to do. In 1999, American teachers were facing increasing pressure to raise test scores, so I often say, only somewhat jokingly, that I went someplace easier to teach. I chose to join the Peace Corps to teach for two years in Burkina Faso, a relatively unknown country in West Africa and the fifth-poorest country in the world, according to the United Nations. I taught the equivalent of middle school and high school mathematics (in French) to classes of seventy-five students each, with essentially no resources other than colored chalk and painted chalkboards. Although the teaching conditions were not exactly like those I had experienced before, some of the commonalities were striking, and I learned many lessons that to this day influence my life and my work.

In 2003, not long after I returned from that incredible experience, I had the honor and good fortune to be elected president of the National Council of Teachers of Mathematics (NCTM). As president, my full-time job for two years was to work with and support teachers of mathematics at all levels across the United States and beyond—an adventure of many dimensions. One aspect of the job was the responsibility for writing a total of eighteen President's Messages for inclusion in NCTM's *News Bulletin*. The staff at NCTM helped me begin thinking about possible topics for those messages, but it quickly became apparent to all of us that I had many issues and topics I was eager to discuss. My first President's Message practically wrote itself; I described my sense of "coming home" as I embarked on what felt like a fantastic job that matched where I was in my career and what I might be able to offer in service. I came to love the kind of writing involved in these President's Messages—short, digestible, sometimes persuasive pieces that might tackle challenging topics, affirm people's best motivations, celebrate great teaching, or challenge limiting habits and beliefs. Most of all, I liked writing messages that might stir things up or stimulate discussion to encourage all of us improve what we do in support of helping every student reach her or his full potential.

During that time, I was surprised, delighted, and humbled when people told me that they enjoyed my President's Messages and that they used them with groups of teachers, administrators, parents, or teacher education students. When Math Solutions approached me about writing a book, my immediate thought was that this kind of book could be a useful resource. I had a long list of topics beyond those I had discussed in my President's Messages. With the help of the Math Solutions staff, I was able to shape the book into what I hope is a useful and thought-provoking resource for teachers, parents, teacher educators, policy makers, and others interested in improving mathematics teaching and learning.

I recognize that it's easier for me to write from outside the classroom than to do the things I advocate. My work today involves issues in schools, districts, communities, states, and beyond, and I regularly face challenges on many levels. But I no longer face one hundred and fifty or two hundred students every week as I once did (or three hundred a week when I taught in Burkina Faso). I still remember from my classroom experience that there were frequently students who frustrated me in their behavior and in their achievement, and who made me confront my own limitations as I tried to help them learn what I knew in my heart they could learn. I also know from the work I do today in schools, school systems, and states how hard it is to reconcile differences of opinion among various stakeholders and how challenging it is to deal with changing expectations from policy makers and the community. We all share the common goal of helping all students develop their mathematical potential. I believe that the critical point of attention for that goal should be what a teacher does with a student to help the student learn mathematics well. I wrote the messages in this book in appreciation of teachers' lifelong commitment to do their work continually better and in recognition of the equal commitment needed by the rest of us to support teachers on this journey.

How to Use This Book

This book consists of forty-one relatively independent messages intended for many audiences—teachers, families, teacher educators, and other leaders. Each message presents a discussion of an issue or challenge related to school mathematics or to the broader system within which we teach at the elementary and secondary levels. The messages are threaded with stories from my experience with teachers and students. My observations and recommendations have emerged from my compelling need to make sense of and put into context what I read, see, hear, and learn from others.

This may not be a book you read from front to back, but I encourage you to read all of it eventually. Feel free to read the messages in whatever order you choose, based on which issues challenge you, which topics resonate with you, or which titles appeal to you at any particular moment. Each of the messages connects to other messages in various ways. You might choose to follow a path suggested by the related messages listed at the end of each piece, rather than reading the messages in numerical order.

The messages are arranged in three parts, each with a slightly different focus. Part I encompasses overarching, global issues especially appealing to a general audience, including policy makers and those outside of education, as well as curriculum developers and school leaders. Part II targets school and community issues relevant for local decision makers and communities. Part III looks more closely at issues of interest in schools and classrooms, especially for teachers. Throughout each part there are messages that reach across all audiences, as we all deal with issues and decisions that affect mathematics teaching and learning in and out of the classroom.

Together, the messages address many of the issues we face in school mathematics, but they are not intended to present a comprehensive overview of the entire area of mathematics education. Rather, they are intended to stimulate personal reflection and interactive discussion, sometimes around delicate topics not always addressed in school settings. Accordingly, each piece concludes with reflection and discussion questions for teachers, families, leaders, and policy makers. To continue the discussion, these questions are followed by the list of related messages, as well as a list of further readings, consisting of books, articles, websites, and so on related to the issues, themes, or stories in the message. In keeping with the emphasis on stimulating reflection and discussion, I have included a range of readings that sometimes present different or opposing points of view.

I hope the reflection and discussion questions help you process the ideas presented in the message, reflect on how you agree or disagree, and consider possible actions to take in your classroom, school, or community. For those who support others in learning and leading, I hope you will also use these questions as you work with groups of teachers, future teachers, teacher educators, coaches, families, administrators, or other educational leaders to challenge the status quo and to consider how we might take action to change the system where it needs to change.

I have proposed many ideas related to the challenges we face in our classrooms, schools, communities, and nation, and many more ideas can be generated as others engage in the discussion. But turning ideas into solutions that work in any particular setting calls for committed and coordinated dialogue, planning, and action. I hope these messages stimulate, enhance, and reinvigorate the work that dedicated educators and citizens undertake to reach the goal of a high-quality mathematics education for every student.

1

Math for a Flattening World

RESHAPING SCHOOL MATHEMATICS
FOR THE 21ST CENTURY

In his 2007 bestseller *The World Is Flat, New York Times* column-ist Thomas L. Friedman proposed the notion that the world is flattening—meaning that around the globe, the competitive playing field is being leveled, especially with respect to jobs. More people in more countries, including those countries once excluded from eco-nomic opportunities, now hold jobs in multinational companies and are raising their quality of living to join the middle class. With the increasing availability of technology, it is no longer necessary for soci-eties to rely on hierarchical structures for access to information. Today, information flows horizontally—available equally to anyone with access to a computer—producing competitors and connecting col-leagues around the world. An international company can have offices in India, China, Malaysia, Brazil, Poland, Russia, or any one of a grow-ing number of nations that can offer well-educated, cost-effective workers. No one would have predicted just a few years ago that Dell Computers would build a facility in Poland, yet the multinational com-pany did just that, giving Poland a significant economic boost. With the spread of this "flattening" phenomenon, the international talent pool of professionals such as computer programmers and other technology specialists is expanding. As mathematics educators, our responsibility is to equip our students with the skills and abilities not just to survive but to thrive in this global village.

What Do Students Need?

For some time, those of us involved in mathematics education have joined with the business sector to advocate for a more mathematically literate population and for programs that prepare more students for careers in science, technology, engineering, and mathematics. Suppose we succeed? Suppose we create a generation of citizens who know mathematics well, with many who can conduct basic research or work in computer programming or design. Even then, it is possible these citizens will not be employable; their salary requirements may price them out of jobs. Professionals in India and China now hold large numbers of basic programming and technical jobs for companies in North America and around the world, but officials in both countries have indicated their commitment to move beyond these basic jobs to prepare to fill higher-level positions in research and innovation. With an eye to the future, India and China, as well as other countries such as Korea, Turkey, and Iran, have invested in educating highly trained technicians, engineers, and computer programmers and in conducting scientific research of their own.

The United States prides itself on having an edge in creativity and innovation. But how long can we maintain this edge in an environment where a commitment born of sheer national will can bring a developing nation into economic prominence?

If scientific and engineering jobs are likely to be outsourced, should we abandon the goal of a high-quality mathematics education for every student? On the contrary. If we are looking toward a global future, we must redouble our efforts to equip our citizens with a working knowledge of mathematics, along with the scientific and economic knowledge that builds on that mathematics. Friedman's book *Hot, Flat, and Crowded* (2008) points out that we are facing an era focused on energy and climate, making it even more urgent to prepare students so they can use mathematics and science to tackle these and other critical problems.

An important element of this kind of education is a commitment to go beyond teaching basic skills, beyond requiring students to know how to perform procedures, and beyond offering recipes for solving problems that look alike. To limit our students to such a narrow view of mathematics is to barely equip them for the bottom tier of jobs the United States now outsources. We need to expect much more of all our students if they are to compete for the kinds of jobs that help businesses and societies solve the problems they face every day—problems no one yet knows how to solve; problems that call for the best creative thinking and problem-solving skills we can bring to the table.

Holding on to the Edge

The United States can still hold onto its competitive edge. This admittedly fragile edge will come, in part, from the advantage of traditional American ingenuity, creativity, and innovation—if we are committed to helping students develop in these areas. But the value of this advantage may diminish as other nations increase their investment in scientific research and their commitment to becoming more innovative. However, Americans have another advantage that has been cited by those who do business internationally. Americans are said to have the ability to see the big picture, understand connections, and build on relationships among people and among ideas. These qualities should be nurtured and developed in our schools if we want to prepare students to solve problems that no one has ever seen before.

What Can We Do?

Our educator colleagues in Japan and other countries often teach with far less *telling* than American educators do. Classroom observations that were part of the Third International Mathematics and Science Study (TIMSS)[1] show that it is more customary for these mathematics teachers than for American teachers to present students with a problem without first telling them all the steps they should follow to solve it (Stigler and Hiebert 1999). Our tendency in the United States is to spoon-feed our students by telling them exactly how to solve a certain type of problem and then asking them to practice solving similar problems. The TIMSS observers found that even when American teachers started with a challenging task, they almost always gave students excessive guidance or intervened as soon as students had difficulty.

In more and more mathematics classrooms on this side of the globe, however, teachers are beginning to realize that they can guide students' learning without doing all the work for them. They are beginning to see the power of letting students struggle a bit to determine how to solve a problem before helping them find the best or most efficient approach(es) to the problem. Many students are not only beginning to have more opportunities for critical thinking but also beginning to have the opportunity to work collaboratively on problems relevant outside of a mathematics textbook. This type of teamwork is becoming a common structure in successful businesses today.

I am convinced that we have the ability to adapt successful strategies from Japan and other countries and perhaps improve on them by tapping into our uniquely American tendencies toward developing creativity, connecting ideas, and understanding relationships. Why not teach in ways that provide students with challenging problems, help them build perseverance, and develop their creativity? This is no small task, but it is well worth the effort if our students are to succeed in the flat world of the twenty-first century.

---

[1]After the Third International Study, TIMSS was renamed Trends in International Mathematics and Science Study to include future studies.

Reflection and Discussion

FOR TEACHERS

- What issues or challenges does this message raise for you? In what ways do you agree with or disagree with the main points of the message?
- How can we change our day-to-day teaching to reflect the changing (flattening) world?
- In thinking globally, what barriers do you face—among teachers, students, or the broader community?
- How can we shift our instructional practice to prepare students for the changing way people work in teams in the workplace?
- How can we help students learn to both ask and answer challenging questions?

FOR FAMILIES

- What questions or issues does this message raise for you to discuss with your son or daughter, the teacher, or school leaders?
- How does the mathematics students need today differ from the mathematics you studied in school?
- How do techniques for teaching mathematics today differ from those used when you were taught mathematics in school?

FOR LEADERS AND POLICY MAKERS

- How does this message reinforce or challenge policies and decisions you have made or are considering?
- How do your policies and priorities reflect a flattening world that looks very different from the world when we went to school?
- How do you accommodate the inclusion of overarching skills like collaboration, critical thinking, and communication in your school(s)?
- How does your mathematics program develop emerging skills like solving complex problems and undertaking in-depth projects?

RELATED MESSAGES

- Message 17, "Constructive Struggling," extends the discussion of challenging our students and eliminating the tendency to tell students everything they need to know in order to solve a problem.

- Message 7, "Not Your Grandpa's Algebra," describes changes in secondary mathematics to better prepare students for today's world.
- Message 5, "Technology is a Tool," looks at how classrooms might adapt to an increasingly technological world.
- Message 3, "Making the Case for Creativity," extends the discussion of helping students develop creativity as part of school mathematics programs.

FURTHER READING

- *The World Is Flat* (Friedman 2007) gives the broader context for the rising middle class around the world and the implications for business, government, education, and society.
- *Hot, Flat, and Crowded* (Friedman 2008) extends the discussion of the flat world and describes the need to focus society's efforts toward an economy centered on energy and climate.
- *The Global Achievement Gap* (Wagner 2008) builds a case for schools to restructure priorities to prepare students for the twenty-first century.
- Partnership for 21st Century Skills (www.21stcenturyskills.org) presents recommendations for a dramatically different vision of education for the twenty-first century from a diverse collaboration of individuals and groups in education, business, and government.
- "What to Learn: 'Core Knowledge' or 'Twenty-First-Century Skills'?" (Toppo 2009) presents a discussion about opposition to the skills called for by the Partnership for 21st Century Skills.
- "The Latest Doomed Pedagogical Fad: Twenty-First-Century Skills" (Matthews 2009) presents Mathews's opposing view to Friedman's, asking whether students who have trouble with today's "nineteenth-century skills in reading, writing and math" are able to learn the skills being called for in the twenty-first century.

2

Untapped Potential

MOVING PAST THE ACHIEVEMENT GAP

Under the spotlight of the sweeping education legislation No Child Left Behind, schools and districts now routinely report mathematics performance for all student populations according to gender, race, language, and socioeconomic status. Although some states and school systems have broken out achievement data in this way for some time, in the past most reports have presented only school or district averages. These average scores don't tell the whole story. When performance data are reported for every population of students, we reveal education's worst-kept and most devastating secret: many of our students, especially in urban and rural schools of poverty, are not learning much mathematics. For years we have raised the cry, "Close the achievement gap!" Yet, with the exception of a few promising examples, achievement gaps have endured.

The term *achievement gap* can make the task at hand seem overwhelming, and it has been used so often that it has begun to lose its impact. Let me offer a new phrase to help us think about this crisis from a different perspective: *untapped potential*. The reality of the achievement gap is that too many students never have an opportunity to develop their mathematical or other knowledge to its fullest potential; too many stars never get to shine.

Our Students

Certainly many students with untapped potential carry the burden of challenges from their lives outside of school; these challenges contribute to their difficulties with learning. But these challenges are often aggravated by conditions within their schools. A look inside schools suggests that it isn't the poverty, the neighborhood, the color, or the home language of these students that is the root cause of their lack of learning.

Even a casual observer can see that our least wealthy schools do not have or provide access to the same level of resources as their wealthier counterparts. Our states, communities, and school systems are forced to distribute too few resources to too many places. Students in high-poverty schools have taken the worst hit, sometimes being taught by teachers teaching out of their field or by long-term substitutes with no mathematics background. Many of these students lack access to high-quality instructional materials. Even basic issues like safety, adequate seating, and the physical condition of school buildings can make learning a constant challenge for these students. Without a reasonable physical environment, a well-qualified mathematics teacher, and appropriate instructional materials, no student has a chance to achieve his potential.

Committed mathematics educators have long known what business and society are beginning to understand: we cannot afford to waste precious human capital by denying some students the opportunity for a high-quality mathematics education simply because of conditions of their birth, heritage, or neighborhood. Whether intentional or unintentional, this kind of institutional inequity reveals a system that hurts students and destines a nation to continually fall short of what it might otherwise accomplish.

Our Expectations

Untapped potential is also found in classrooms and schools outside of poor or urban areas—in low-level classes where some students are expected to learn less because they have never achieved in the past at the same level as their schoolmates. Students with untapped potential can sit almost invisibly in mainstream classes; they tune out what a teacher has to say for several reasons—because they don't see the usefulness of what is being taught, because they have no confidence in their ability to do mathematics, because they are distracted by issues outside of school, or because they simply aren't engaged in what is happening in the classroom.

Facing Reality

How can a state, community, or school reach its full potential? It must begin by taking a hard look at reality. When a school's or district's mathematics performance differs significantly from group to group, the system has a problem not with an underachieving group but with its mathematics program. When a state or a school system can predict mathematics performance by looking at a map, the system has a problem not with one place or another but with its mathematics program. And when a person can walk down the hall of a school and identify whether a math class is low, medium, or high level just by looking in the window, the system has a problem not with "those" students but with its mathematics program.

Tapping untapped potential does not mean that we must invest all our resources in helping our lowest-achieving students. Students deserve, and society demands, that we also support and advance our most able students. But what if, given the right learning conditions, some of our presumed low-achieving students might one day be recognized as some of our most able students? What if an unchallenged, unrecognized, and unsupported student languishing in a neglected classroom might be the person who could help solve one of society's great problems of the future? What if some of our greatest talent is sitting untapped in classrooms across the nation?

What Can We Do?

Realizing untapped potential (and in the process closing the achievement gap) means operating on two levels. First, we must do what some call *raising the floor*, to ensure that every student learns challenging mathematics to a higher level than we have ever expected. Second, as we accomplish this ambitious task, we will discover far more stars than we ever imagined, so that we might also *raise the ceiling*. Schools may choose to offer something extra to support their brightest students and to let them soar. But first let's make sure we know who these students are.

WHAT ELSE CAN WE DO?

- We can continue to proclaim the importance of teaching all our students.
- We can commit to ending low-level tracking, endless remediation, and other practices and policies that sentence some students to fall ever further behind.
- We can advocate for all schools to receive adequate funding and appropriate resource allocation at the local, state, and federal levels.
- We can support practices and programs that strengthen the mathematics knowledge and teaching skills of all teachers.
- We can expand our accountability measures to assess what we value and take a stand against making high-stakes decisions based on a single test score.
- We can use our professional community as a forum for discussing delicate issues frankly and openly, exchanging successful practices, and sharing what we learn.

Many teachers are already accepting these challenges, and their students are accomplishing great things. On behalf of all their students, their communities, and the nation, we owe them our sincere gratitude, appreciation, and support.

Reflection and Discussion

FOR TEACHERS

- What issues or challenges does this message raise for you? In what ways do you agree with or disagree with the main points of the message?
- In what ways are you successful in helping students succeed who have previously been unsuccessful in learning mathematics?
- Have you discovered a star in an unlikely place? How do you nurture that star?
- What are some of your greatest challenges in teaching all students?
- How can we maintain high expectations in the face of the real challenges in dealing with diverse groups of students, including many who have significant learning gaps?

FOR FAMILIES

- What questions or issues does this message raise for you to discuss with your son or daughter, the teacher, or school leaders?
- How do you help your daughter or son believe that she or he has unlimited potential?
- Have you communicated with the teacher to find out where your son's or daughter's strengths lie? How can you encourage the development of these strengths?

FOR LEADERS AND POLICY MAKERS

- How does this message reinforce or challenge policies and decisions you have made or are considering?
- How well do the demographics in your advanced mathematics classes or tracks match the demographics in your lowest-level mathematics classes? How well do both reflect the demographics of your school and district?
- What alternatives to tracking practices might allow teachers to support students who are behind or struggling?
- What types of intervention programs, rather than remediation, do you have in place (or can you consider), including providing extra time and support before students who might be struggling fall too far behind?
- What alternatives to retention do you offer in order to help students who are behind without simply putting them through the same experience that was ineffective the first time?

RELATED MESSAGES

- Message 32, "Yes, but . . . ," challenges us to examine our assumptions and expectations for students.
- Message 3, "Making the Case for Creativity," sheds light on an underdeveloped aspect of school mathematics, potentially one where underachieving students might shine.
- Message 37, "Boring!," reminds us of the consequences when students are not engaged in school or in mathematics class.

FURTHER READING

- *A Mind at a Time* (Levine 2003) looks at how some students are disadvantaged in school and focuses on using different approaches to teaching to students' varied strengths.
- *The Shame of the Nation* (Kozol 2006) is a challenging book that takes a hard look at lingering inequities in our schools as we enter the twenty-first century.
- *English Language Learners in the Mathematics Classroom* (Coggins et al. 2007) provides insights and strategies to help students whose first language is not English reach their potential in mathematics.
- The Education Trust (www.edtrust.org) provides a variety of reports about inequities in schools and identifies schools that break expected low achievement patterns with high performance.
- *Mathematics Success and Failure Among African-American Youth* (Martin 2000) provides insights into how to support African American students in achieving their mathematical potential.
- *Take It Up: Leading for Educational Equity* (Becerra and Weissglass 2004) offers activities for educators and leaders to address educational inequities.
- *The Global Achievement Gap* (Wagner 2008) reminds us that our current emphasis on high-stakes testing can mask a student's most important abilities and can reinforce incorrect decisions about which students are most likely to succeed.

www   This message is also available in printable format at mathsolutions.com/fasterisntsmarter.

3

Making the Case for Creativity

AN OVERLOOKED ELEMENT IN SCHOOL MATHEMATICS

I n the competitive world of the twenty-first century, report after report identifies innovation and creativity as critical factors in tomorrow's economy. Within a rich description of how employers must innovate to survive, *Tough Choices or Tough Times*, from the National Center on Education and the Economy (2008), describes three particular qualities of successful workers for the future: top academic performance, the ability to learn quickly, and creativity. These three qualities translate into important emphases for schools. Certainly, we all recognize the significance of academic knowledge for all students. And we strive for students to learn how to learn—to be adaptable and to develop a willingness to take on new tasks. The development of creativity, however, is a goal that we seem to have pushed into the background. In our current era of accountability tied to high-stakes, large-scale tests, what is tested (and how it is tested) tends to be what is taught (and how it is taught). Testing creativity is simply too difficult and too expensive for most states to take on as part of their accountability system. With the tremendous amount of information to be learned every year, there does not appear to be room in the instructional day for teachers to help students develop their creativity.

Yet if innovation is central to a nation's and an individual's future, then certainly the development of creativity should be central to a student's education. There is growing consensus that creativity can be learned, or certainly enhanced. In fact, new interpretations and an update of Bloom's taxonomy put *creating* at the highest level on the list of learning behaviors (Anderson et al. 2001). In today's schools, however, the subject areas most likely to focus on developing creativity are increasingly squeezed out of a crowded instructional program. Programs in the arts, in particular, have become nearly invisible in elementary and middle schools. Worse, within the basic-skills disciplines of reading, writing, and mathematics, the emphasis seems to fall on measurable, often mechanical, procedures, with students acquiring a set of facts and skills related to what is already known, rather than developing other parts of their brains that might help them *create* what is not yet known.

The Nature of Creativity

In a background paper commissioned for *Tough Choices or Tough Times*, Karlyn Adams (2006) describes a model of creativity developed by Teresa Amabile of Harvard Business School. Amabile conceptualizes a person's creativity as a blend of three key aspects: what the person knows (knowledge), how the person approaches problems (critical thinking or problem-solving skills), and the person's motivation to be creative (especially intrinsic interest and passion). In my conversations with mathematics teachers, they consistently report to me that the aspect they spend the most time on is dispensing knowledge, with some attention to specific problem-solving strategies (even these may be a series of learned steps) and little time to stimulate interest in and passion for mathematics.

Developing Creativity

Teaching students how to think creatively means doing more than having them solve traditional word problems. This means going beyond George Polya's four classic principles for problem solving: understanding the problem, devising a plan, carrying out the plan, and reviewing and extending (2004). These simple and elegant principles can be used to tackle basic word problems commonly found in textbooks. But these same principles can also provide students with a structure to learn how to approach more complex problems that don't fit previously learned patterns. As students extend their experience to deal with increasingly rich and multifaceted problems, they strengthen their thinking in ways that help them synthesize what they know and develop creative ways of thinking about nonroutine situations. Regardless of how well students apply what they know in predictable, often formulaic problems, if they are to develop the kind of imaginitive thinking that will serve them in the future, they need the opportunity to wrestle with, talk about, and think through problems they don't know how to solve.

Beyond problem solving, developing creativity means giving students interesting tasks that engage their minds and stimulate their interest in mathematics. In an earlier time, some of the best mathematics teachers often used mathematically relevant puzzles, games, and even theatrics to *sell* mathematics, stimulate interest, and engage students in learning. In today's high-pressure schools, most mathematics teachers don't feel they have the time or luxury to engage in anything that strays from their prescribed curriculum plan. Rather, they are pushed to *cover* material in preparation for annual tests or interim benchmark tests. Students identified as being behind or struggling are at even more risk than other students of having their mathematics learning limited to routine, low-level skills without the opportunity to develop their creativity. Yet offering them the opportunity to develop creatively not only can enhance their learning but also can tap into learning styles not often addressed in mathematics classes. Developing a student's creativity may eventually even support the student's learning of more routine skills. As any student develops confidence and motivation to succeed in mathematics, she is more likely to be able to build on that foundation to access higher-level mathematics and other knowledge that depends on mathematics.

What Can We Do?

The *Tough Choices or Tough Times* report provides specific suggestions for refocusing our efforts in schools toward developing a more knowledgeable and creative workforce. Among other recommendations for K–12 education, the report calls for

- teaching students about creativity and how it develops;
- addressing the three aspects of creativity (knowledge, creative thinking, and motivation);
- helping students find their passion;
- developing students' confidence, persistence, and tolerance for risk taking;
- increasing problem-based and project-based learning;
- incorporating creativity into the testing system; and
- integrating enjoyment into education.

Thinking creatively, solving problems, enjoying learning—surely this is a great recipe for helping all students ignite their passion, develop their creativity, and learn the mathematical thinking they need for their future.

Reflection and Discussion

FOR TEACHERS

- What issues or challenges does this message raise for you? In what ways do you agree with or disagree with the main points of the message?
- How can you offer all students the opportunity to extend their problem-solving skills beyond routine word problems?

(continued)

- How open are you to accepting solutions from students that might be different than the solution you originally thought would work?
- How can you incorporate more enjoyment into your mathematics classroom?
- How can you provide opportunities and thoughtful support for students to wrestle with challenging mathematical ideas or problems?
- How can you challenge your own expectations about what students can do so that you can provide an opportunity for every student to develop creativity and use that creativity to tap into higher-level mathematics?

FOR FAMILIES

- What questions or issues does this message raise for you to discuss with your son or daughter, the teacher, or school leaders?
- How can you challenge your daughter or son to try problems she or he doesn't know how to solve in advance? How open are you to the possibility that a little struggling over a challenging problem may be OK?
- How can you communicate to the teacher and school officials the importance of helping students develop creativity as they learn mathematics?
- How can you encourage your local school board or community to ensure the development of creativity? How can you challenge them when they implement policies and programs that get in the way of this development?

FOR LEADERS AND POLICY MAKERS

- How does this message reinforce or challenge policies and decisions you have made or are considering?
- How well do you incorporate the critical skill of creativity into the work of the school, district, or state to accompany student learning on more routine skills?
- How can you advocate for programs that encourage students to think and try problems they don't know how to solve in advance?
- What programs do you have in place for special populations of students to ensure that all students have an opportunity to develop creativity, instead of preparing some students for a future of only low-level participation in work and society?

RELATED MESSAGES

- Message 17, "Constructive Struggling," challenges us to let students tackle a challenging problem or interesting task without first spoon-feeding them the steps they should follow to get an answer.

- Message 33, "Engaged in What?," looks beyond the superficial activity in the classroom at what it takes to deeply engage students in interesting tasks.

- Message 23, "The Power of Patterns," explores a few of the many patterns that can be found in mathematics.

FURTHER READING

- Sources of Innovation and Creativity: A Summary of the Research (Adams 2006), a background paper prepared for *Tough Choices or Tough Times*, provides an overview of research about innovation and creativity and how these traits are developed, including a discussion of Teresa Amabile's vision of creativity.

- *The Global Achievement Gap* (Wagner 2008) reinforces the importance of creativity and complex thinking in the twenty-first century.

- *Sparks of Genius: The Thirteen Thinking Tools of the World's Most Creative People* (Root-Bernstein and Root-Bernstein 2001) looks at creativity and makes recommendations for transforming schools to respond to today's demanding and complex world.

- *Out of Our Minds: Learning to Be Creative* (Robinson 2001) reinforces the need for our educational system to address the development of creativity.

- *A Whole New Mind* (Pink 2006) builds on brain research to look at the kinds of intelligence we need to nurture in students for the twenty-first century.

4

Good Old Days

LEARNING FROM THE ROADS WE'VE TRAVELED

A s the twenty-first century flies by, many American communities are engaging in intense discussions about how (and whether) school mathematics should be reformed. For some in these communities, the discussions stimulate a sense of déjà vu; haven't we been here before? Haven't we tried something like that? The short answer is, yes. Perhaps there are lessons to be learned through an admittedly oversimplified look back at a few waves of school mathematics reform since the Second World War.

The 1940s—a Decade of Complacency

As World War II drew to a close, the United States had successfully survived a terrible conflict and the nation was viewed as a world leader. Americans could comfortably rest in the knowledge that the economy, the educational system, and the future were headed in the right direction. A high school education may not yet have become the norm, but most students went to school for at least some time. It would be years before many people would become concerned that some students in the nation were not receiving the same level of education as others, nor the level of education they needed for a successful future.

The 1950s—a Decade of Awakening

As the nation moved into the 1950s, the contentment of the late 1940s was reflected in an idealized American family life shown in television shows like *Father Knows Best* and *Leave It to Beaver*. Families were stable, children were basically good kids who went to school (even though they might have been mischievous), and life was predictable. But in 1957, a dramatic world event began a shift in American thinking that would change how we would approach school mathematics through the end of that decade and well into the next. In 1957, the Soviet Union launched a space satellite called Sputnik. Suddenly, Americans began to worry that the United States' greatest political enemy was surpassing us in terms of science and technology. The potential imbalance in science and in world leadership was obvious even to the average U.S. citizen—the nation had to do something to catch up.

The 1960s—a Decade of Drastic Change

In the wake of Sputnik, and in concert with President Kennedy's goal to land a man on the moon by the end of the decade, the United States made an unprecedented commitment to improve mathematics and science from elementary school through advanced graduate programs, with a focus on creating a new generation of scientists and engineers. As part of this *new math* movement, dramatically different textbooks and instructional materials were developed for elementary and secondary education, often guided by mathematicians and scientists. New math offered many positive new directions, and for some students (including me), it presented a new and expanded picture of what mathematics could be. But the era of new math also taught us that making dramatic change is nearly impossible to manage on a large scale and a short time line without significant support. Many excellent in-depth teacher institutes offered through the National Science Foundation provided some teachers with a stronger mathematics and science background than any previous generation of teachers. But many other teachers, especially elementary teachers, did not have the support they needed to teach the mathematics they were now expected to teach, and parents were left in the dark as to how to help their children on homework that didn't resemble anything they'd ever seen before. Meanwhile, thanks to a commitment of national will, the energy of the decade met the challenge once thought unreachable: the United States landed a man on the moon, accompanied by an unprecedented focus on math, science, engineering, and education.

The 1970s—a Decade of Overreaction

As new math rolled through the 1960s, a mounting backlash led to a drastic pendulum swing in the other direction. Many of the textbooks published during the 1970s (and continuing into the 1980s) represented a return to a narrower view of mathematics as part of a *back to basics* movement. Rather than emphasizing the intricacies and depth of mathematics represented by new math, some of these programs emphasized practice on arithmetic computation. This return to familiar territory temporarily appeased some parents and community members. But many found this narrow vision of mathematics too limited for a space-age generation interested in more than low-level jobs.

The 1980s—a Decade of Reports

Amid growing frustration over the state of American schools, the 1980s ushered in a wave of reports from groups within and outside of education. One after another, the reports called for raising standards and increasing accountability, and highlighted the need to improve school mathematics and science. Among the reports, *A Nation at Risk* described a "rising tide of mediocrity" in schools, noting that the nation had "squandered the gains in student achievement made in the wake of the Sputnik challenge" (National Commission on Excellence in Education 1984). Two particularly noteworthy reports on school mathematics emerged in 1989. The National Research Council published *Everybody Counts*, making a compelling case for raising expectations for every student and calling for K–12 mathematics to prepare students for a variety of future paths. And the National Council of Teachers of Mathematics (NCTM) published its landmark document *Curriculum and Evaluation Standards for School Mathematics*, providing a model for other disciplines by offering standards for what students should know and be able to do.

The 1990s—a Decade of Dialogue

The era of reports continued through the 1990s, but as the decade began, NCTM called for a "decade of dialogue." The organization urged the nation to use its standards as a starting point to engage in discussions and activities about overhauling K–12 mathematics. Several national efforts focused on convening schools, states, and other professional communities in conversations on how to use the NCTM standards as a tool to support positive change. Many innovative instructional materials were also developed; state after state identified and raised standards and expectations for all students.

The 2000s—a Flat New Millennium

The new millennium is perhaps best described with language from *The World Is Flat* by Thomas L. Friedman (2007). Echoing themes from the 1957 Soviet launch of Sputnik and the indictment of *A Nation at Risk* from 1984, Friedman laid out the rapidly changing global dynamic characterized by outsourcing of jobs, instant around-the-world communication, and broader participation in the economy by a growing middle class in more countries than ever before. At the beginning of the millennium,

NCTM released *Principles and Standards for School Mathematics* (2000), which reinforced, clarified, and extended its earlier mathematics standards. Overall, the new millennium seems to demand yet another ramping up of what is expected of all students and their teachers, especially in the areas of science, engineering, and mathematics.

Yesterday, Today, and Tomorrow

It is comforting to imagine that each generation learns from the challenges, successes, and failures of previous generations, even when the evidence in education does not always show a strong track record in this regard. We know more now than we did in the 1940s about how students learn. Some students and teachers have access to excellent materials and many teachers use effective and engaging approaches to teach students. Yet resistance to change seems to be a natural human quality, and real, lasting, nationwide change has been hard to come by. In spite of our general acceptance that we can improve what we do, memories of how it used to be seem to morph into a romanticized recollection of a saner, better day sometime long ago.

What Can We Do?

I believe we can learn from where we have been, from both successes and unfulfilled possibilities. We can tap into the confidence of the 1940s. We can pay attention to major scientific breakthroughs around the world, as we were called to do in the 1950s. Learning from the 1960s, we can take aggressive steps to emphasize science and mathematics and learn about how to support these aggressive steps in every way possible so that they succeed. From the overreaction of the 1970s, we can learn to moderate the swings of the pendulum. We can pay selective attention to the dozens of reports like those from the 1980s and ever since, so that we focus attention on the parts of the education system that need it most. We can continue the dialogue from the 1990s and make sure that all voices speak and are heard. And we can recognize that the world of the 2000s is never the same from one day to the next, and that we must prepare students with a different kind of education than ever before.

If we are smart (and lucky), what we have learned will enable us to create the kind of mathematics learning experience for every student that has been described by NCTM for many years and called for in the reports and books that lay out the many challenges we face as families, communities, states, and a nation. We lack not the knowledge, but perhaps only the national will, to put what we know into action in ways that make sense for every school in the country and, especially, for every student.

Reflection and Discussion

FOR TEACHERS

- What issues or challenges does this message raise for you? In what ways do you agree with or disagree with the main points of the message?
- What lessons can we learn from the generations of mathematics programs and textbooks of the past fifty years?
- How can we build on those lessons to create a relevant, rigorous mathematics education for every student?
- How open are you to the possibility that even the best of what we did forty, twenty, ten, or even five years ago may not be adequate for preparing our students for the world they will face tomorrow?

FOR FAMILIES

- What questions or issues does this message raise for you to discuss with your son or daughter, the teacher, or school leaders?
- How open are you to the possibility that even the best of what we did forty, twenty, ten, or even five years ago may not be adequate for preparing our students for the world they will face tomorrow?
- How can you find out more about your school's mathematics program to understand its purposes, content, and approaches (going beyond labels like *reform*, *traditional*, or *back to basics* and beyond the title of the textbook being used)?

FOR LEADERS AND POLICY MAKERS

- How does this message reinforce or challenge policies and decisions you have made or are considering?
- As you respond to increased calls for higher standards, how can you ensure adequate time for teachers and others to make changes?
- How can you engage teachers and others in the decision-making process so that perspectives of all stakeholders are considered before you make drastic changes?
- How can you ensure that teachers and the community do not experience the next new thing as yet another swing of the pendulum?

- How can you recognize and find out more about cycles, fads, and pendulum swings related to school mathematics and education in general? How can you serve the role of moderating and filtering these fads for teachers so that they can continue the steady, long-term work of improving mathematics teaching and learning without unproductive distractions?

RELATED MESSAGES

- Message 12, "Beyond Band-Aids and Bandwagons," looks at educational fads and considers how lasting change can be made.
- Message 13, "Seek First to Understand," calls for collaboration across communities to improve programs for sustainable change.

FURTHER READING

- *Sensible Mathematics: A Guide for School Leaders* (Leinwand 2000) presents an overview of the landscape of mathematics reform and provides practical guidelines for improving a mathematics program at the local level or on a larger scale.
- "Mathematics Education Then and Now: The Need for Reform" (Findell 1996) considers today's efforts for reform in school mathematics within the broader perspective of previous efforts.
- "Facing Facts: Achieving Balance in High School Mathematics" (Steen 2007) looks back at mathematics reform efforts over the past fifty years and makes recommendations for designing high school mathematics programs in the twenty-first century.
- *Everybody Counts: A Report to the Nation on the Future of Mathematics Education* (Mathematical Sciences Education Board and National Research Council 1989) makes a compelling case for providing all students with appropriate, challenging, relevant mathematics, remarkable for its lasting insights that continue to resonate today.
- *Curriculum and Evaluation Standards for School Mathematics* (NCTM 1989) provides the first professional recommendations for what should be included in school mathematics.
- *Principles and Standards for School Mathematics* (NCTM 2000) refines, clarifies, and extends NCTM's landmark 1989 standards.

5

Technology
Is a Tool

CHANGING MATHEMATICS IN A TECHNOLOGICAL WORLD

Computers and calculators were invented to save humans time and to allow us to solve more challenging problems more easily than we could otherwise. The pace of technological advances today is staggering. Potential applications for technology are increasing exponentially and the cost and availability make some forms of technology accessible to nearly everyone. Calculators, computers, and a growing array of technological innovations have become important tools for doing mathematics, joining the ranks of the compass, straightedge, pencil, and (in earlier days) the slide rule and trig tables. Yet it's been noted that some school mathematics curricula seem like efforts to make technology obsolete—they essentially pretend that technology does not exist.

Today's technology is not a panacea for transforming the teaching and learning of mathematics, but neither is it the source of all the difficulties in mathematics classrooms. Instead of discussing whether particular forms of technology are good or bad, we need to discuss how we can capitalize on these tools to help every student learn more mathematics, not less.

The Influence of Technology on Curriculum

Technology is here to stay, and it generates at least three important effects on the school mathematics curriculum. First, some mathematics is now *more important* than in the past because it plays a role in the design and use of technology. For instance, discrete mathematics topics such as matrices take on new significance in light of their use to organize information in the rows and columns that form the basis for spreadsheets. Matrices are now routinely used as technological tools to help us solve many problems in fields such as manufacturing, travel, and marketing. Furthermore, the ability for technological tools to deal with mathematical data in many forms means that students now need to be more proficient than in the past in translating from one form to another, moving among numbers, symbols, graphs, and tables, as they choose which representation can help them solve a particular problem. Even the basic task of changing fractions to decimals and vice-versa takes on new importance as students interact with calculators or software that may deal more directly with decimals than with fractions. All of these topics and skills are more important in this technological age than in the past.

At the same time, technology makes some mathematics *less important*. This idea is controversial—some fear computation will disappear from the school curriculum since calculators can perform certain types of basic operations quickly and accurately. However, even in an age of technology, it remains important for students to know how to add, subtract, multiply, and divide mentally and with a pencil and paper. But we must determine how much valuable instructional time we should devote to helping students become proficient with lengthy or tedious calculations. Determining how long a divisor is long enough in the study of long division, for example, is now an important educational decision. While some proficiency with multidigit procedures is preferred in most communities, the relative priority of this type of work is worthy of discussion. In the typically crowded American mathematics curriculum, often described as a mile wide and an inch deep, deciding what to omit is crucial, especially as emerging topics vie for inclusion.

The third and most important way in which technology affects the mathematics curriculum is that it makes some mathematics *possible* for the first time. Using calculators, students at all levels can tackle real problems that might arise from planning a field trip or from interpreting a recent news story, for example, even if the numbers involved might make the problem unwieldy with only a pencil and paper. Middle school students can analyze data using a wide range of statistical tools, thus developing quantitative reasoning abilities far beyond what was once possible. Graphing calculators allow students to see the connections between visual and symbolic representations of mathematical situations. These multifaceted calculators can be a useful tool for modeling a variety of problem situations. We are just beginning to scratch the surface of the potential of computerized algebra systems and other emerging forms of technology. These are but a few examples of how technology can help all students tackle complex problems not otherwise accessible to them, in the process raising their level of mathematical creativity and thinking.

Teaching with Technology

The teacher is a key decision maker in using technology effectively in the classroom. Teachers' most important technology decision is to determine when students should use technological tools and when they should not. Students need to learn when to do something in their heads, when to reach for a pencil, and when to use technology. Technology decisions, just like other instructional decisions, call for teachers to have a solid knowledge of mathematics and a working knowledge of available technological tools. There is nothing wrong with students knowing more than their teacher about how to use some features of a calculator or a piece of software. But there is something wrong if a teacher prohibits or limits the use of technology because of his or her own discomfort, or if a teacher allows unlimited use of technology without helping students master essential mental tools (including number sense, operation sense, estimation skills, and thinking skills). Teachers need to know how to help students access higher-level mathematics using the tools available, and not relegate the use of tools to only checking answers or repeating procedures students have already done by hand.

Who Gets Access to Technology?

Ensuring that all students have access to technology for both in-school use and for homework is the responsibility of schools and school systems; it should not be left solely to students and their families. Ensuring such access can carry significant budget implications that call for serious ethical discussions among educators. But it is not reasonable to expect all students to buy graphing calculators that may cost more than their shoes or to expect every family to have a home computer with online access. Requiring such a burden of families means that some students will have access to sophisticated tools and others will not. If we allow this burden to become the norm, society will face a digital divide greater and more dangerous than any economic gap we have yet seen in schools. The same can be said if some students have access to computers or other sophisticated technologies outside of school while other students do not. Neither is it acceptable for students in poor communities to be denied the opportunity to access higher-level mathematics because their school cannot afford appropriate tools or does not prioritize the purchase of such tools. Furthermore, it is not acceptable that some schools have access to only outdated hand-me-down technology.

What Can We Do?

Mathematics can no longer be the cheapest subject in the school budget. What was once done with little more than chalk or overhead pens now calls for a significant and ongoing investment in technology. In times of tight budgets, this can be a real challenge. But if we are serious about all students learning rigorous and challenging mathematics, then we must get serious about the task of ensuring access to reasonable resources for all students, regardless of where they live.

We must question not whether to use technology, but how to use it in ways that support the mathematics learning of every student. If students do not learn appropriate ways to use technology in school, they will surely find inappropriate ways to use it outside of school. Our responsibility, then, is to ensure not only that students have access to technological tools, but also that we take full advantage of these tools to help students learn the complex quantitative and thinking skills they will need as they enter our technology-driven workforce.

Reflection and Discussion

FOR TEACHERS

- What issues or challenges does this message raise for you? In what ways do you agree with or disagree with the main points of the message?
- What challenges do you face in using technology to support student learning?
- How can you address the financial and equity issues related to providing all students with technology? How can you handle related management issues, like keeping equipment in working order and accounted for?
- In what ways do you effectively use technology to raise the level of mathematics your students learn?
- How do you support teachers in being selective and strategic about when students may use calculators and when they should not? How do you make such decisions?
- How can you learn about how to use emerging technologies that might be useful and appropriate for students to raise their level of mathematics learning?

FOR FAMILIES

- What questions or issues does this message raise for you to discuss with your son or daughter, the teacher, or school leaders?
- What mathematical skills did you learn in school that may no longer have the same importance? What mathematical topics are important today that you did not learn in school?
- What questions can you ask at school to learn more about when and how the teacher expects students to use calculators or computers both in school and outside of school?
- What can you do if you don't have the resources to provide your son or daughter with the kind of technology he or she might need? How can you find out what resources or assistance the school can provide?

(continued)

FOR LEADERS AND POLICY MAKERS

- How does this message reinforce or challenge policies and decisions you have made or are considering?
- How can you provide access for all students to technology, including computers, appropriate calculators, and other emerging technologies that might be recommended by your mathematics teachers?
- In making decisions about what mathematics to teach, how can you take into account recommendations for changes in standards and expectations based on the rapidly changing world outside of school, especially with respect to the use of technological tools?

RELATED MESSAGES

- Message 20, "Putting Calculators in Their Place," deals with how calculators can coexist with the teaching of computational skills.
- Message 30, "Crystal's Calculator," tells a personal story about the role calculators can play in support of a student's learning of both high-level mathematics and lower-level skills, if accompanied by high expectations and engaging tasks.

FURTHER READING

- "Students as Contributors: The Digital Learning Farm" (November 2008) describes how students can interact with technology in support of their learning.
- *Using Technology and Problem Solving in Middle and High School Mathematics: Investigations Using Scientific and Graphing Calculators, Spreadsheets, and The Geometer's Sketchpad* (Goldberg 2006) presents ideas on using wide-ranging types of technology in secondary mathematics classrooms.
- *Explorations: Integrating Handheld Technology into the Elementary Mathematics Classroom* (Olson, Schielack, and Olson 2002) provides activities for using technology to improve student learning at the elementary grades.

6

"Teach Harder!" Isn't the Answer

IMPROVEMENT TAKES MORE THAN TEACHER EFFORT

Over the years, we have learned a lot about how students come to know mathematics and about how to teach for lasting learning. We have learned from looking at what other countries do, and we have learned by looking in our own backyard. Students learn challenging mathematics when they have opportunities to engage in rich problems and when a knowledgeable teacher guides their learning and helps them connect the classroom activities they do with the mathematics that underlies the activities.

Nevertheless, some administrators, policy makers, and communities have resisted supporting the use of promising teaching practices and materials that might be different from what they themselves experienced in school, claiming that they are too difficult to implement or have no long-term data proving their effectiveness. Instead of looking for new approaches designed to make high-level mathematics accessible to all students, they call for a return to *traditional* methods, emphasizing skill development and calling for teacher lecture as the primary means to accomplish it. They ask teachers to just do a better job of what we used to do.

The Way We've Always Done It

We have considerable evidence from national and international assessments that the traditional approach of teachers lecturing to students has not served most of our students. Data show that many students have not learned the mathematics we wanted them to learn, either in the past or more recently. Although I respect the motivation and commitment of all those involved in discussions on improving mathematics education in the United States, I question whether doing more of the same is the answer for the challenges we face. Where we once sought to educate a third of our students for study beyond high school, we now strive to educate *all* students to high levels, regardless of whether they are headed for higher education or for jobs with a future in the workforce. Today many more students will pursue some kind of postsecondary instruction. Even students who go straight into the workforce from high school often need a basic understanding of algebra, geometry, physics, and electronic tools. Most of all, we know that the kinds of problems that employers, workers, and professionals now handle are often far more complex than those that were common during the agricultural and industrial times that shaped our traditional educational system. Simply stated, today's citizens and workers need a far deeper knowledge of mathematics and greater quantitative abilities than at any time in the past. If we are to dramatically raise the bar for all students, we need to consider approaches other than those we have traditionally relied on.

I suggest, therefore, that it is oversimplified, unrealistic, and unfair to try to raise students' achievement in mathematics simply by putting pressure on teachers to teach harder with old methods, old textbooks, and old tools. To assume that teachers aren't already teaching hard enough is grossly inaccurate. Across the board, teachers want students to achieve at high levels, and they do whatever they can to help them learn. But to accomplish the ambitious goal of a high-quality mathematics education for every student, educators, policy makers, and communities will have to make significant, fundamental changes in the educational system, not just exhort teachers to try harder to satisfy accountability structures imposed on what has always been done.

What Can We Do?

We have to make hard choices about curriculum at every level, choosing to focus at each grade on fewer more connected goals and making a commitment to engage students in those important topics so that they both understand what they are learning and also learn how to do the procedures involved. We need to invest in our teaching force by recruiting potential teachers, mentoring new teachers, nurturing and respecting teachers at every stage of their careers, and offering all teachers high-quality professional learning opportunities that help them continue to develop their mathematical knowledge and their understanding of teaching and learning mathematics. We need to allocate adequate resources for students, regardless of their school setting, and especially in high-poverty areas. This includes making sure that every student has access to a well-qualified teacher of mathematics. We need to teach in ways that engage students in doing mathematics and solving challenging problems instead of simply watching a teacher demonstrate mathematics. Finally, we need to make sure that our system offers opportunities for working across grades and school levels and that the components of the system are well aligned around challenging and appropriate goals. These can be important, systemic, lasting changes that go far beyond teaching harder. To do less is to deny teachers the tools, resources, and support they need to make a real difference in the mathematics every student learns.

When we do institute significant changes, we need to commit to following through and supporting those changes over time to allow teachers to refine what they do and to allow student growth to develop. One of the worst things many school systems do is to change course early in the implementation of a new program or new initiative. This kind of scattered, short-term thinking sets up both teachers and students for failure, as what is done one year in no way supports what comes next. Teachers come to believe that there is no reason to invest their time and energy in the next new thing that comes along, since they know from experience that what comes in one day might be gone the next. And students cannot build a strong and connected knowledge base of mathematics when the direction changes every year or two. We may implement different strategies to accomplish our goal of a high-quality mathematics education for every student. What we cannot do is discard good programs just because they are difficult to implement or because we don't see immediate results or because a new administration has something different in mind. What we need to do in order to serve our students is to do our homework, take whatever steps are necessary to support significant change in how we teach, and work together collaboratively in sustained efforts based on the best teaching practices and materials we have, toward the goal of a high-quality mathematics education for every single student.

Reflection and Discussion

FOR TEACHERS

- What issues or challenges does this message raise for you? In what ways do you agree with or disagree with the main points of the message?
- What are the challenges you face in implementing new programs and in helping every student meet high expectations?
- Where can you go to learn how to shift your teaching toward practices that help a changing student population prepare for a changing world?

FOR FAMILIES

- What questions or issues does this message raise for you to discuss with your son or daughter, the teacher, or school leaders?

(*continued*)

- How can you find out more about current teaching practices that may be different from those you recognize?
- How can you support the school system's implementation of improvement efforts?

FOR LEADERS AND POLICY MAKERS

- How does this message reinforce or challenge policies and decisions you have made or are considering?
- How prevalent is lecture-based teaching in your school(s)? How can you help teachers expand their repertoire of teaching approaches to provide more varied and engaging experiences for students?
- How can you build in adequate supports for teachers and students and a reasonable time line to implement improvements in your policies and programs?

RELATED MESSAGES

- Message 4, "Good Old Days," examines swings of the pendulum over time with respect to changing visions of school mathematics.
- Message 12, "Beyond Band-Aids and Bandwagons," looks at educational fads and considers how we can make lasting change.
- Message 13, "Seek First to Understand," suggests involving teachers with mathematicians, administrators, and others to shape mathematics program improvements.

FURTHER READING

- *Inside Teaching: How Classroom Life Undermines Reform* (Kennedy 2006) considers the reality of implementing school reform in classrooms today and offers suggestions for those designing reform programs.
- *What's Math Got to Do with It?* (Boaler 2008) describes some of the challenges facing American mathematics education and offers insights on how we can improve.
- *Leading the Way: Principals and Superintendents Look at Math Instruction* (Burns 1999) offers suggestions for leaders in implementing improvements in mathematics teaching and learning.
- *The Courage to Teach: Exploring the Inner Landscape of a Teacher's Life* (Palmer 2007) provides insights into teaching and the life of a teacher and recognizes the critical role of teachers in improving school programs.

7

Not Your Grandpa's Algebra

PREPARING ALL STUDENTS FOR COLLEGE AND THE WORKFORCE

In previous generations, algebra was a high school course that consisted of rote practice using x and other variables to solve different kinds of equations. Students were subjected to dozens, if not hundreds, of word problems or story problems and expected to use the various types of equations they had been taught to solve the problems. Students might have been asked to find the age of someone's uncle, the amount of cashews in a container of mixed nuts, the digits in a three-digit mystery number, or what time two trains would run into each other. Thankfully, many of today's students begin to learn algebra with understanding throughout elementary and middle school and they solve problems from a much richer array of mathematical and non-mathematical contexts than what their grandparents experienced. This shifting vision focuses on using algebraic thinking to represent relationships in a range of situations, not all of which fall into predictable categories. Yet unfortunately, too often when today's students arrive at high school mathematics, especially as they enter higher-level courses such as Algebra 2, they still find themselves confronting a largely traditional vision of mathematics that may not meet the needs of all students preparing for many different career paths.

The Mathematics We Need Today

Workers of tomorrow need a richer, deeper, and fundamentally different education than those of the twentieth century. In *The World Is Flat*, Thomas L. Friedman (2007) describes today's rapidly changing twenty-first-century world as *flattening*. A growing middle class of well-educated workers in countries both rich and poor, many holding jobs in multi-national companies, reflect the technological and political shifts that are leveling the global playing field. Technology has rendered many jobs obsolete, and new workers find themselves facing a dramatically different workplace than just a few years ago. Predictions of continuing demographic, political, and technological shifts foretell a global job market subject to continuing changes. Experts from business and education agree with Friedman and the authors of numerous reports, including *Tough Choices or Tough Times* (National Center on Education and the Economy 2008), *Rising Above the Gathering Storm* (Committee on Prospering in the Global Economy et al. 2007), *Tapping America's Potential* (AeA et al. 2005), and *Before It's Too Late* (National Commission on Mathematics and Science Teaching for the Twenty-First Century 2001) that students need more mathematics than before. Specifically, recommendations now cluster around the expectation that, regardless of whether students are headed toward higher education or planning on entering the workforce straight out of high school, they will need a common level of mathematics education that includes the equivalent of Algebra 1, Geometry, and Algebra 2. The argument is that this level of mathematical expertise not only prepares students for college, but also is necessary for workforce training programs that will enable a worker to hold a good job with the potential for advancement.

However, I would argue that the Algebra 2 expectation is based primarily on employers' assertions that workers need to have studied considerable mathematics in high school, through at least three years of challenging mathematics, rather than on a strongly held belief that the particular content of an Algebra 2 course is necessary for today's (or tomorrow's) jobs. A typical Algebra 2 class today has changed very little from the abstract, symbol-intensive course of two generations ago. Many Algebra 2 textbooks reflect the goal of that time to prepare some students for a calculus path leading to mathematically intensive college majors. In the small but growing number of states that have adopted statewide standards for courses at this level, the standards tend to reflect this increasingly out-of-date purpose and limited audience. Yet rather than prepare only *some* students for calculus, high school mathematics at the Algebra 2 level today needs to prepare *all* students for a range of futures, where high-level quantitative reasoning and mathematical thinking will enable them to deal with numerical data and statistical information. Yesterday's Algebra 2 course cannot simply be retrofitted for today's students who are preparing for tomorrow's jobs.

The Long-Term Goal

At least two solutions to the shortcomings of Algebra 2 in meeting the needs of all students may be helpful—one for the long term, and one for the short term. The ideal solution for the long term is to build a high school mathematics program that connects to the pre-K–8 mathematics program to form a continuous pre-K–12 experience. Many school systems are succeeding in redefining a more connected and focused elementary and middle grades mathematics program; there is no reason why we cannot also create programs for grades 9, 10, and 11 that develop the algebraic, geometric, and statistical knowledge and skills all students need today, with a small number of well-defined options for grade 12. Some students might be carefully accelerated into such a program sooner than grade 9, if that meets their needs. Such an integrated program allows for the purposeful incorporation of emerging topics and skills such as discrete mathematics (used in many computer-based applications) and statistics (used regularly in reports in the media).

Several integrated high school programs have been developed since the late 1980s. While many of these programs are effective in their own right, each of them focuses on different topics at different grade levels, making it difficult, if not impossible, for states to write high school mathematics standards calling for an integrated approach. Standards, and accompanying end-of-course tests, would have to be written either for one particular program or else for no program. Neither of these alternatives is acceptable to most state-level policy makers. But with a long-term national commitment to developing a coherent pre-K–12 program, educators could develop broad consensus around a few particular content emphases at each grade level. With identified goals, program developers could revise existing programs or develop new ones to target this content. Much as the National Council of Teachers of Mathematics (NCTM) focal points (2006) have provided a starting point for discussions about grade-level priorities for prekindergarten through grade 8, such an approach to an integrated mathematics experience at high school could provide school systems and states clear guidance for defining priorities that extend from these grades to high school.

What Can We Do?

Meanwhile, for the short term, wherever the traditional courses of Algebra 1, Geometry, and Algebra 2 are taught, we should continue to find ways to incorporate the emerging content and skills identified as important for today's workplace and everyday life. Specifically, similar to the shifts that have already taken place in Algebra 1 in a few states, all of these courses need to incorporate more relevant uses of algebra and geometry to model relationships and real-world situations, more use of technology to represent algebraic and geometric relationships, and more opportunities for all students to develop reasoning and thinking skills. We should also seek ways to incorporate appropriate content on statistics, although such an effort means carefully examining other topics as to their relative importance in a rigorous mathematics program for all students. This could include considering whether any topics in the current Algebra 2 course (or the Geometry course) might satisfactorily be addressed in a later course, such as Precalculus.

Also for the short term, two or three courses should be developed to follow these basic three years of high school mathematics, whether organized as traditional courses or an integrated alternative. Some students will need to continue their study of mathematics with precalculus, leading to calculus, depending on when they start their study of high school mathematics. However, many students need opportunities to study considerably more statistics and data analysis than has been typically addressed in high school in order to make sense of the deluge of data and quantitative information in the media every day. They need experience with selected topics from discrete mathematics, such as using matrices or understanding networks and counting techniques. They also need sophisticated and deep knowledge of financial situations beyond basic consumer topics, including understanding investments and debt. Several states and school systems are developing courses that address some of these topics as stand-alone courses in a combined fourth-year course experience. When states and school systems work together around a few well-defined options, materials developers will be more likely to develop instructional materials to support such courses.

As schools implement these changes, some mathematicians may fear that high schools are shifting their focus away from preparing future mathematics majors. However, students moving toward mathematics or a math-intensive field at the university level should be able to study many of the abstract elements of mathematics they will need for college in precalculus and calculus. Simply tweaking the status quo might make Grandpa happy, but it is unacceptable today: If we leave the system unchanged, most students will not learn what they need to learn for their varied futures in a changing marketplace. What society needs now is the national will and commitment to transform high school mathematics as part of our work to strengthen the pre-K–12 mathematics program for all students. What students need now is to graduate from high school ready for any path they might follow in their rapidly flattening world.

Reflection and Discussion

FOR TEACHERS

- What issues or challenges does this message raise for you? In what ways do you agree with or disagree with the main points of the message?
- How can you support at your grade level the pre-K–12 development of algebraic thinking and the use of mathematics to represent relationships?

- How can you work within your school system or state to move toward a more coherent pre-K–12 program in which each year builds on the year before?
- How can you help students make smooth transitions from elementary school to middle school to high school?
- If you are a high school teacher, how open are you to moving toward an integrated mathematics program if you don't already teach such a program? What barriers or challenges do you see that need to be addressed in order to make such a long-term transition? How do you think you and your colleagues could address these challenges?
- If you are a high school teacher in a program consisting of Algebra 1, Geometry, and Algebra 2, how can you enrich the program you teach to be more relevant and useful to all students, regardless of their future path? In what ways might you change the content and the approach(es) that you use?

FOR FAMILIES

- What questions or issues does this message raise for you to discuss with your son or daughter, the teacher, or school leaders?
- How open are you to the possibility that high school mathematics could be structured differently today than it was when you were in school?
- How can you work with your school leaders and other families in the community to advocate moving toward a more coherent pre-K–12 program that builds continuously from elementary school through middle school and high school?

FOR LEADERS AND POLICY MAKERS

- How does this message reinforce or challenge policies and decisions you have made or are considering?
- How can you move toward a long-term vision of pre-K–12 mathematics that is coherent and connected across grade levels? How open are you to considering an integrated high school mathematics program if your school(s) do(es) not already use one?
- How can you enrich the teaching of traditionally titled courses like Algebra 1, Geometry, and Algebra 2 so that all (or more) students learn powerful and useful mathematics, regardless of their future path?
- What options do you have (or can you develop) for students after completing the first three common years of high school mathematics through approximately Algebra 2, such as courses in precalculus, statistics, discrete math, and financial literacy?

RELATED MESSAGES

- Message 1, "Math for a Flattening World," makes a case for changing how schools prepare students for the twenty-first century.
- Message 25, "Pushing Algebra Down," looks at the pros and cons of accelerating some or all students into high school mathematics prior to high school as a tool for equity and access.
- Message 37, "Boring!," reminds us of the consequences when students don't see the relevance of what they are taught.

FURTHER READING

- *The World Is Flat* (Friedman 2007) gives the broader context for the rising middle class around the world and describes the implications for business, government, education, and society.
- *Everybody Counts: A Report to the Nation on the Future of Mathematics Education* (Mathematical Sciences Education Board and National Research Council 1989) makes a compelling case for providing all students with appropriate, challenging, relevant mathematics, remarkable for its lasting insights that continue to resonate long after its original publication.
- "Facing Facts: Achieving Balance in High School Mathematics" (Steen 2007) looks back at mathematics reform efforts over the past fifty years, as well as making recommendations for designing high school mathematics programs in the twenty-first century.
- *Windows on Teaching Math: Cases of Middle and Secondary Classrooms* (Merseth 2003a) and *Windows on Teaching Math: Cases of Middle and Secondary Classrooms: Facilitator's Guide* (Merseth 2003b) describe cases—scenarios for stimulating analysis and discussion among teachers to shift and improve their practice in secondary math classrooms.
- Fourth-Year Capstone Courses (Charles A. Dana Center and Achieve, Inc. 2008) provides descriptions and information about a variety of fourth-year mathematics courses developed by various groups to follow Algebra 2 (www.utdanacenter.org/k12mathbenchmarks/resources/capstone.php).
- High School Fourth Year Mathematics Courses (The University of Arizona Institute for Mathematics and Education 2008) provides information on efforts to develop relevant mathematics courses to follow Algebra 2 (http://ime.math.arizona.edu/2007-08/1013_fourthyear.html).
- Math Is More (www.mathismore.net) advocates change in mathematics, including presentations from a 2008 conference on the future of high school mathematics.

8 More Math, More Dropouts?

HOW WE RAISE THE BAR MATTERS

More and more states are calling for all high school graduates to complete at least three or four years of academically rigorous mathematics, often through the level of Algebra 1, Geometry, and Algebra 2, or their equivalent in Integrated Mathematics 1, 2, and 3. Recommendations for twenty-first-century skills from numerous reports continue to emphasize this level of mathematics as essential for dealing with our quantitative world and for preparing for emerging job categories. Countering these recommendations are serious concerns that if requirements increase, even more students will drop out of high school. We are already faced with alarming statistics on dropouts from many schools, especially in urban areas and among minority and economically disadvantaged students. The question is whether potential gains for students from increasing expectations across grades pre-K–12 outweigh a potential increase in the dropout rate. The answer is neither clear nor easy.

When Students *Don't* Graduate

To put the issue of dropouts into perspective, we can look at the negative impact on a student of not completing high school. The most obvious problem of not having a high school education is the greatly diminished opportunity to find a job. Even if a high school dropout succeeds in finding a job, the income will likely be so low that the student (and family) will face a lifetime of poverty, barely getting by from month to month. Opportunities for advancement will be limited, unless the student goes back to school for at least a GED.

When Students *Do* Graduate

So we can make a strong case that a student needs at least a high school diploma in order to have a chance for success in the workplace. But the diploma is just a piece of paper—a gatekeeper. The level of education behind the diploma is what opens doors. How well will a high school diploma serve students in their day-to-day lives if it doesn't represent a significantly higher level of education than in the past? Fewer than twenty years ago, high school mathematics courses with names like General Math, Basic Math, Functional Math, Fundamentals of Math, or Consumer Math were considered adequate for high school graduation, addressing at best middle school mathematics skills and at worst a sampling of elementary school arithmetic. A student might have been expected to complete one or two years of such courses unless the student was designated as college-bound. In that case the student would be expected to complete two or three years of mathematics including Algebra 1 use Arabic number for consistency. A small number of advanced students completed higher-level courses that might lead to a precalculus or calculus course offered as part of the College Board's Advanced Placement program or the International Baccalaureate program.

Under that previous system of minimal high school expectations for some students, any student encountering difficulty or falling behind might be tracked into remedial courses as early as elementary school. These students were destined to experience a mathematics program consisting almost entirely of basic arithmetic skills, falling ever further behind throughout elementary school and middle school as they headed toward more of the same at high school. Thus even a high school graduate might have accomplished only low-level numerical skills, even though he had received the credential of a high school diploma. Jobs for students with only a high school diploma have always been limited. But today, many of these low-level jobs are rapidly disappearing, including jobs like those of assembly-line workers. Or these jobs have greatly changed in scope or need, like those of secretaries working in businesses that once relied on communication via typed letters. Yesterday's vision of a high school diploma and the level of education it represented simply do not serve today's young people entering the workforce in a technology-intensive, knowledge-based information society where every worker is likely to have access to a computer or hand-held technological tool of some kind that manages information and communication.

The vast majority of jobs today (and the anticipated jobs of tomorrow) call for a far higher level of high school education than in the past. An increasing number of today's jobs demand some kind of education after high school. ACT and Achieve Inc. report that even blue-collar jobs now call for training that goes beyond a high school diploma. For example, Achieve notes on its website (www.achieve.org) that two-thirds of new jobs created by 2010 will require education beyond high school, such as a two-year degree or technical training. The argument for a more rigorous high school education is driving increased graduation expectations, especially in mathematics, in every state in the nation.

The Balance

There is a delicate balance between implementing higher requirements and supporting students so that more of them do not choose to leave high school without graduating. Many schools, districts, and states have recognized this need as they implement various types of student support structures at the elementary and middle school levels to better prepare students for high school. They may also rely on summer bridge programs—programs that provide some students with extra support over the summer months to help them successfully enter grade 9. They may offer in-school support programs such as enriched or intensive double-period Algebra 1 (or extended time for other basic subjects, like English). However, just because a school offers some type of special program does not mean that students will be more likely to succeed. No matter what structure a program takes, if it does not engage students in relevant tasks—if it simply repeats strategies that have failed students in the past or provides extra time for the same approach—then students will be no better served than they would be without the program; they will only be more bored, more disengaged, and more convinced that math is not their thing. Students need real support structures that lead to learning, not simply new vehicles that repackage unsuccessful approaches to learning. While we don't have universal, fool-proof answers to these challenges, many schools are finding success with their efforts to support students in meeting increased expectations. We can look forward to evidence and research that may help guide our work in the future. Meanwhile, providing effective support that helps every student meet increased expectations today calls for a commitment of policy makers, teachers, instructional leaders, parents, and students themselves. This level of comprehensive commitment and support is not easy, cheap, or fast.

The alternative to supporting students in meeting higher expectations is not, however, to keep high school graduation requirements low. If states and districts give in to pressures to lower expectations in the name of keeping more students in school, the very meaning of a high school education should be questioned. What good does it do students to stay in school and graduate if they leave high school without meaningful knowledge and usable skills for dealing with the quantitative demands of the workplace? How does it serve students to give them a piece of paper that says they have a high school education if that education represents minimal preparation for the shrinking number of low-level service jobs in our increasingly competitive job market?

What Can We Do?

Our compassion for students who might drop out cannot be allowed to overrule our good judgment and the growing evidence that every young person needs more education now than in the past. For most students today and, especially, tomorrow, this begins with high school graduation; it should not end there. This beginning needs to represent a broader and more solid foundation than ever before, including ensuring that students have strong quantitative and reasoning skills, a well-balanced knowledge of all subject areas, critical reasoning skills, and the ability to apply what they have learned in knowledge-intensive collaborative work environments as well as in their day-to-day lives. This calls for supporting students in meeting rigorous and relevant expectations in whatever ways it takes at every level of education, not caving in to fear by holding on to an outdated, low-level model of school that has been proven not to work for too many students.

Reflection and Discussion

FOR TEACHERS

- What issues or challenges does this message raise for you? In what ways do you agree with or disagree with the main points of the message?
- What is your role in making high school mathematics worthy of the course title for which a student gets credit?
- Regardless of the grade level you teach, how can you teach in engaging and supportive ways that allow students to meet the rapidly increasing expectations for high school graduation?
- What options might you explore for the future to help all students meet increased expectations and stay in school?

FOR FAMILIES

- What questions or issues does this message raise for you to discuss with your son or daughter, the teacher, or school leaders?
- How can you help your daughter or son understand the importance of a high school education and the value of some kind of additional education after high school?
- How can you express your high expectations for your son or daughter in constructive and positive ways, providing support for him or her to meet those expectations?

FOR LEADERS AND POLICY MAKERS

- How does this message reinforce or challenge policies and decisions you have made or are considering?
- How do you deal with the challenges involved in raising expectations for all students, especially students likely to drop out of school?
- How do you ensure that all high school graduates have an education worthy of a twenty-first-century high school diploma that prepares them for the future?
- What programs and connections are in place or might you consider to support students in selecting their future path after high school, including preparation for certificate programs, technical training, or postsecondary study?

RELATED MESSAGES

- Message 1, "Math for a Flattening World," looks at the changing demands of today's society.
- Message 17, "Constructive Struggling," makes a case for offering students an opportunity to work hard and wrestle with challenging problems.
- Message 31, "Do They Really Need It?," describes the author's challenge in raising expectations for all students, regardless of their future path.

FURTHER READING

- *The Silent Epidemic: Perspectives of High School Dropouts* (Bridgeland, Dilulio, and Morison 2006) provides descriptive data and information on the nation's dropout problem and makes recommendations on decreasing the dropout rate.
- *Fires in the Bathroom: Advice for Teachers from High School Students* (Cushman 2005) presents students views about high school, including their views about challenge, expectations, and relevance.
- *Ready for College and Ready for Work: Same or Different?* (ACT 2006) reports on the knowledge required for entry into job programs and for college admissions.
- American Diploma Project (ADP) Network (www.achieve.org) includes information, reports, and resources about college and workforce readiness.

9

Increasing Access or Ensuring Failure?

POLICY MAKERS THROW A HAMMER THROUGH THE WALL

The trend on the part of many states and districts to increase the level of mathematics required of all students is both exciting and terrifying. On the surface, it seems to be exactly what many of us in mathematics education have advocated. Finally, we can put an end to the practice of sending a nonrepresentative portion of our students down a mathematical dead end. Finally, we say, we can put an end to low-level courses that serve no purpose other than to ensure that these students will hate mathematics, find school irrelevant, and leave school ill-equipped to deal with the world. The movement to raise the bar seems to hold the potential to dramatically change our view of what it means to be a high school graduate, especially for those least well served by the system, like our students of color and students of poverty.

If we look beyond the surface, however, more disturbing concerns emerge. Simply de-tracking students or changing the courses in which they are enrolled does not change the underlying problems their previous placement was intended to address. Many of our students have been unsuccessful in school mathematics year after year, in terms of developing both functional proficiency in traditional computation skills and meaningful problem-solving skills to deal with real situations in a dramatically changing technological society. Further, concerns peak when students are enrolled in high school mathematics, usually Algebra 1, in eighth grade or earlier. In spite of a small but growing number of exceptional examples, high school algebra continues to consist primarily of a sequence of abstract mechanical procedures largely lacking any real-world context. Unfortunately, most teachers have never been shown how to teach in a way that engages a diverse student population in a variety of interesting and important learning activities. Their students are not likely to develop the inherent critical thinking and problem-solving abilities to succeed in an algebra course. Rather, most school systems have tried to "retrofit" traditional courses like Algebra I or Geometry, once designed to prepare the college-bound elite, to now fit all students. To do so, they use teaching techniques tailored to students already successful in mathematics classrooms taught in traditional ways.

Unfortunate Scenarios

By simply enacting a state or district mandate to teach all students at or above grade level, we are in danger of being lulled into a sense of false satisfaction that we have solved the critical and complex problems of access, equity, and meaningful mathematics instruction for all of our students. When this practice is implemented without substantial support from a number of directions, one or both of two scenarios is likely to result as students move into high school math courses:

- Students who have never experienced success in mathematics will be placed into academically challenging courses like Algebra and Geometry. Some students will blossom in the hands of well-prepared, caring teachers who engage students in mathematics by using teaching strategies that differ from traditional mathematics teaching. Other teachers will continue to teach the kind of algebra they have always taught in ways they have always taught, even though their audience is drastically different. These teachers may say that they have tried to raise their expectations for their "low" students—that they have taught the material but that the students just can't handle it, aren't motivated, or don't do their part. Without extensive support, many, if not most, students in these classrooms will fail, and their teachers' beliefs will persist that some students just cannot deal with higher-level mathematics.

- In other districts, compassionate teachers concerned about the potential for students to fail algebra, or teachers pushed by administrators concerned about high failure rates, will see to it that algebra becomes accessible to all students by watering down the content of their traditional course. They may even slow it down, taking a year of abstract, irrelevant, high-level algebra and spreading it out to two years of slow, abstract, irrelevant, low-level algebra or spending two class periods a day doing the same thing they would normally do in one. They may desperately adopt whatever current textbook or program promises to solve their problem—the program that guarantees that their students will drill until mastery on the abstract recipes of algebra or the elusive proofs of geometry. Students may indeed pass these courses, but to what end? These students will reaffirm their view of mathematics as useless to their lives and their view of themselves as nonmath students. Worse, they will enter the world ill-equipped to handle any quantitative situation.

Four Key Steps

These scenarios do not mean that policy makers are wrong to eliminate low-level high school courses or to expect more of students at every grade level. Rather, it means that by expecting more, our work has just begun. In order to increase the likelihood that we can serve a broader population of students with higher-level mathematics, we *must* take several steps at the same time.

1. ENGAGE IN PROFESSIONAL DEVELOPMENT

Teachers need substantial ongoing professional development. For most teachers, even some with mathematics degrees, this may include learning the deep conceptual foundations of school mathematics, learning more about statistics, and learning how to use algebra and geometry to model a variety of authentic situations. For all teachers, this professional development should include expanding their repertoire of instructional approaches with new strategies to increase student engagement, develop lasting understanding, and provide meaningful opportunities for students to use what they have learned.

2. RECONSIDER WHAT WE TEACH

High school courses need to become more integrated (blending and connecting Algebra, Geometry, Statistics, and more) and more technology based. Courses need to incorporate critical thinking in order to meet the needs of an increasingly diverse student audience and in order to prepare students to deal with the complex problems they will face in tomorrow's workplace.

3. SHIFT HOW WE TEACH

We need to develop new kinds of instructional delivery and support systems. We should continue to explore alternative delivery structures, especially double-period algebra, or explore variations on traditional schedules. However, there is growing evidence that this type of structure won't succeed if teachers continue to use traditional lecture-based instructional approaches or leave students to learn on their own with individualized, computerized tutoring. Students likely to have difficulty need a more engaging and interactive kind of mathematics instruction than that which has not served them in the past.

4. BROADEN HOW WE MEASURE SUCCESS

Program and student evaluations should include meaningful measures of student success that go beyond standardized tests or a state's accountability test. End-of-course assessments may be valuable, but only if they address mathematical thinking, reasoning, and problem solving as well as course content. This means using other forms of assessment besides multiple-choice tests, such as open-ended questions or portfolios containing samples of student work from throughout the course.

The next several years will provide much insight into appropriate next steps to serve all students in rigorous mathematics at every level from early childhood through high school. Unfortunately, some of that insight may arrive too late to help today's students. We cannot wait for this retroactive insight before we take action; the concrete steps described here, at a minimum, can be taken now.

The Hammer in the Wall

It may be shortsighted to believe that a mandate eliminating low-level courses can force a fundamental change in beliefs, curriculum, or teaching practice. A recent personal experience has caused me to see this kind of policy move from a different perspective, however. Not long ago, my family undertook a major home remodeling project. In one of many discussions with our contractor, we asked him what he thought we should do with a particular wall in our kitchen. We had already procrastinated about making a decision, and we were continuing to vacillate as we talked to him, claiming that we were not yet adequately prepared to make the right choice; we needed more time to look at magazines and talk to other people. The contractor decided to finalize our decision—he walked across the room, took out his hammer, and knocked a large hole through the wall in question. Against the backdrop of our gasps and whimpers, he announced that we would now *have* to deal with the wall.

Policy makers have hit our wall with a hammer. As caring professional educators, we might think that we are working our way toward solving our problems, that the hammer is unnecessary. However, mandates and legislated actions calling for students to complete certain courses and meet certain expectations have hammered a hole in the wall, and we have to deal with it—now.

What Can We Do?

This is a wonderful opportunity to continue to improve students' pre-K–8 mathematics foundation and to revamp the high school mathematics program we claim builds on that foundation. Let us not waste this opportunity. Let us commit to concrete, long-term solutions based on our best professional judgment, experience, and research. From policy makers, we need mandates to be accompanied with reasonable implementation time lines and a commitment to support the practitioners responsible for making the changes reality. From practitioners, we need a commitment to act in responsible ways that may challenge our expectations for some students. Without a serious commitment from both policy makers and practitioners, we will certainly lose many of our students.

Let us allocate the resources to follow through with what needs to be done. Let us build a powerful network of concerned educators and citizens committed to truly providing access to high-level mathematics for all students. Let us finish knocking down the wall, and let us build in its place a real future for every one of our students.

Reflection and Discussion

FOR TEACHERS

- What issues or challenges does this message raise for you? In what ways do you agree with or disagree with the main points of the message?
- How can you accommodate students' previous gaps and deficiencies in mathematics without holding them back from more engaging mathematics?
- How can you incorporate engaging and supportive teaching approaches into your classroom that are consistent with rigorous course goals?
- What tools do you need in order to teach to higher goals and to prepare students with the tools they'll need in order to succeed?

FOR FAMILIES

- What questions or issues does this message raise for you to discuss with your son or daughter, the teacher, or school leaders?
- Have you embraced the notion that your daughter or son might be able to succeed at a higher level of mathematics than you might have previously thought? How have you communicated your high expectations to her or him?
- Regardless of previous achievement (high or low), what kinds of positive messages can you put forth regarding the importance of perseverance for success in mathematics and your son's or daughter's potential for success?
- Have you recognized that increasing acceleration of a successful student may or may not be the best path to prepare a student for the future? In considering placement, acceleration, and course-selection decisions, how can you take into account what your son or daughter will learn, what he or she might miss, and how he or she will be best served over time?

FOR LEADERS AND POLICY MAKERS

- How does this message reinforce or challenge policies and decisions you have made or are considering?
- How can you support teachers and students in meeting increased expectations including providing a reasonable implementation time line and appropriate support structures for students who may struggle or have gaps in their mathematical knowledge?
- How can you support teachers in terms of appropriate professional learning experiences that help them fundamentally change their teaching for the increasingly diverse audience they are expected to serve?
- How can you connect work across pre-K–12 (or pre-K–16) to address challenges early in a student's mathematical career?

RELATED MESSAGES

- Message 8, "More Math, More Dropouts?," considers implications of raising expectations for students at high school.
- Message 2, "Untapped Potential," discusses the need to raise expectations and support students in meeting those expectations.
- Message 25, "Pushing Algebra Down," addresses the issue of accelerating middle school students into high school mathematics courses.

FURTHER READING

- *Ready for College and Ready for Work: Same or Different?* (ACT 2006) discusses the need for all students to reach a level of Algebra 2 for high school graduation in order to be ready for either higher education or workforce training programs.
- *Tough Choices or Tough Times* (National Center on Education and the Economy 2008) is a comprehensive report by a group largely outside of education that advocates raising the bar on what we expect of students and shifting our view of what education should provide to prepare workers and citizens for the twenty-first-century workforce.
- *Windows on Teaching Math: Cases of Middle and Secondary Classrooms* (Merseth 2003a) and *Windows on Teaching Math: Cases of Middle and Secondary Classrooms: Facilitator's Guide* (Merseth 2003b) describe a series of cases—scenarios for stimulating analysis and discussion among teachers to help them shift and improve their practice in secondary math classrooms.

10

It's Not Just About Math and Reading

THE NEED FOR A WELL-BALANCED CURRICULUM

In the 1980s, significant education reform efforts that were beginning in a few states included a mandate for a well-balanced curriculum. Recognizing that not all students were receiving the same breadth of education, some of these reforms required that elementary and middle school students receive instruction in reading, writing, mathematics, social studies, science, physical education, art, music, and more. High school graduation requirements were expanded to become more comprehensive as well as more rigorous. These moves recognized the importance of access for all students to a full and meaningful education.

In the twenty years since these early efforts to improve education, priorities across the United States have shifted. Now, in the wake of the federal No Child Left Behind legislation, the emphasis in most states has shifted to reading and mathematics, with science possibly to be addressed in the future. With significant decisions and sanctions at stake for states, schools, teachers, and students, it has become unacceptably commonplace to find elementary schools where students spend the vast majority of their school day in reading (especially) and mathematics classes to the exclusion of almost all other content areas.

In high school, increasing graduation requirements in mathematics, science, and other academic disciplines can squeeze out electives, especially as students race to accumulate Advanced Placement courses or hurry down other pathways to college credit. And middle school—once recognized as the place where students could explore many options to discover what interested them—is caught in a squeeze. Middle school instructional programs are now forced to make up for a lack of exposure to some school subjects in elementary school, while also offering algebra and other high school classes so that students can begin the process of accruing credits for high school.

A well-balanced education seems to have fallen victim to questionably good intentions in an era of high-stakes, basic-skills accountability and the race to college. Worse, this is happening at a time when students need a broad, deep, and rich education more than at any other time in history.

Clarifying Priorities

Accountability is a laudable goal; the public needs to know that students are learning. But putting too much emphasis on test results, especially results on a single multiple-choice test that addresses only part of what students should know, is now showing us what many educators feared and warned about years ago. Forces at every level of the educational system are pushing teachers to shorten their view and narrow their focus toward limited types of questions addressing a limited number of content areas. Simply put, they are teaching to the test. Students are developing the notion that learning matters only for the next big test, embracing strategies exactly the opposite of the lifelong learning approach necessary for tomorrow's jobs in a knowledge-based economy.

Certainly, we can agree that the most important aspect of education is helping students learn to communicate—to read, write, and speak. Without these basic tools, a person can only be a passive recipient of a small slice of what society has to offer, but never a full or active participant. These communication abilities open the door to everything else that education comprises as well as day-to-day functioning in a twenty-first-century society.

And we might also agree that today there are compelling reasons why students need more mathematics than ever before. Technological advances allow the generation of unlimited quantitative data and information that is overwhelming to process meaningfully without sophisticated quantitative reasoning skills. Statistical studies are reported (and misreported) in the media daily, and mathematics is needed to make sense of all kinds of numerical and scientific information in everyday life. Mathematical knowledge and skills are also increasingly expected at all levels of the workforce. New careers in mathematics-dependent fields abound as the twenty-first century moves in technology-intensive, knowledge-intensive directions. Report after report calls for more individuals ready to move into such fields, from basic technician levels to advanced graduate study.

Meanwhile, science also has an urgent calling, bringing its importance in the curriculum to renewed prominence for every student. There is significant movement along social and political dimensions toward an economy based on new forms of energy and a green lifestyle. Issues of science underlie every aspect of this kind of society as we deal with the convergence of energy, climate, and economic issues with the urgency to take care of the planet we inhabit. Social issues regarding science and research appear on election ballots, and science is applied in fields of work as diverse as health care, home construction, and the auto industry.

And More . . .

While there is growing support for these few core content areas, it is not hard to argue that within these subject areas we may be limiting the education our students receive to that which is likely to be assessed on accountability tests. And what of the rest of the curriculum that may not be taught at all? In a 2007 op-ed piece in the *Wall Street Journal*, Chester Finn and Diane Ravitch warn that our current infatuation with the STEM (science, technology, engineering, and mathematics) fields and the narrow focus of the federal No Child Left Behind legislation have the collective potential to limit our students' education in dangerous ways. They make a compelling case that *the STEM needs leaves and flowers*.

In today's global society, awareness of history, geography, and world events is critical if we are to understand the rest of the world and have any chance of making sense of the continuing geopolitical shifts among nations. Yet social studies, while generally considered a core academic subject, is often receiving less and less instructional time as schools scramble to spend more time on reading and math.

Beyond the four basic subjects (English language arts, mathematics, science, and social studies), enrichment subjects have taken an even harder hit in recent years, struggling for attention as core requirements increase and budgets shrink. Yet it may be that when students study art and music, it helps them develop their creativity, a critical twenty-first century skill in an economy that highly values innovation. Physical education cannot be shortchanged if we are to turn the tide on an increasingly unfit population. And learning languages other than English is more important than ever in our shrinking global community, where countries around the world interact daily in business and government. Research is strong that learning languages is far easier for young children than for teenagers or adults. Meanwhile, many of the most relevant technical skills in demand today are taught through career and technical education courses many students never have an opportunity to pursue.

What Can We Do?

Most of all, beyond the subject names that appear in a school schedule, students need opportunities to connect what they learn across subject areas. Students can learn science in their reading class as they read material about energy, climate, and animals. Students can reinforce the mathematics and statistics concepts they learn as they interpret social studies surveys or conduct simple studies in other content areas. In a school program with limited time, educators need to take advantage of opportunities to help students make such connections. In doing so, they also give students something important in its own right: the ability to call on knowledge from all disciplines to solve complex problems that don't look like the questions at the end of the chapter in any textbook.

This century calls for a renewed emphasis on education, and it raises the importance of mathematics and science as part of that education. But let us not allow a well-balanced education to become a casualty of a narrow emphasis on accountability around a few core content areas. If we are serious about raising the bar on the education we provide every student, then we also must be serious about what that education includes. Every student today deserves a full range of knowledge within a rich program addressing all content areas and tying together what he or she knows through reasoning, critical thinking, and communication.

Reflection and Discussion

FOR TEACHERS

- What issues or challenges does this message raise for you? In what ways do you agree with or disagree with the main points of the message?
- How can you ensure that students' education includes a well-balanced curriculum?
- In what ways can you help students connect what they learn across content areas (such as looking for common threads in how problems are solved in science, mathematics, and social studies or giving students complex problems that cross disciplines)?

FOR FAMILIES

- What questions or issues does this message raise for you to discuss with your son or daughter, the teacher, or school leaders?
- How can you help your daughter or son explore all the subject areas of the school curriculum, especially those that may not be receiving much attention at school?

FOR LEADERS AND POLICY MAKERS

- How does this message reinforce or challenge policies and decisions you have made or are considering?
- How well do you provide students the opportunity to learn the four core content areas—language arts, mathematics, science, and social

(continued)

studies—while continuing to provide learning in other disciplines, including the arts, physical education, other languages, and electives?

- How do you help teachers understand that they should use their professional judgment to teach in ways that go beyond an emphasis on preparation for a large-scale test?

RELATED MESSAGES

- Message 1, "Math for a Flattening World," describes what students need to succeed in the twenty-first century.
- Message 35, "Putting Testing in Perspective," looks at issues around high-stakes testing and teaching to the test.
- Message 3, "Making the Case for Creativity," discusses the need to help students develop their creativity within and outside of mathematics class.

FURTHER READING

- "Not By Geeks Alone" (Finn and Ravitch 2007b) makes a case for teaching more than STEM fields in schools.
- *Hot, Flat, and Crowded* (Friedman 2008) considers the critical role of science (especially climate and energy) and complex problem solving to address the major issues of the twenty-first century.
- Partnership for 21st Century Skills (www.21stcenturyskills.org) presents recommendations for a dramatically different view of education for the twenty-first century by a diverse collaboration of individuals and groups from education, business, and government.
- "What to Learn: 'Core Knowledge' or 'Twenty-First-Century Skills'?" (Toppo 2009) presents a discussion about opposition to the skills called for by the Partnership for 21st Century Skills.
- *Comprehending Math: Adapting Reading Strategies to Teach Mathematics, K–6* (Hyde 2006) describes an approach to teaching that incorporates reading comprehension, mathematical problem solving, and thinking.
- *Beyond the Basics: Achieving a Liberal Education for All Children* (Finn and Ravitch 2007a) describes the need for a broad education.

11 Weighing Hens

LOOKING AT BENCHMARK TESTING

In today's era of extreme accountability, we seem to be obsessed with test scores, yet held hostage by the tests themselves. Most school systems today find themselves focused on the results of large-scale accountability tests. Test scores can determine whether teachers and schools will face sanctions, and a student's test scores can drive critical decisions such as whether the student will be promoted or in what class the student will be placed. A concern once voiced by a few is now voiced by many: *Are we losing sight of learning in the interest of test scores?*

As if the larger-than-life high-stakes accountability test isn't enough, many policy makers, because of the pressure to raise test scores, have turned to even more testing. In particular, many schools now require *interim tests*—often called *benchmark tests*—which are administered one to six times a year. These tests are intended to determine whether a student is on track to perform satisfactorily on the year-end accountability test. In some cases, benchmark tests may be a useful part of a school system's comprehensive assessment system. If used appropriately, they can give us helpful information for evaluating a program or provide a basis for productive common conversations among educators. But such assessments also have the potential to interfere with student learning, rather than improve it. In some systems, benchmark tests take precious time away from instruction while contributing little or nothing to student learning. The preparation, administration, scoring, and analysis of such tests can also place a considerable burden on teachers. It is our responsibility to carefully consider whether the costs involved with these tests outweigh the potential benefits.

Five Important Questions

The Aspen Institute's Education and Society policy program published an insightful brief around the topic of interim assessments. The report suggests that policy makers consider five questions before implementing a system of interim testing:

1. What do we want to learn from this assessment?
2. Who will use the information gathered from this assessment?
3. What action steps will be taken as a result of this assessment?
4. What professional development or support structures should be in place to ensure the action steps are taken and are successful?
5. How will student learning improve as a result of using this interim assessment system and will it improve more than if the assessment system was not used? (Perie et al. 2007, 3)

Answering these questions helps us identify the ways in which valuable information from a well-designed assessment might help a teacher guide instruction and improve student learning. The questions also call attention to what is involved in using assessment results to improve student performance and how much support both teachers and students may need if real improvement is going to take place.

In addition to these five essential questions about *why we should use this assessment* and *what we should do with the results*, two related questions about the potential costs of the assessment might also be asked:

6. How much instructional time will the assessment require?
7. How much teacher time will be involved in preparing for, administering, scoring, and analyzing the results?

These two questions focus on one of the biggest concerns associated with interim testing: Will a program of frequently administered standardized assessments improve student learning, or will it exact a cost far greater than its benefit? If a mandatory assessment takes away students' learning time and also creates an excessive burden on teachers, any potential gain in information about a student's progress may be overshadowed by these human costs.

There is a saying (some attribute its origin to Australia) that reads: "You don't make a hen fatter by weighing it more often." The obvious connection is that we don't improve student learning simply by administering more tests. Our challenge as educators is to make sure that whenever we "weigh" student learning, we also make a contribution to "fattening," or improving it. Benchmark tests often fail this challenge if not used with great care within a comprehensive system of instruction and ongoing classroom assessment.

For example, we need to recognize that benchmark tests, like the large-scale tests they are designed to precede, are not designed to be diagnostic. Benchmark tests may be able to point a teacher in the direction of where to look more closely at a student's work. But a knowledgeable teacher with an understanding of learning and assessment can do an even more efficient and effective job of diagnosing student difficulties through the day-to-day classroom assessment used as part of instruction. This may or may not involve a test. In many cases a review of a student's project presentation, an observation of a student at work, or even a simple conversation with a student about a particular math problem can provide important information a skillful teacher can use to redirect student's learning. This information can be far more valuable to a teacher (and therefore to a student) than a benchmark test administered after the fact over cumulative learning outcomes. Students lose no instructional time when this kind of ongoing assessment is incorporated into instruction, and they avoid the often negative experience of taking yet another formal test.

The critical factor in the success of either benchmark testing or ongoing classroom assessment is how educators use the assessment to adjust instruction and improve student learning. Once educators have internalized such knowledge and implemented it into instructional practice, we might question whether benchmark testing is even necessary.

What Can We Do?

It may well be that thoughtful development of an interim testing program can be helpful to improving student learning, especially if teachers are involved in designing the system or in making decisions about whether or how often to use the system. But if benchmark tests are used simply to see how students might do on their year-end accountability test—if we just want to weigh the hen—then we should carefully measure the value to student learning according to the questions listed earlier. Without careful attention to how and why we are using such tests, we may find more teachers and students experiencing what one teacher described to me: two to three days lost from instruction out of every six weeks, solely for the preparation and administration of the benchmark test.

We don't have time in schools to assess students in ways that don't contribute to improved student learning. Let's avoid falling victim to the notion that weighing hens makes them fatter and commit instead to using common sense in making decisions about how and how often we measure student learning. Let us commit to using a wide range of classroom assessment tools to help us guide student learning. And let us also commit to involving teachers in making decisions about the kinds of tests we impose. Not only does this involvement value and take advantage of the collective knowledge and expertise of professional teachers, but it also benefits all of our students.

Reflection and Discussion

FOR TEACHERS

- What issues or challenges does this message raise for you? In what ways do you agree with or disagree with the main points of the message?
- How comfortable are you with your knowledge and use of ongoing assessment in your mathematics program?
- What learning opportunities are available to improve your knowledge and use of assessment to guide instruction and improve learning?

FOR FAMILIES

- What questions or issues does this message raise for you to discuss with your son or daughter, the teacher, or school leaders?
- What discussions have you had (or can you have) with teachers and school leaders about the time and value of any systemwide or schoolwide testing in the mathematics program?
- How can you use results of your daughter's or son's math tests to talk about what she or he has learned?
- As you look at daily work and the results of assessments, what are some constructive ways you can communicate to the teacher any areas where you think your son or daughter might still be struggling?

FOR LEADERS AND POLICY MAKERS

- How does this message reinforce or challenge policies and decisions you have made or are considering?
- If you have a system of interim testing in place, or are considering such a system, how can you ensure that the potential benefits will outweigh the likely costs?
- How can you help teachers improve their knowledge of assessment as a tool to improve student learning?

RELATED MESSAGES

- Message 19, "Embracing Accountability," describes the role of accountability in improving mathematics learning and takes a practical look at large-scale assessment.

- Message 12, "Beyond Band-Aids and Bandwagons," looks at educational fads and considers how lasting change can be made.

- Message 35, "Putting Testing in Perspective," considers how teachers can become better at using and balancing various types of assessments in support of student learning.

FURTHER READING

- The Role of Interim Assessments in a Comprehensive Assessment System: A Policy Brief (Perie, Marion, Gong, and Wurtzel 2007) lays out a clear case around issues in using interim assessments, including a discussion of potential benefits, problems, and considerations when choosing to use such instruments.

- *The Mismeasure of Man* (Gould 1996) is a scathing indictment of standardized tests and the assumptions underlying the "bell-shaped curve."

- *Mathematics Assessment: Myths, Models, Good Questions, and Practical Suggestions* (Stenmark 1991) is a great resource for teachers in designing and administering a variety of classroom assessments. It includes sample items and scoring rubrics.

12

Beyond Band-Aids and Bandwagons

MAKING REAL CHANGE

There is little argument today that education can be better than it is, and that mathematics teaching, in particular, needs significant attention. Many schools and school systems are in the process of undertaking efforts to improve mathematics teaching and learning. But a look at schools across the nation shows that some of our attempts to implement improvement fall short of what is needed. Too much of this work falls into one of two categories—Band-Aids and bandwagons.

Band-Aids

Band-Aids is a label we can use to describe those efforts that address an issue in a piecemeal fashion or undertake a short-term solution. It includes approaches that seem to prevent wounds from getting worse but do not really target the source of the problem. For example, some school systems or states have chosen to limit class size or mandate how much time should be spent teaching particular subjects or topics within a subject. Yet without fundamentally changing how instructional time is used with students, both of these efforts are unlikely to make a positive difference in student learning. If a teacher lectures to thirty students or to twenty-seven students or even to twenty-four students, the students are not necessarily any more likely to learn than those in a larger class if nothing else changes. And students might receive sixty minutes of mathematics instruction rather than forty-five minutes, but if that additional time is not spent engaged in doing meaningful mathematics, gains are likely to be small or short-lived.

Likewise, a state or local mandate to eliminate the practice of social promotion does not ensure that all students will learn. This Band-Aid may address some of the problems caused by moving students along without any consideration of what they have learned, but it doesn't take into account more serious concerns related to why students have not achieved or, more important, how they will make up lost ground. We have decades of evidence showing that most students retained in the same grade eventually drop out before graduating from high school (Jimerson 2001).

Other popular Band-Aids include adopting new textbooks, changing school leaders, adding a few conceptual questions to lesson plans or instructional materials, or asking teachers to attend short-term staff development sessions related to a particular issue or approach. If these actions are undertaken in isolation, they are likely to simply distract teachers and students, rather than transform how teachers teach or what students learn.

Bandwagons

Too often, policy makers choose to adopt the latest educational fad that promises to fix whatever is wrong with a school, a program, an instructional approach, or *those* students. These decisions are often driven by passion or desperation to improve how teachers teach and how students learn. Although we all feel the urgent need to improve mathematics performance, we must be careful about recklessly jumping on a bandwagon.

Education, especially mathematics education, has sometimes been criticized for not implementing research-based programs. In general, I find this to be an unfounded criticism. A number of excellent programs are built on principles and practices validated by an extensive base of research about how children learn mathematics and how we can teach it. But the criticism is quite valid in terms of our tendency in education to adopt the next big thing, the quick fix. Too often policy makers or school leaders hear about something that appears to be working in another school or state and decide it is just the thing they need to improve their students' test scores. Unfortunately, what seems to work somewhere else may not have any long-term evidence of effectiveness over time, may rely on the personal charisma of one or two teachers or leaders, may not be scalable beyond a few classrooms or a single school, or may not be based on sound instructional practice or what we know about learning.

In recent years, most teachers have seen more than one bandwagon or fad pass by. A long list of programs that became popular rather quickly might include objectives-based instruction, standards-based teaching, benchmark testing, data-driven decision making, individualized instruction, effective schools, assertive discipline, the small schools movement, charter schools, the 5E model, the seven-step lesson plan, formative assessment, mastery learning, early college high schools, and much more.

Like some of the Band-Aids mentioned earlier, not all bandwagons are bad ideas or lack supporting evidence. Just as some Band-Aids address urgent equity issues, like repairing school facilities or replacing outdated textbooks, some bandwagons or movements in American education are based on serious work done by teachers, leaders, and researchers and are well supported for long-term sustainability. If a teacher with fewer students in class and more class time is able to provide students more opportunities to engage in rich mathematics tasks, struggle with challenging problems, and interact in constructive ways with the mathematics, then this work is more than a Band-Aid. If a district implements an innovative program to provide support for students who are falling behind in ways that advance the students through previous learning and onto grade level, then doing away with social promotion may be a good step. If school administrators and teachers use data that include more than test scores, such as extended samples of student work and qualitative information from students and teachers, then basing decisions on data may be an important undertaking, and not just the next bandwagon.

What Can We Do?

Often schools get caught up in adopting something just enough to use its label, rather than implementing the critical attributes or underlying research-based philosophy intended by that label. Not only can such a superficial implementation shortchange students, but the label itself can sometimes ignite opposition. This alone is one reason for leaders to consider avoiding labels in favor of description. Instead of saying that the school system is adopting *reform mathematics*, why not talk about building a balanced program of conceptual understanding, problem solving, and skill development? The district or school initiative need not be labeled with the title of a controversial textbook, but might instead be discussed as simply the district or school mathematics program. This kind of language can help teachers within the school as well as community members outside of the school understand the components and philosophy of what is being adopted rather than reacting to a label they may have seen elsewhere. To make a change that is positive, real, and lasting, consider a few other basic steps, described below.

ENGAGE THE STAKEHOLDERS

Consider involving early in the decision-making process those who will implement a new program, as well as other stakeholders, and keep them engaged throughout the adoption of the program.

DO THE HOMEWORK

If possible, look for a sound research base (different from marketing statistics) for any program being adopted, as well as some evidence that it can be implemented on a manageable scale and is likely to help students both now and in future years, or at least look for a research-based instructional approach.

INVEST UP FRONT

Be idealistic, but also realistic, in terms of what *can* be done and what *must* be done within a reasonable time frame, and provide adequate preparation and support prior to implementation.

BACK UP THE INVESTMENT

Develop varying levels of support for both teachers and students that may evolve over time during implementation.

STAY THE COURSE

To the extent possible, make a long-term commitment to support the implementation, recognizing that some course correction along the way may be necessary, but commit to not jumping ship too soon.

In an era of extreme accountability based on student test scores, many leaders and policy makers are understandably eager to do something immediate and tangible to make a positive difference. We must be careful, however, that the something is not just a quick fix or a potential distraction that overrules our common sense and thoughtful practice.

Reflection and Discussion

FOR TEACHERS

- What issues or challenges does this message raise for you? In what ways do you agree with or disagree with the main points of the message?
- What Band-Aids or bandwagons might you be implementing or considering for your classroom or school? How might you rethink ideas that might not be well grounded or practical? How can you further support those efforts with potential for success?

FOR FAMILIES

- What questions or issues does this message raise for you to discuss with your son or daughter, the teacher, or school leaders?
- How can you make teachers, leaders, and policy makers aware of your interest to be part of the decision-making process?
- How can you expand your understanding of school programs and instructional issues so that you can provide the best input possible?

(continued)

FOR LEADERS AND POLICY MAKERS

- How does this message reinforce or challenge policies and decisions you have made or are considering?
- What Band-Aids or bandwagons might you be implementing or considering for your school(s) and how might you either rethink or build adequate support for such efforts?
- As you think about new directions you might like to undertake, how willing are you to commit to building an infrastructure that will increase the likelihood of lasting success?
- What stakeholders will you need to involve in forthcoming program decisions and what form might that involvement take?

RELATED MESSAGES

- Message 4, "Good Old Days," looks back at several waves of reform in school mathematics.
- Message 13, "Seek First to Understand," calls for collaboration across professional communities in planning for educational improvements.

FURTHER READING

- *Adding It Up: Helping Children Learn Mathematics* (Kilpatrick, Swafford, and Findell 2001) is an important resource for teachers and leaders that describes the research behind effective mathematics teaching and learning.
- *The New Meaning of Educational Change* (Fullan 2007b) is a discussion of how change happens in educational settings and the role of the change facilitator.
- *Implementing Change: Patterns, Principles, and Potholes* (Hall and Hord 2005) presents an analysis of the change process and recommendations by well-respected experts in educational change.
- *Mathematics and Science for a Change: How to Design, Implement, and Sustain High-Quality Professional Development* (Weiss and Pasley 2009) presents a research-based discussion of effective mathematics and science professional learning programs to improve teaching and learning.
- *The Fifth Discipline: The Art and Practice of the Learning Organization* (Senge 2006) proposes principles for organizations based on learning, teamwork, and vision, all of which are based on concepts of learning that can and should provide guidance for educational systems.

13

Seek First to Understand

COLLABORATING TO IMPROVE MATHEMATICS
TEACHING AND LEARNING

I n his bestseller *The 7 Habits of Highly Effective People* (2004), Stephen R. Covey states that effective people "seek first to understand, then to be understood." In a discussion of this habit, Covey notes that we sometimes complain that someone else does not understand our point of view, and he challenges us to consider trying to understand the other person first as a bridge.

In school settings, understanding, communicating, and working together across communities can help us generate better ways of providing every student with the highest-quality mathematics education possible. Students, in particular, benefit when mathematics educators work collaboratively with mathematicians, scientists, policy makers, school administrators, businesspeople, and families of students. Likewise, in their efforts to improve mathematics education, it is crucial that these groups stay connected to those who work with students on a daily basis.

Five Ways to Understand Each Other

Mathematicians can help educators stay focused on mathematical content as we work to improve our mathematics teaching. Educators can help mathematicians understand that learning and proficiency can be developed in many ways. Mathematics education researchers can offer insights that help mathematicians understand why certain approaches may be instructionally preferable to others that seem more mathematically defensible. Policy makers and businesspeople can help educators realize the importance of documenting student achievement and can raise awareness about the future that students face. Families can give those who are working to improve mathematics education a more complete view of students' particular needs and challenges.

Building on the commonalities and respecting important differences within these and other points of view can help us shape a stronger vision for school mathematics. We must reach out within and across our communities if we are going to improve students' mathematical learning. As we make these connections, the following guidelines may prove useful.

1. ACKNOWLEDGE DIFFERENCES OF OPINION

Not everyone within a community thinks the same way. Among mathematicians, there are as many differences of opinion as there are among educators; the same is true among policy makers, among parents, and among administrators. Discussions about how to improve mathematics teaching inevitably involve more than two sides with two distinct points of view.

2. CLARIFY FOR UNDERSTANDING

As you listen, let the other person know that you have heard not only the words but also the underlying concerns and ideas being communicated. In particular, clarify specialized language that you may use or understand differently from others, such as *curriculum* or *standard*. Describe with examples instead of using a label (such as *constructivist* or *traditional*), especially when the label may communicate an extreme or loaded point of view that may or may not represent what you or someone else is trying to say.

3. SUGGEST RATHER THAN CRITICIZE

No program, test, or classroom will ever be perfect, whether it reflects what you recommend or something different. Focus on constructive suggestions for what can be done instead of focusing on errors or shortcomings of what is currently being done.

4. NOTICE DIFFERENCES IN COMMUNICATION STYLE

Trust among collaborators evolves over time. Some mathematicians and scientists argue with each other as a routine part of their academic discourse. Some businesspeople and policy makers want short, direct, immediate solutions to problems. Some educators want to broaden discussions to include factors beyond mathematical content. Some people strive for consensus and others thrive on opposition. Recognizing and adjusting to such differences in style can help ensure that both those sending messages and those receiving them do not become disengaged or offended by someone else's approach.

5. CONSIDER BALANCE AND EMPHASIS

Avoid advocating for absolutes or extremes. What you support does not have to be an all-or-nothing proposition. Likewise, what someone else suggests may not be absolute. Perhaps more important than whether to include a particular topic in the math program, for example, are issues of how to engage students in learning the topic, how students can connect it to other knowledge, and how students will develop the depth of learning and the methods of thinking necessary to solve problems.

Moving Forward

In our work to improve school mathematics, we must understand and respect the voices of mathematicians, educators, and students. To inform and ground our discussions, we must also understand and respect the perspectives of parents, policy makers, and the public at large. Understanding does not mean giving up what we believe; it is not realistic to think that we all can or should agree. Healthy differences of opinion are not only inevitable but also valuable, especially when we are committed to learning from each other with an eye to our shared goal of better mathematics for all students.

So let us meet together, talk with each other, listen to each other, and learn from each other. Let us seek to understand as we work side by side. Let us voice our differences constructively, come to consensus where possible, and agree to constructively disagree when necessary. Let us not make the status quo a life sentence for our students because of our inability to communicate. Let us, rather, commit to the goal of constantly improving what we are doing. Understanding each other is where we begin.

Reflection and Discussion

FOR TEACHERS

- What issues or challenges does this message raise for you? In what ways do you agree with or disagree with the main points of the message?
- What do you know about mathematics teaching that you learned from someone who has knowledge or a background that is different than yours?
- How can you reach out to parents or others in terms of finding out what is most important to them?

FOR FAMILIES

- What questions or issues does this message raise for you to discuss with your son or daughter, the teacher, or school leaders?

(continued)

- What opportunities do you have to interact with teachers, school leaders, and policy makers regarding issues related to your daughter's or son's education?
- How can you learn more about what teachers and school leaders value and what decisions they are making?

FOR LEADERS AND POLICY MAKERS

- How does this message reinforce or challenge policies and decisions you have made or are considering?
- What collaborations can you form that might support improving the way that mathematics is taught in your school or district?
- How can we overcome barriers that interfere with working across communities?

RELATED MESSAGES

- Message 26, "Beyond Pockets of Wonderfulness," calls for collaboration and articulation among colleagues and across grades.
- Message 27, "A Math Message to Families," reminds us of the importance of reaching out to families and communities.
- The Afterword, "The Sum of the Parts Is Greater than Some of the Parts," calls us to work together toward improving mathematics teaching and learning at all levels.

FURTHER READING

- *The 7 Habits of Highly Effective People* (Covey 2004) describes habits common to many effective people and makes recommendations for effective communication and understanding.
- *Failure Is Not an Option™: Six Principles That Guide Student Achievement in High-Performing Schools* (Blankstein 2004) provides inspiration and practical ideas on transforming schools systemically, including the importance of collaboration and engagement of the broader community.
- The Vermont Mathematics Initiative (www.uvm.edu/~vmi/) is a long-standing and highly recognized professional learning program for developing K–8 mathematics leaders, building on a powerful collaboration of mathematicians, educators, classroom teachers, leaders, and the broader community.

14

Balance Is Basic

A 21ST-CENTURY VIEW OF A BALANCED
MATHEMATICS PROGRAM

E ven though much has changed about the nature of mathematics
students need and the depth of mathematical thinking called for
today, the fundamentals of a balanced mathematics program
remain much the same as they have for years. Essentially, we want all
students to

1. *make sense of math:* understand mathematical concepts and ideas
   so they can make sense of the mathematics they do;

2. *do math:* know mathematical facts and perform mathematical
   skills; and

3. *use math:* solve a wide range of problems in various contexts by
   reasoning, thinking, and applying the mathematics they have
   learned.

However, even though we may agree on the broad categories, arguments abound over what exactly each of these pieces comprises and
over the relative weight and importance of each. People are often
quick to categorize opposing views, applying labels like *back to basics*
or *reform*. For example, some people fear that students in a program they
label as *reform* might not receive the emphasis on computation they see
in more traditional programs. Others fear that if students focus exces-
sively on computational procedures without adequate understanding, their
proficiency will be superficial and short-lived. Still others argue that
if students cannot solve particular types of problems, ranging from
routine word problems to complex problems with no known solution,
they will not be prepared for the world outside of school. It's time to
get past these arguments, move beyond the labels, and look at what we
mean when we discuss the components of a balanced mathematics
program.

Making Sense of Math: Conceptual Understanding

Without conceptual understanding, learning skills is meaningless. Many students acquire skills (with varying degrees of success), only to find that they lack the understanding that would help them apply what they have learned. For example, in solving a problem involving fractions, a student may know the rules: how to *go straight across* (when multiplying fractions), *turn upside down and then go straight across* (when dividing fractions), or *find a common denominator* (for adding and subtracting fractions with unlike denominators). But what if a student doesn't understand the operations the rules represent or how they relate to the problem at hand? In such a case, every encounter with fractions results in a guessing game: Which strategy should I use? Even students skilled in procedures will be lost if they don't understand the meanings of the operations well enough to determine which procedure might be appropriate.

On the other hand, if a student has a strong understanding of what a fraction represents, and also a solid understanding of what it means to add, subtract, multiply, or divide, the act of adding fractions becomes far less complex—and less of a guessing game. Students with both skills and conceptual understanding are likely to more easily form mental images of mathematical concepts they might recognize in problem situations. As a result, a student can see in her mind how to put the fractions together for the situation a problem presents. She has no reason to be tempted to choose an incorrect rule because she knows what operation(s) might be helpful and which procedure(s) could therefore be useful.

Doing Math: Skills, Facts, and Procedures

Understanding mathematical ideas and concepts is powerful. But without also knowing how to perform the necessary skills, understanding alone is insufficient. If taught well, proficiency with mathematical skills can contribute to mathematical understanding. Both components—skills and understanding—are especially critical when tackling challenging problems.

In today's highly technological world, there is debate as to the extent of computational skills a student needs. We all want students to know how to add, subtract, multiply, and divide whole numbers, decimals, and fractions for both positive and negative numbers. But we must also be realistic about when students should be able to compute mentally, when they should perform computation with a pencil, and when they might rely on a calculator or other technological tool. It may be that being able to use a pencil and paper to do a long-division exercise with a four-digit divisor is not as critical as it once was. Perhaps students have as much proficiency with the tool of division as they need if they can perform pencil-and-paper division exercises through two-digit divisors, for example, and longer or more complex division exercises with a calculator. Students might be expected to estimate results of most division exercises mentally, and even determine exact answers to certain types of basic division exercises in their heads. These shifts don't make computational skills unimportant. Rather, the shifts help us make room for the rest of a balanced program that includes the solid understanding described earlier and what is arguably the most critical feature of a balanced mathematics program—problem solving.

Using Math: Problem Solving

If students have a sound understanding of mathematical ideas and some level of skills mastery, they have certainly gained important mathematical knowledge. But there is a difference in knowledge that is useful for an exercise in a mathematics textbook and knowledge that is needed to solve authentic, multifaceted problems in other contexts. For a student's knowledge of mathematics to truly come together, we must also focus on the third component of a balanced mathematics program: problem solving. Solving problems requires that students consider the many tools they have acquired and select which one(s) might be useful for a wide range of problems at varying levels of complexity and in many different contexts. Solving problems is the most visible indicator of how well a student has assimilated the knowledge he has acquired and how comprehensive a set of mathematical tools the student has built.

Beyond the Big Three

What constitutes a balanced mathematics program has been the subject of significant work in mathematics education for more than thirty years. The National Council of Supervisors of Mathematics released a statement about *new basics* in 1977, supporting the teaching of an expanded set of basic skills that calls for (among other things) a focus on problem solving and the incorporation of appropriate uses of technology. Shortly after, in 1980, the National Council of Teachers of Mathematics (NCTM) produced its call to action entitled *An Agenda for Action*, which outlines priorities for school mathematics. These priorities center on problem solving and call for the use of tools like calculators and computers. NCTM took an even bolder step at the end of the same decade in launching their landmark publication, *Curriculum and Evaluation Standards for School Mathematics* in 1989, in which a comprehensive mathematics program for grades K–12 is outlined, elaborating what mathematical content and processes all students need. In 2000, NCTM further refined the agenda with the publication of *Principles and Standards for School Mathematics*. All of these publications reinforce the importance of a balanced program of conceptual understanding, skills, and problem solving, while also reflecting shifts in emphasis within each of these. These publications also recognize the growing importance of what we might consider the connective tissue of a coherent mathematics program—mathematical habits of mind, flexible thinking skills, and strong quantitative reasoning. These critical abilities mirror the twenty-first-century skills now called for in report after report from the business and policy sectors. In continuing to expand our thinking about priorities we now realize the importance of helping students show or represent mathematical situations in different ways (using words, objects, pictures, graphs, tables, numbers, and symbols). As students move fluently among these, they solidify their understanding and, potentially, their proficiency. We also now recognize how important it is for students to communicate the mathematics they know. Presenting or explaining an idea or a solution to a problem can help a student reinforce what he knows or, alternatively, can help him realize (and correct) errors in his thinking.

In *Adding It Up* (Kilpatrick, Swafford, and Findell 2001) and its partner booklet, *Helping Children Learn Mathematics* (Findell and Swafford 2002), the authors use the metaphor of a rope to define mathematical knowledge. The five strands of the rope represent understanding, computing, applying, reasoning, and engaging. The first three of these strands reflect the three components of balanced mathematics discussed in this message. The last two—reasoning (and the various types of mathematical thinking associated with it) and engaging (including habits of mind such as persistence and a willingness to take on a challenging problem)—reflect the connective tissue previously described.

What Can We Do?

Whether you prefer the metaphor of a rope or the notion of three building blocks with connective tissue, the fact is that all students need it all. They need a balanced program of understanding, skills, and problem solving and they need a flexible set of thinking and reasoning tools they can call on to pull all of these pieces together. From a mathematical standpoint, each piece needs to support the other pieces. Students need to connect understanding with doing and using mathematics. They need to use tools of communication, representation, reasoning, and thinking to make mathematics useful beyond the classroom. Whenever we omit part of a balanced mathematics program for any student, whatever is left falls apart. Whether intentional or unintentional, whether guided by good intentions or low expectations, whether targeted at one student or at a group of students, the student without a balanced and comprehensive knowledge of mathematics has no foundation upon which to build future mathematical success.

It only makes sense, from a mathematical perspective and from a moral and ethical perspective, for schools to absolutely commit to providing all students a deep, connected, comprehensive, balanced mathematics program that will allow every student to meet the increasing demands of twenty-first-century society and the workplace.

Reflection and Discussion

FOR TEACHERS

- What issues or challenges does this message raise for you? In what ways do you agree with or disagree with the main points of the message?

- How can you connect the skills students learn with their understanding of what the skills represent?

- How can you help students develop mathematical habits of mind such as the willingness to take on challenging tasks or the perseverance to spend time on a hard problem?

- Which components of a balanced mathematics program do you feel you are most effectively providing for your students? Which components might you more effectively target in the future?

FOR FAMILIES

- What questions or issues does this message raise for you to discuss with your son or daughter, the teacher, or school leaders?

- How can you work together with your daughter or son to communicate how important it is to understand or make sense of the procedures she or he is learning?

- What messages can you convey to your son or daughter about the importance of connecting the pieces of mathematics being learned? Make a point to ask your son or daughter to explain to you a skill he or she is learning and how it connects or relates to the learning of the previous week.

- In what ways might you ask your daughter or son to show you another way to think about a problem or situation she or he is working on? Consider the use of pictures, models, a table, and so on.

(continued)

FOR LEADERS AND POLICY MAKERS

- How does this message reinforce or challenge policies and decisions you have made or are considering?
- How balanced is your mathematics curriculum, and how well do your textbooks or instructional materials reflect a comprehensive and connected blend of understanding, skills, and problem solving? How well does your program incorporate the critical connective tissue that includes reasoning and mathematical thinking? Addressing these issues in the curriculum will likely call for careful study by knowledgeable mathematics teachers or other mathematics educators.
- How can you help your teachers teach in ways that help students develop mathematical habits of mind?

RELATED MESSAGES

- Message 4, "Good Old Days," looks back at several waves of mathematics reform that included differing views of what is basic.
- Message 1, "Math for a Flattening World," makes a case for changing how schools prepare students for a twenty-first-century world.
- Message 20, "Putting Calculators in Their Place," considers the role of calculators when teaching computation and discusses how much technology is appropriate in a math classroom.

FURTHER READING

- *Helping Children Learn Mathematics* (Findell and Swafford 2002), the partner document to *Adding It Up* (Kilpatrick, Swafford, and Findell 2001), is a short booklet for a broad audience of readers that highlights the rope model described in this message and presents clear recommendations for teachers, families, and leaders to improve mathematics teaching and support mathematics learning at school and at home.
- *A Research Companion to Principles and Standards for School Mathematics* (Kilpatrick, Martin, and Schifter 2003) summarizes the research behind the recommendations for a balanced mathematics program as described in *Principles and Standards for School Mathematics* (NCTM 2000).
- *Elementary and Middle School Mathematics: Teaching Developmentally* (Van de Walle, Karp, and Bay-Williams 2009) is a widely recognized elementary and middle school mathematics

methods textbook for preservice teachers that includes a beautiful development of numbers and operations and also comprehensively develops other topics in a well-balanced mathematics program.

- *Sensible Mathematics: A Guide for School Leaders* (Leinwand 2000) presents an overview of the landscape of mathematics reform, including some of the terms used in discussions about mathematics reform and provides practical guidelines for improving a mathematics program at the local level or on a larger scale.

- *Principles and Standards for School Mathematics* (National Council of Teachers of Mathematics 2000) refines, clarifies, and extends NCTM's landmark 1989 standards and describes the richness and depth of a comprehensive and balanced mathematics program.

- "Math Homework Is Due Tomorrow—How Can I Help?" (NCTM 2006b) is a downloadable brochure on NCTM's Family Resources page (http://nctm.org/resources/families) that helps families make sense of the math they see coming home from school.

- NCTM's Family Resources page (http://nctm.org/resources/families) also includes links to three documents that answer questions about the changing nature of mathematics today, calculator use in math classrooms, and the use of timed skills tests.

www   This message is also available in printable format at
      mathsolutions.com/fasterisntsmarter.

15 Less Can Be More

RETHINKING THE SPIRAL CURRICULUM

A mile wide and an inch deep. This arguably well-earned label for the United States math curriculum has stuck for more than a decade, from at least the time the results of the Third International Mathematics and Science Study (TIMSS) were published (TIMSS International Study Center 1995). The label describes the uniquely American phenomenon of breaking down mathematics knowledge and skills into long lists of small pieces of knowledge for teachers to teach and students to learn. The metaphor calls attention to dramatic differences between this approach used to organize school mathematics in the United States and more focused approaches used by high-performing countries like Singapore, Japan, and Finland.

A Redundant Spiral

The United States has a historical affinity for organizing mathematics content using a *spiral curriculum,* in which students revisit topics each year, allegedly extending in each grade what they have learned in the grade before. The premise is that if students develop a strong foundation one year, they can build on and expand that foundation the next year. In the United States, however, that intended expansion has too often degenerated into redundancy—doing nearly the same thing every year as the year before, but perhaps with one more digit or an uglier denominator.

For many years, in the name of a well-balanced math curriculum, we have tried, beginning in kindergarten, to teach students a little bit about everything there is to know about mathematics—not only numbers and how to put them together but also basic notions of shape, measurement, data, and algebraic thinking. In first grade we revisit these same topics as we teach students a little bit more about everything there is to know about mathematics, and likewise in each grade throughout elementary and middle school. Sometimes it seems that each year we teach essentially the same things as the year before, but with larger or more difficult numbers. More and more educators and researchers are beginning to question how much difference there is in asking students to subtract two four-digit numbers one year and two five-digit numbers the next. This creeping redundancy results in every grade level being crowded with too much content. Teachers are expected to cover a long list of topics and rarely have the time they need to teach any topic in depth. Worse, students become numb to mathematical topics they have seen many times before, potentially killing their interest in mathematics and lowering their motivation to learn anything well the first time. Students eventually come to think, "It's no big deal if I don't get it this time—it'll be back next year!" Each year teachers observe that many students have not learned the previous year's content well, probably for lack of adequate time on any given concept or skill. So it should come as no surprise that many teachers believe that the mathematics program should essentially repeat most of what has already been taught.

The issue is not whether it is important to teach all the strands or themes of mathematics. It is absolutely important to do so as part of a balanced mathematics program. Students need to develop the seeds of algebra and geometry, as well as the management of data throughout their mathematics experience, beginning in the earliest grades. The issue instead is whether we have to teach something about every important idea within those strands at every grade, as if filling in all the boxes in all the rows and columns of a pre-K–8 or pre-K–12 matrix of grades and mathematical strands. Do we have the time to cover more and more small topics at the expense of learning deep mathematics? Does it work for students to try to learn long lists of small and isolated bits of knowledge? Might we be willing to let students tackle bigger chunks of learning than we thought they could handle in the past?

To Review or Not to Review

It is a natural tendency for teachers to want students to remember everything they have learned (or that we wish they had learned). If students don't seem to remember something right away, it's also a natural tendency for teachers to want to review it. But review can be handled in ways that don't undermine new learning. Families can help with reviewing computational facts and skills, both written and mental, that we want students to keep fresh in their minds. Teachers can help identify what is most important for families to work on with their students at any point in time. In school, review can be integrated into new content being learned in mathematics or other subject areas. And whenever and wherever review is done, we should remember that a little review at fairly frequent intervals can serve students extremely well and alleviate the need for excessive repetition that often leads to students losing interest in mathematics.

Focusing to Learn

In the process of putting review in its place and reining in the out-of-control spiral, we might be able to work with our colleagues at other grade levels to determine at which one or two grade level(s) the emphasis on a certain topic might take place. In doing so, we can eliminate some of the small bits of this repetitive knowledge we currently expect of students at other grade levels. Instead, perhaps we can help students connect what they are doing to bigger ideas of mathematics. We can support students in turning the small things they are learning into a larger, more cohesive and useful body of knowledge. Surveys by the Center for the Study of Mathematics Curriculum (Reys 2006), addressing state mathematics standards, show that there's a wide range in the number of small pieces of mathematics learning that different states expect of students at each grade. In some states, a fourth grader, for example, might be asked to learn seventy or more objectives, expectations, or bits of knowledge. Many of those bits involve small extensions of previously learned material, such as the notion of performing a computation with numbers one digit larger than the year before.

This trend is beginning to shift. In the wake of the National Council of Teachers of Mathematics' *Curriculum Focal Points for Prekindergarten through Grade 8 Mathematics: A Quest for Coherence* (2006), several states are revising their mathematics standards, with a growing tendency toward focusing on fewer topics at each grade level. The goal is to help students learn well the mathematics they study. When teachers teach efficiently for meaning, proficiency, and problem solving, and when students learn with depth, fluency, and understanding, they do not need to revisit the same topics in the same way year after year. Rather, they can accomplish what the spiral curriculum originally intended—they can build on what they know as they go on to expand their learning with new mathematics.

What Can We Do?

Simply covering less material is not enough. In today's high-accountability, rapidly changing world, students need to learn much more than ever before if they are to be prepared for success. But when we eliminate repetition from grade to grade, and then teach in meaningful, focused, and efficient ways that deepen student understanding, less can be more. Covering fewer topics can allow students to understand more of what they study. Teachers can capitalize on the time gained to teach rich, engaging content that develops meaningful ideas and high-level mathematical reasoning. Students with a deep understanding of fractions, for example, will become comfortable with what fractions mean and how fractions relate to each other, and they will be able to use fractions to represent a variety of contexts, situations, and problems. These students are likely to be able to move smoothly at the appropriate time to proficiently learn how to add, subtract, multiply, and divide fractions with lasting understanding and without the need for later review and remediation, even when they encounter an ugly denominator. Teaching thoroughly and well the first time is always an investment, yielding big dividends as students go on to learn higher-level and more complex content the next year instead of ending up in an endless spiral of redundancy.

Reflection and Discussion

FOR TEACHERS

- What issues or challenges does this message raise for you? In what ways do you agree with or disagree with the main points of the message?

- How well do your state's standards provide for teaching in depth, rather than teaching small increments of previously learned material?

- What opportunities can you find to work with colleagues at other grade levels to determine where there might be unnecessary overlap from grade to grade? How can you work together to identify the highest priority topics or skills for each grade?

- How can you call on families or outside programs to provide some of the review you might want so that you can devote more time to new content?

FOR FAMILIES

- What questions or issues does this message raise for you to discuss with your son or daughter, the teacher, or school leaders?

- How can you help your daughter or son review and extend what is learned in school, especially for computation? Can you provide some of the review and practice teachers might not have time to do, keeping in mind that a little bit of review goes a long way?

(continued)

- In what ways might you work with the teacher so that you know what are the most important topics, skills, and ideas you can reinforce outside of school?

FOR LEADERS AND POLICY MAKERS

- How does this message reinforce or challenge policies and decisions you have made or are considering?
- How well do your state standards prioritize mathematical content and minimize redundancy so that teachers have adequate time for in-depth teaching on new topics?
- What kinds of support (or permission) can you provide teachers so that they can put review in proper perspective and spend more time on identified priorities?

RELATED MESSAGES

- Message 34, "Forgetting Isn't Forever," reminds us that just because a student doesn't immediately recall something, we shouldn't assume the student doesn't know it or couldn't retrieve it with a brief reminder or appropriate stimulus.
- Message 16, "Hard Arithmetic Isn't Deep Mathematics," considers the need to look beyond lengthier computational skills to provide students with a comprehensive mathematics program.
- Message 18, "Faster Isn't Smarter," considers the preoccupation we sometimes have with timed tests as a measure of mathematical knowledge.

FURTHER READING

- *Splintered Vision* (Schmidt, McKnight, and Raizen 1997) looks at the redundancy in the American mathematics curriculum compared to mathematics programs in other countries.
- *The Intended Mathematics Curriculum as Represented in State-Level Curriculum Standards: Consensus or Confusion?* (Reys 2006) surveys state standards to look at various features of the standards, including the number of pieces of learning, or student expectations, called for in various states (current as of the date of the surveys).

16 Hard Arithmetic Isn't Deep Mathematics

TEACHING MORE THAN COMPUTATION

The kind of mathematics that adults need today goes far beyond what once was sufficient. In the past, it might have been enough to know how to read, write, and do the basic measurement and arithmetic they might use in everyday life. In the past, it might also have been enough for students who were going to college to master a set of algebraic tools that enabled them to enroll in higher-level mathematics or science courses. But today's world is characterized by rapid change and pervasive technology. More of our students are likely to participate in some kind of postsecondary education than ever before, and the jobs in demand now didn't even exist five years ago.

In this environment, how do we raise the bar on the mathematical proficiency that we expect of all students, regardless of what path they might pursue after high school? What kind of mathematics do all students need? And how likely is it that all students can achieve the goals that we set?

The Meaning of Depth

We can begin to raise the bar on mathematical proficiency by eliminating some of the endless repetition in our curriculum. We can choose to focus on fewer topics at each grade level, distributing important mathematical ideas across the grades rather than superficially teaching a little bit about many topics in each grade. In this way, students have a chance to learn mathematics deeply, so that they don't need to be taught the same topics year after year. Depth means that students know a lot about multiplication before they deal with an algorithm for performing multiplication. Depth means that when we introduce fractions, we teach students what fractions represent, in what kinds of situations fractions might be useful, how fractions compare to one another, how they relate to what students know about whole numbers, what it means when the numerator or denominator increases or decreases, and so on. Depth means that before students confront the rules for operating with fractions—what students remember as going straight across, turning upside down, or finding a common denominator—we ensure that they know a lot about fractions and a lot about operations. Depth means that when students study ratios, they go well beyond solving proportions to recognize and utilize proportional relationships in many apparently different settings (like scale drawings, percent increase, sales tax, maps, multiplicative growth and even early notions of mathematical functions), in the process helping them connect mathematical ideas from prekindergarten through grade 12. Depth also means that students earning credit for a high school algebra course not only know how to solve equations but also have built a strong base of algebraic thinking and have developed a diverse set of algebraic tools with which they can represent, model, and solve many kinds of problems—both within and outside of mathematics.

WHAT DEPTH IS NOT

Depth does not mean making all students master arithmetic procedures faster, earlier, or with more digits. A school system whose standards include the mastery of fraction operations earlier than the standards of another system does not necessarily have a more rigorous curriculum. Depth does not mean narrowing our curriculum to numbers and operations alone at the expense of measurement, geometry, and data analysis, where those numbers and operations are actually used and where students learn critical non-numerical ways of thinking as well. Depth does not necessarily mean more exercises. Focusing on more or longer arithmetic procedures at the expense of deeper explorations and problem solving is not the same as raising our expectations for all students. And depth does not have to be painful or boring.

WHERE DEPTH IS SHALLOW

Some of the students least likely to experience deep mathematics are those identified as members of special populations. Students whose first language is not English, students who have learning disabilities, students with physical limitations, students in special education programs, and students who lag behind for whatever reason too often receive the narrowest mathematics teaching we have to offer, usually limited to numerical facts and procedures. Often, compassionate teachers determine that students who have difficulty dealing with language should be limited to working on strictly numerical exercises involving no words. Consequently, many of these students never see a challenging problem or an engaging context simply because their teachers have determined that it would be too frustrating for them. We cannot be surprised when such students perform poorly on tests of higher-level thinking if their experience has never prepared them to think. These students, especially, need strong support and nurturing that goes well beyond arithmetic, even hard arithmetic.

What Can We Do?

While visiting schools, I have found wonderful examples of classrooms where students are learning mathematics in depth. In these classrooms, students experience mathematics taught with strong understanding. They are actively engaged in meaningful and challenging mathematics that may include but go well beyond arithmetic. In these schools, the door is open for every student to meet rigorous mathematics expectations, and students are naturally more engaged in the problems they see and the mathematics they learn.

Depth is not the same as hard arithmetic. Depth comes when students get it. This means that students need to see the contexts in which mathematical ideas arise, need to wrestle with those ideas in problems that take some time to solve, and need opportunities to represent and communicate what they learn.

If we define our mathematics curriculum—the standards that states adopt and test—in ways that focus on students knowing, understanding, and using mathematics, and not just doing hard arithmetic, we can achieve this depth. If we also make shifts in how we structure our classrooms and engage our students, we can ensure that all students can achieve the high goals we set as we raise the bar on what it means to know and be able to use mathematics well.

Reflection and Discussion

FOR TEACHERS

- What issues or challenges does this message raise for you? In what ways do you agree with or disagree with the main points of the message?
- If your state or school system is shifting its curriculum and standards toward deep mathematics rather than hard arithmetic, how can your teaching support this shift? If the curriculum and standards are not changing, in what ways can you help your students make a shift toward deep mathematics?

(continued)

- What will it take to help all students meet high standards for rich mathematics? What barriers might keep students from reaching these standards, and how can you tackle these barriers?

FOR FAMILIES

- What questions or issues does this message raise for you to discuss with your son or daughter, the teacher, or school leaders?
- In what ways can you support your daughter or son at home in learning more than hard arithmetic?
- What kind of problems might you present to your son or daughter that require the use of thinking and reasoning skills?
- How can you support the teacher or school in teaching deep mathematics?

FOR LEADERS AND POLICY MAKERS

- How does this message reinforce or challenge policies and decisions you have made or are considering?
- How well does your mathematics program incorporate more than hard arithmetic, especially for students who are behind or who have special needs?
- What kinds of professional learning opportunities and support can you provide to help teachers strengthen the roots of their knowledge of mathematics and expand their teaching repertoire to go beyond numerical skills?

RELATED MESSAGES

- Message 32, "Yes, but . . . ," considers the reasons why we think some students do not reach high standards.
- Message 15, "Less Can Be More," looks at the problems with our overly repetitive mathematics curriculum.

FURTHER READING

- *Curriculum Focal Points* (National Council of Teachers of Mathematics 2006a) suggests three areas of instructional emphasis for deep mathematical knowledge and numerical proficiency at each grade level from prekindergarten through grade eight.
- *The Schools Our Children Deserve: Moving Beyond Traditional Classrooms and "Tougher Standards"* (Kohn 2000) addresses issues related to recent trends to focus on basics and tests, including a chapter with the subtitle "Confusing Harder with Better."

- *Math for All: Differentiating Instruction, Grades K–2* (Dacey and Salemi 2007), *Math for All: Differentiating Instruction, Grades 3–5* (Dacey and Lynch 2007), and *Math for All: Differentiating Instruction, Grades 6–8* (Dacey and Gartland 2009) is a three-book series that offers tasks, strategies, and research-based guidance for teaching deep mathematics to students of varying abilities, interests, and learning styles.

- *Accessible Mathematics: Ten Instructional Shifts That Raise Student Achievement* (Leinwand 2009) suggests classroom shifts teachers can make that lead to deeper student learning in mathematics.

- *Beyond Arithmetic: Changing Mathematics in the Elementary Classroom* (Mokros, Russell, and Economopoulos 1995) helps teachers examine and improve their mathematics teaching around richer problems that engage students more than traditional exercises, including guidance on evaluating or assessing this different kind of teaching and learning.

17 Constructive Struggling

THE VALUE OF CHALLENGING OUR STUDENTS

A merican teachers are soft. That's the message I heard when I started my service in the Peace Corps. I was assigned to teach mathematics (in French) in Burkina Faso, a small West African country unknown to most Americans. Throughout our eleven weeks of training, our Burkinabè teacher trainers explained to us that American teachers tend to want all students to succeed and that we grade students too high. "Your students won't respect you if you are too soft," Sou and Salam reminded us on more than one occasion. Over time, I learned to put that message in perspective. I observed that the Burkinabè system was based on a philosophy that seemed to be aimed largely at eliminating students from the school system—a totally opposite goal from that in the United States, and a goal that carried its own challenges. But this experience caused me to take a closer look at what we expect of students in U.S. mathematics classrooms. I began to wonder whether our compassion for students and our desire for all students to succeed might in fact be disadvantaging them. It is now clear to me that in too many cases we are not expecting enough of our students. In fact, most mathematics teachers report to me that their students are not willing to try hard problems that they can't immediately see how to solve.

Over and over again, we hear that U.S. math students deal with less challenging mathematics than students in other countries. The content of international tests like TIMSS[1] and PISA[2], and the performance of U.S. students on those tests, reinforce the notion that our students may

---

[1]Trends in International Mathematics and Science Study, formerly the Third International Mathematics and Science Study (http://timss.bc.edu)
[2]Programme for International Student Assessment, administered by the Organisation for Economic Co-operation and Development (OECD; www.pisa.oecd.org)

not be dealing with the same level of complexity in mathematics as students in other countries. I don't advocate that the United States should copy the programs of other countries; there are too many cultural and societal differences and too many challenges for any program to be successful on a large scale when it is transported in its entirety to a different setting. But I strongly support our close examination of practices used elsewhere that might inform our work to improve mathematics teaching and learning in this country.

Spoon-Feeding Our Students

In *The Teaching Gap*, Jim Stigler and Jim Hiebert (1999) report the results of classroom observations that were part of the 1995 TIMSS. This particular part of the study sent observers to eighth-grade classrooms in the United States, Germany, and Japan. Observers categorized the level of mathematics evident in classrooms in these three countries. They noted that in U.S. classrooms, students typically dealt with a much lower level of mathematics content than students in other countries. Observers also noted that our students had far fewer opportunities to develop new mathematical learning; instead, they were simply being told what to do. Worse, observers reported that on the few occasions when American teachers chose mathematically complex tasks, their teaching approach tended to remove the complexity and reduce the difficulty of the tasks.

It appears that in the interest of having students succeed, we sometimes spoon-feed our students too much information and ask too little of them in return. We tell them what approach or tools they can use to solve a problem, or we guide them in a directed fashion that makes one path obvious, thus removing the challenge. In essence, we tell them how to solve a problem before they have a chance to tackle it themselves. Somewhere along the way, we seem to have decided that students shouldn't struggle with mathematics.

The Need for Complexity

One of the most important lessons we can learn from other countries is that sometimes mathematics is hard, and sometimes we have to struggle to figure things out, especially with problems that are complex. When we introduce complexity in the problems we ask students to solve and challenge them beyond what they think they can do, we give them the opportunity to struggle a bit—an opportunity that many students never experience in mathematics from elementary school through high school. A look at those American classrooms where teachers and students invite complexity shows that the kind of mathematics problems students can really sink their teeth into (and consequently might struggle with) are often more interesting and engaging than the problems we have traditionally provided in math classrooms. It turns out that offering students a chance to struggle may go hand in hand with motivating them, if we do it right.

Constructive Struggling

Some teachers and parents may be concerned that students will become frustrated or fall behind if they are given mathematics problems that seem too hard. I offer a new way to think about this by advocating *constructive struggling*, not pointless frustration. Constructive struggling can happen when a skillful teacher gives students engaging yet challenging problems. Constructive struggling can take place when a teacher decides that one demanding, possibly time-consuming problem will likely provide more learning value than several shorter but more obvious problems. Constructive struggling involves presenting students with problems that call for more than a superficial application of a rote procedure. Constructive struggling occurs when an effective teacher knows how to provide guiding questions in a way that stops short of telling students everything they need to know to solve a problem. Constructive struggling can build from the elementary grades through the rest of a student's education as teachers continually balance the types of problems they give students. An effective teacher provides problems that range from straightforward applications of recently learned mathematics to more complex problems that require critical thinking and the connection of more than one mathematical concept, skill, or idea. As students engage in the constructive struggling needed for some of these problems, they learn that perseverance, in-depth analysis, and critical thinking are valued in mathematics as much as quick recall, direct skill application, and instant intuition.

What Can We Do?

Of course we want students to succeed, and we don't want students to dislike math class. Perhaps the way to help them most, both in terms of success and attitude, lies in the counterintuitive notion of finding the right level of struggle or challenge—a level that is both constructive and instructive. The business community tells us that the ability and willingness to tackle a problem that is not easily solved is one of the most important traits of a well-educated adult in the twenty-first century. If we do our job well and make students think just a little harder, we can prepare them to take on some of the most difficult problems we face today as well as the unknown problems we are likely to face tomorrow.

Reflection and Discussion

FOR TEACHERS

- What issues or challenges does this message raise for you? In what ways do you agree with or disagree with the main points of the message?

- What teaching actions or strategies do you think support or inhibit students' willingness to accept the struggle that goes with solving a challenging problem?

- How long do you allow your students to wrestle with a complex problem before you offer increasingly guided assistance? How frequently do you provide such an opportunity?

- How can you determine the right amount of frustration and struggle for any given student on any given task?

- How can you help your students develop the confidence and persistence necessary to persevere through a challenge?

FOR FAMILIES

- What questions or issues does this message raise for you to discuss with your son or daughter, the teacher, or school leaders?

- How can you help your daughter or son understand that it's OK to struggle with a math problem sometimes?

- In what ways can you help your son or daughter with math homework without spoon-feeding all of the steps needed in order to solve a challenging problem?

- How can you help your daughter or son develop confidence and persistence in tackling hard mathematics problems? How can you support the teacher's efforts in developing student confidence and persistence?

FOR LEADERS AND POLICY MAKERS

- How does this message reinforce or challenge policies and decisions you have made or are considering?

- How can your mathematics program support students in learning the value of working through a hard or complex problem?

- What kinds of professional learning opportunities can you offer teachers to help them learn how to determine and incorporate appropriate levels of struggling in their mathematics teaching?

RELATED MESSAGES

- Message 16, "Hard Arithmetic Isn't Deep Mathematics," makes the argument that mathematics must include more than computation.
- Message 32, "Yes, but . . . ," examines some of the reasons we think students don't learn challenging mathematics.
- Message 2, "Untapped Potential," reminds us that many students can do much more challenging work than we currently expect of them.
- Message 31, "Do They Really Need It?," discusses the value of letting students tackle challenging mathematics, even if we aren't sure whether or when students will use it.

FURTHER READING

- *The Teaching Gap: Best Ideas from the World's Teachers for Improving Education in the Classroom* (Stigler and Hiebert 1999) considers differences between American mathematics teaching compared to mathematics teaching in other countries, including differences in how students may be encouraged to struggle with hard problems.
- *Professional Standards for Teaching Mathematics* (National Council of Teachers of Mathematics 1991) remains one of the richest descriptions of the nature of worthwhile tasks and classroom discourse that pushes students' thinking and develops mathematical understanding.
- NCTM's Illuminations website (http://illuminations.nctm.org) provides a rich online source of student activities to develop mathematical thinking and understanding.
- *Exemplars: Standards-Based Assessment and Instruction* (www.exemplars.com) provides a variety of tasks for several subject areas, including mathematics. The tasks cover a range of difficulty levels and are designed to challenge students' thinking.
- My website on Burkina Faso (http://csinburkinafaso.com) includes photos and stories about life and teaching during my Peace Corps assignment from 1999 through 2001.

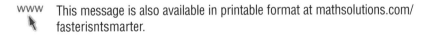 This message is also available in printable format at mathsolutions.com/ fasterisntsmarter.

18 Faster Isn't Smarter

THE TRAP OF TIMED TESTS

It's a widespread belief that to be good at math means to be fast at computation. But this belief may in fact do more harm as good. Some of the world's greatest thinkers, scientists, and mathematicians have not been fast at arithmetic, even though they were tremendously successful in working with higher-level mathematics. Dr. Emma King has noted her poor performance on rote arithmetic computation, in spite of her highly recognized work in the scientific field of cosmology. Numerous scientists and scholars from around the world could tell similar stories.

Certainly as part of a complete and balanced mathematics program it is useful to be able to add, subtract, multiply, and divide quickly, and it is important to know basic addition and multiplication facts without having to figure them out or count on your fingers. But asking students to demonstrate this knowledge within an arbitrary time limit may actually interfere with their learning. While computational recall is important, it is only part of a comprehensive mathematical background that includes more complex computation, an understanding of mathematical concepts, and the ability to think and reason to solve problems. Measuring this one aspect of mathematics—fact recall—using timed tests is both flawed as an assessment approach and damaging to many students' confidence and willingness to tackle new problems.

A Classroom Story

The pressure and potential damage of timed tests became especially evident to me several years ago when a seventh-grade teacher invited me to visit her class. It was September, and the teacher was spending two weeks reviewing multiplication facts before going on to seventh-grade material. The teacher explained to me that each day she was testing a different set of facts. The day I visited, the class was taking a timed test on the "four timeses." The students became increasingly anxious as the teacher passed out short fact tests face down on their desks. All eyes were watching the second hand on the clock; students knew that until it reached 12, they were safe. Then the second hand hit 12 and the teacher said, "Begin!" The boy I was sitting next to ground out a few answers. He was gripping his pencil so hard that it broke in the process. It seemed an eternity, but finally the three minutes were up. I looked at the boy's paper. He had not come close to finishing, and the few answers he had so painstakingly attempted to write were wrong. If his performance was similar to others in the class, I had to conclude (as the teacher had) that these seventh graders did not know their facts.

The teacher collected the papers and handed out a puzzle-type worksheet for the students to complete while she graded the tests. The puzzle worksheet was on the same facts the students had just seen on the test. I sat quietly as the same boy now used his broken pencil to calmly and correctly complete all the facts on the worksheet. He got the correct answer to the puzzle, put down his pencil, and got out a book to read. A few minutes later, the teacher read the names of the students who had passed the timed test. Of course, the boy seated next to me was not on the list.

The lessons from this story are obvious. Some students respond well to competitive and timed situations, thriving on the pressure to bring out their best; others have quite a different reaction. This particular boy received a clear message that some students are good at math and some are not—and he knew which group he was in. He also was prevented from finishing the test, something that causes some students tremendous frustration. Furthermore, the teacher was led to believe, incorrectly, that this student did not know his multiplication facts. Consequently, and perhaps worst of all, the boy was placed in a special group to receive remediation on low-level arithmetic, robbing him of the opportunity to move into more interesting problems and engaging work involving seventh-grade mathematics.

Alternative Scenarios

When I tell this story, sometimes teachers share other approaches to helping students develop speed in computation. For example, if a teacher or school chooses to include speed as a mathematics priority, the teacher might offer students the option to work toward their best time during a six- or nine-week grading period, designating a specified block of time one day a week for this type of work. When a student is ready to try to improve his previous time, he can request to take the test. Students record their starting and ending times, doing their best to complete the test quickly and beat their best time, but always finishing and competing against only themselves. This type of self-administered assessment carries much less stress and allows each student to complete the test without competing against other students.

What Can We Do?

Even if we use other practices to evaluate speed, we need to weigh the importance of this aspect of mathematics within the entire program. Overemphasizing fast fact recall at the expense of problem solving and conceptual experiences gives students a distorted idea of the nature of mathematics and of their ability to do mathematics. Some students never survive this experience and they turn away from mathematics for years, sometimes forever. Having experienced timed tests when they were students, many adults believe that accurate, fast computation is the most significant part of mathematics. When pressed, many of these adults who dislike or fear mathematics attribute these negative feelings to experiences from their school years, especially the use of timed tests. In determining how much to value speed in arithmetic, we must consider the costs and benefits: If teachers highly value speed in mathematics, what are the potential gains for student learning? The potential barriers?

For some students, their success at being fast at computation opens doors to allow them access to higher-level mathematics. But as Marilyn Burns has stated, "Speed with arithmetic skills has little, if anything, to do with mathematical power" (1989). We are now discovering that being good mathematical thinkers or problem solvers is at least as important as being good at computation and can also pave the way to higher-level mathematics. At a time when we want to help every student learn challenging, rigorous, and relevant mathematics, we must look for ways to tap into each student's strengths, not fall into the trap of believing that timed tests are the way we identify our good mathematics students.

Reflection and Discussion

FOR TEACHERS

- What issues or challenges does this message raise for you? In what ways do you agree with or disagree with the main points of the message?
- What value do you put on speed in your classroom, and how can you evaluate speed in positive ways that support student learning?
- If your school or district mandates timed tests, and if you disagree with this mandate, how can you work aggressively to change this practice?

(continued)

- How can you use a variety of assessments that go beyond timed computation or fact recall in order to find out how well students are learning mathematics?

FOR FAMILIES

- What questions or issues does this message raise for you to discuss with your son or daughter, the teacher, or school leaders?
- How can you help your daughter or son understand that it is useful to be able to perform mathematical procedures efficiently, but that this is not the only measure of success in mathematics?
- Realizing that support at home can be tremendously useful in fact recall, how can you help your son or daughter learn, practice, and reinforce basic facts and mental procedures so that these become automatic, without using timed tests or sending negative messages about mathematics that could affect his or her developing confidence as a learner of mathematics?

FOR LEADERS AND POLICY MAKERS

- How does this message reinforce or challenge policies and decisions you have made or are considering?
- In particular, if your school or district endorses, encourages, or mandates the use of timed computation or fact recall tests, how might you redirect this policy?
- How can you find out whether teachers support the use of timed tests? How can you make teachers aware of the potential negative consequences of using timed tests?
- How can you help teachers develop a robust set of assessment tools and strategies to inform their teaching and to find out what mathematics students know?

RELATED MESSAGES

- Message 16, "Hard Arithmetic Isn't Deep Mathematics," discusses what rigorous mathematics looks like.
- Message 24, "Do It in Your Head," makes a case for including the teaching of mental math as part of a balanced mathematics program.
- Message 35, "Putting Testing in Perspective," looks at the types of assessments teachers can use in support of student learning.

FURTHER READING

- "The Need for Speed in Mathematics" (Gilliland 2001) looks at why timed skills tests may not be helpful for students.

- *About Teaching Mathematics: A K–8 Resource* (Burns 2007a) covers many aspects of school mathematics, including a discussion on misconceptions about the value of timed tests.

- *Overcoming Math Anxiety* (Tobias 1995) looks at the role of negative school experiences, including timed tests, in the development of math anxiety in adults.

- The Family Resources page of the National Council of Teachers of Mathematics (www.nctm.org/resources/families) includes, among other resources, links to documents that answer questions about the changing nature of mathematics today and the use of timed skills tests.

www This message is also available in printable format at
mathsolutions.com/fasterisntsmarter.

19 Embracing Accountability

SURVIVING THE TEST WHILE TEACHING GOOD MATHEMATICS

More than two decades of increasingly demanding state and local accountability systems, accentuated by the high-stakes No Child Left Behind legislation, have focused attention on controversial large-scale tests and student test scores. Being accountable for students' learning is indeed our professional responsibility, but real accountability involves more than just test scores. I suggest that as teachers of mathematics and those who support teachers and learners of mathematics, we should not complain about accountability; rather, we should embrace it. If we are committed to embracing accountability in support of a high-quality mathematics education for all students, then we have both a responsibility and an opportunity to influence accountability practices in three ways—practice, participation, and advocacy.

Day-to-Day Practice

For many years now, the United States mathematics program has been appropriately labeled as *a mile wide and an inch deep*, referring to the practice of revisiting topics year after year and crowding too many isolated bits of learning into each grade. This overcrowded mathematics curriculum has allowed little or no time for building a foundation of understanding and proficiency. But in an increasing number of schools, caring and competent teachers have been working to move their mathematics programs toward more focus, more depth, and more coherence. Guided by the standards from the National Council of Teachers of Mathematics (NCTM), innovative curriculum materials, research about effective practices, and their own experience, these teachers have helped students learn mathematical skills, make sense of what they are learning, and engage in challenging mathematical problems. Not only have the best students demonstrated these abilities, but students no one ever thought could learn mathematics have also found success in these classrooms.

Yet just when these teachers are beginning to see the results of their hard work, many of them now feel pressured to sidetrack their effective programs. The demand to produce results in the form of student test scores on large-scale accountability tests causes many communities and school systems to adopt shallow, quick-fix programs and test-preparation tricks that take up inordinate amounts of instructional time. Teachers who recognize the dangers of this kind of superficial, short-term thinking nevertheless feel required to do what they are asked to do.

One of the greatest challenges facing teachers is finding a way to withstand these pressures and teach a well-articulated mathematics program. I have seen teachers, schools, and school districts stand their ground, as difficult as this may be. They have shown that by teaching a solid, well-balanced, excellent mathematics program, students' test scores improve. This seems to be true even where tests disproportionately assess lower-level skills that represent only a small part of a comprehensive mathematics program.

This does not mean that we should ignore preparation for tests. Rather, it means that in our day-to-day practice, we must find time-efficient, commonsense ways to improve students' test-taking skills and test readiness without derailing or diluting an effective balanced mathematics program.

Participation in the Process

Often, states involve teachers and other mathematics educators in the design and implementation of standards and tests. From within this structure, teachers and other educational leaders can use what they know about teaching and learning mathematics to influence standards and tests. Mathematics education professionals can work to ensure that state standards represent a balanced and well-aligned program of skills, understanding, and problem solving that promotes students' mathematical thinking. Unfortunately, assessment measures rarely go beyond multiple-choice tests to assess the complete scope of a state's standards, as they tend to be tend to be costly to develop, administer, and score. But even in a tough budget environment, active input from knowledgeable educators can shape tests so that they support the full breadth of state standards as closely as possible.

When the call comes for committee nominations, reactions to draft documents, or testimony before state policy makers, it is our responsibility as educators and citizens to answer in positive and constructive ways. Depending on where we live, such avenues for input may be well publicized or we may need to seek them out. Whatever it takes, we need to make our participation in the process a priority or we have no excuse when the schools we value head in directions we decry.

Advocacy for Students

We should work from within the system whenever possible. But it is our moral imperative to express opinions about actions that we believe are not in the best interests of all students. If particular practices tend to disadvantage or disenfranchise any student, we must raise our voices to change the system where it needs to be changed. When the system is shifting in harmful ways for any student, it is our ethical responsibility to speak up.

Speaking up is appropriate from any educator or citizen, but it can be especially helpful from teachers, leaders, and community members in schools and school systems where student test scores are high. Since their students are succeeding, such teachers can hardly be viewed as complaining. Yet these teachers can have considerable influence when they join with colleagues from other settings in which test-preparation practices may be more harmful. Fortunately, many people still care about and pay attention to the voices of professional educators and knowledgeable citizens.

What Can We Do?

Our decisions and actions can influence students more than any single state or federal initiative. If mathematics teachers are to be respected as professionals, we must embrace accountability. We must insist on being held accountable for producing results—showing the public that our students are learning challenging mathematics. We must also take action and speak up when students' mathematics learning is at stake. We cannot afford to complain about an unjust system without working to address its problems. Nor can we accept without protest an inadequate and unjust system that sacrifices mathematics learning for the sake of expediency and the possibility of increased test scores. Our responsibility is to teach mathematics well to all students and to embrace the opportunity to demonstrate to the public that our students have also learned it well.

Reflection and Discussion

FOR TEACHERS

- What issues or challenges does this message raise for you? In what ways do you agree with or disagree with the main points of the message?
- How can you work within the accountability system to support students' mathematics learning?
- How do you help students and families make sense of accountability test scores as part of a bigger picture of student mathematics learning?
- What success stories do you know of professional mathematics educators who have helped influence and shape their accountability system?

FOR FAMILIES

- What questions or issues does this message raise for you to discuss with your son or daughter, the teacher, or school leaders?
- How can you make sense of the test results you receive for your daughter or son, including annual accountability tests, ongoing classroom assessments, and teacher observations?
- How can you work with the teacher or school to use test results to help your son or daughter learn mathematics?

FOR LEADERS AND POLICY MAKERS

- How does this message reinforce or challenge policies and decisions you have made or are considering?
- How does your school or district place large-scale assessment results into a broader context of assessment and instructional information to improve teaching and learning and to inform families about student progress?
- In what ways do you value, respect, and support information teachers gather about students beyond accountability tests?
- How can you help teachers continue to improve their knowledge and use of a range of assessment measures?

RELATED MESSAGES

- Message 12, "Beyond Band-Aids and Bandwagons," looks at the dangers of adopting fads at the expense of effective teaching and student learning.

- Message 11, "Weighing Hens," considers limitations of interim testing and looks at other types of assessments.

- Message 35, "Putting Testing in Perspective," considers how teachers can become better at using and balancing various types of assessments to improve student learning.

FURTHER READING

- NCTM's Large-Scale Assessment Tool: A Framework to Evaluate Large-Scale Assessments of Mathematics page (www.nctm.org/resources/content.aspx?id=10796) provides a comprehensive framework that describes criteria of effective use of large-scale mathematics assessments.

- *Mathematics Assessment Literacy: Concepts and Terms in Large-Scale Assessment* (Romagnano 2006) presents an overview of large-scale testing in mathematics to help teachers make sense of both the assessment process and the results.

20 Putting Calculators in Their Place

THE ROLE OF CALCULATORS AND COMPUTATION IN THE CLASSROOM

The question is not whether or not to use calculators in elementary classrooms. The question is what responsibilities educators have to help students develop appropriate understanding and skills about numbers and computation, while also teaching when and when not to use technology as a tool.

Outside of school, technology plays a role in every aspect of our lives. New technological tools and new uses for those tools appear almost every day. Yet inside schools it sometimes appears as if we are pretending that technology doesn't exist. In many schools and communities, we cannot agree about whether we should allow students to use calculators, in particular. Few would argue that we should abandon the teaching of all computational skills just because we can add, subtract, multiply, and divide on a calculator. But beyond that fundamental agreement, there are considerable differences of opinion as to how the availability of calculators fits with the development of number and computation skills.

Ideally, we need to capitalize on the appropriate use of technology to enhance students' mathematical understanding, recognizing that the purpose is not to make learning mathematics easier, but to make students' mathematics experience stronger and deeper. This will occur only when teachers incorporate appropriate uses of technology into their teaching and thoughtfully determine when, and when not, to call on these tools.

Number and Operation Sense

All students need to develop number sense. *Number sense* refers to a deep knowledge and understanding of what numbers are, what they represent, the order and relationships among them, how they can be put together and taken apart, and so on. Much of this development will occur without the use of a calculator. For example, as students become more familiar with recognizing 7 as being made up of 3 and 4 or of 2 and 5, they not only understand "seven-ness" better, they also build a foundation for understanding addition and subtraction and they begin to acquire mental math skills. Likewise, as students learn the meaning of fractions and explore the relationships among different fractions, they build a critical foundation that will eventually allow them to solve problems in situations where fractions naturally arise. In support of the development of number sense, elementary teachers can selectively use calculators and other technology to show how numbers can build other numbers, as well as to investigate relationships and patterns with numbers.

Students also need to develop an understanding of what it means to add, subtract, multiply, and divide. On the surface, it may appear that this learning should happen without technology. But developing an understanding of these operations is far more complex than learning how to perform them. Sometimes the procedures themselves can get in the way of understanding what an operation means and when it might be useful. Consider especially the case of long division. Cognitive scientists have identified as many as twenty-seven separate steps involved in long division, and most of these steps have little to do with knowing what it means to divide (Wesson 2008). We must be careful not to confuse proficiency in procedures with knowing about the operation involved. Students who may have a fragile understanding about the operation they are performing at any given time (for example, division) are far less likely to remember how to do the procedure than if they know what it means to divide, have a mental picture of division, and recognize situations in which division might be helpful. Again, teachers can find appropriate and engaging ways to use calculators as part of a comprehensive set of approaches to support the development of operation sense. In developing number and operation sense, as with other topics in mathematics, teachers need to spend as much time learning when *not* to use calculators as learning when to use them.

Pencil-and-Paper Computation

Even in today's increasingly technological society, written mathematical procedures continue to be an important part of school mathematics programs, including computational procedures at the elementary grades and more symbolic algebraic procedures in later grades. All students should become proficient in carrying out basic procedures. However, students do not have the same need today to perform procedures with lengthy or tedious numbers as they might have had in a previous era where technology was not available. Teachers and policy makers need to carefully consider how far students need to go in terms of written computation with unwieldy numbers. Technology can be useful in dealing with the kinds of lengthy computations that might arise in problems involving cumbersome numbers. Using technology in this way allows students to tackle mathematically sophisticated problems even before they have mastered the underlying arithmetic, thus helping them develop higher-level thinking skills even as they continue to develop computational skills. The use of technology in these cases can free up instructional time to address more complex problems and other topics in the mathematics program.

Estimation and Mental Math Skills

Of even more importance than written computation, however, students need a strong set of estimation and mental math skills. Estimates are often preferable to computed answers for certain situations. Estimates also help students interpret calculator outputs to determine if they are of a reasonable magnitude for a particular problem or calculation. Students should become proficient at using mental math shortcuts, performing basic computations mentally, and generating ballpark answers for situations calling for estimates of size, distance, and magnitude.

Putting It All Together

Calculators and other technological tools (including those that don't yet exist) can have powerful and appropriate uses at all grade levels. Their use can comfortably exist with the development of written and mental numerical skills and quantitative understanding. A choice not to use calculators out of fear that students will not learn written skills is shortsighted and it limits the mathematics students might be able to learn. There is no question that students will use calculators outside of school. If they have not learned appropriate purposes and uses for calculators in school, they will surely misuse them outside of school, reaching for an electronic crutch instead of remembering a simple fact or doing a quick mental calculation.

What Can We Do?

It is our responsibility to help students develop decision-making skills to determine when it is both helpful and appropriate to use a calculator and when it is inappropriate or time-consuming to do so. Furthermore, when a teacher uses calculators appropriately and well, students are able to learn far more challenging mathematics than what they would otherwise spend their time on. The mathematics we want students to learn should be the driving force behind the lesson and behind the choice of what tools to use, not the other way around. When we put mathematics first, and choose our tools based on the task at hand, all students can have the opportunity to learn rich and challenging mathematics in ways that will serve them well in a technology-based world.

Reflection and Discussion

FOR TEACHERS

- What issues or challenges does this message raise for you? In what ways do you agree with or disagree with the main points of the message?
- How can you use calculators to enhance the development of students' number and operation sense? Where can you go to learn new ways to use calculators for this purpose?
- Beyond the use of calculators, how can you help students develop number sense in terms of building numbers, taking them apart, ordering them, and exploring relationships among them?
- How can you help students create mental pictures of addition, subtraction, multiplication, and division?
- How can you help students develop mental math skills, including, but not limited to, estimation and computational shortcuts?
- What kinds of teaching strategies can you use to help students acquire both an understanding of the operations and the ability to perform the related procedures?

FOR FAMILIES

- What questions or issues does this message raise for you to discuss with your son or daughter, the teacher, or school leaders?
- How open are you to the possibility that there may be an appropriate role for technology, like calculators, for students in elementary as well as secondary grades?
- In what ways can you help your daughter or son develop number sense, operation sense, and mental math skills? What opportunities do you have to work together to practice finding number combinations that make ten, talk about different ways to make seven, talk about the mathematics behind different situations you may encounter, estimate answers to problems ahead of time, and so on?
- How can you communicate to the teacher and school leaders your support for the selective use of calculators in appropriate ways?

FOR LEADERS AND POLICY MAKERS

- How does this message reinforce or challenge policies and decisions you have made or are considering?
- How do your policies and programs support, entrust, and empower teachers in using calculators appropriately within a strong and balanced mathematics program?
- What opportunities can you provide to help teachers learn to use calculators effectively in support of students' mathematical development?
- How do your policies and programs support the development of strong number sense and operation sense, beyond the computational procedures that are more obvious measures of students' mathematical skills?
- How do your policies and programs support the development of estimation and mental math skills?

RELATED MESSAGES

- Message 5, "Technology Is a Tool," describes how technology can support the learning of good mathematics.
- Message 14, "Balance Is Basic," describes the importance of addressing computation and understanding within a balanced mathematics program.
- Message 24, "Do It in Your Head," makes the case for emphasizing mental math and discusses how mental math fits within an effective math program.
- Message 30, "Crystal's Calculator," tells the personal story of a student whose background in fraction computation was weak, but who went on to succeed in advanced mathematics.

FURTHER READING

- *Explorations: Integrating Handheld Technology into the Elementary Mathematics Classroom* (Olson, Schielack, and Olson 2002) considers how teachers can incorporate the use of calculators within the teaching of a comprehensive mathematics program and provides sample activities.
- *Learning Math with Calculators: Activities for Grades 3–8* (Sparrow and Swan 2001) discusses issues related to using calculators in elementary and middle school mathematics classrooms and provides a variety of examples of teaching activities.

- The Family Resources page of the National Council of Teachers of Mathematics (www.nctm.org/resources/families) includes, among many other resources, links to documents that answer questions about the changing nature of mathematics today and calculator use in math classrooms.

- Early writing done while serving as National Council of Teachers of Mathematics (NCTM) President inspired parts of this message. My writing was part of the development of NCTM's position statement entitled Computation, Calculators, and Common Sense (2005; www.nctm.org/about/content.aspx?id=6358), which lays out a concise argument about using common sense to balance the use of calculators with the teaching of computation.

- "Calculators in K–5 Textbooks" (Chval and Hicks 2009) presents an overview of and recommendations for how calculators can be used in elementary mathematics classrooms to support student learning.

21

No More Pilgrim Pie

THE CHALLENGES OF INTEGRATING MATHEMATICS WITH OTHER SUBJECTS

Thanksgiving arrives. Because of a district-wide push for teachers to develop integrated instructional units, a group of elementary (or middle school) teachers have designed an integrated unit centered on Thanksgiving. This unit naturally addresses learning objectives for social studies related to American history and the early settlers. In order to tie in the unit to other subjects, students write a story about the early settlers, make an art project of a turkey, sing a song about Thanksgiving, and bring in math and science (and a bit of home economics) with a hands-on lesson involving doubling or halving a recipe to make Pilgrim pie. Is this a successful attempt at connecting content across the disciplines or just a collection of activities? The answer calls for serious consideration of the potential value of integrating subject areas and the challenges of trying to do so in a meaningful way.

Connecting Content

Reinforcing the connections among the disciplines is a worthwhile goal. If done well, students come to see mathematics, as well as science, social studies, English, and the arts, not as separate school subjects, but as subjects that connect to each other and to life outside of school. However, integrating instruction well can be challenging and time-consuming—and it may not always be the best way for students to learn the content of any one discipline.

When students work with fractions in recipes, such as in the Pilgrim pie lesson above, it helps them see that fractions are part of the world outside of school. But if the only math skills students experience in lessons outside of math class fall into a few predictable low-level categories, they may develop a narrow and superficial view of how mathematics is used. Too often, especially if teachers are not specialists in mathematics, connections to mathematical topics in integrated lessons involve a small set of skills often contrived to fit the theme of the lesson. In such lessons, students might be asked to double or halve a recipe, identify or draw shapes in pictures of a turkey or other thematic objects, measure something with a ruler, work with money, or draw a bar graph of a simple data set.

These situations are fine as far as they go, but even young children in a comprehensive mathematics program can move quickly past the basic skill and recognition level to engage in richer tasks and solving complex problems. If simple mathematical tasks in interdisciplinary units come to represent students' primary view of how mathematics is used in the world, they might miss the opportunity to make meaningful connections that show how mathematical thinking, reasoning, and habits of mind can serve them in many situations both in and outside of school.

Success Stories

Some schools have found great success in developing rich, integrated teaching experiences that cross content lines. In one well-established, successful high school in Virginia, all ninth-grade students enroll in an integrated course addressing English, biology, and technology. Throughout the year, students develop research skills in a project-based environment where they use technology to explore ideas and concepts from biology. They also discuss, argue, write about, hypothesize, defend, and present their research findings. In a small, experimental high school in Texas, teachers from science, mathematics, English, and social studies routinely plan in-depth projects for students that address the state's standards for the various subject areas. Students work collaboratively, over time, on projects they ultimately present to a community panel.

In both of these schools, teachers are very knowledgeable about their particular disciplines and they spend considerable and intense time working together to plan these integrated units, guide students as they progress, and evaluate students' work. These teachers go to great lengths to make sure that all of their state standards for particular subjects are incorporated, or they determine how they will address those that fall outside the scope of the integrated projects. The schools are structured to carefully select and then mentor and support new teachers, to ensure that incoming teachers can successfully utilize these unique instructional models as part of their school's team.

In some elementary and middle schools I have visited, teachers plan one or two short but rich integrated units during the year. Students might conduct a basic survey in science or social studies and use quantitative reasoning and communication skills to analyze the results, describe their conclusions, and present their reports. The key to their success is that these units are not intended to cover a year's worth of work, and not all content areas are forced into every unit. Rather, the units present opportunities for students to see the connections between what they are learning and other subject areas.

Where Integration Falls Short

These success stories have worked in part because committed teachers devote considerable time to work together in designing rich, appropriate, connected activities. However, many efforts to integrate instruction fall short of the ambitious goals of the educators and policy makers who push for them. Problems associated with efforts to integrate content areas are numerous.

TRIVIALIZING CONTENT

Teachers look for the most obvious way to tie in a subject area, too often trivializing the subject as only incidental to the central content of the integrated lesson or unit. Art is more than tracing your hand to make a turkey, and mathematics is more than doubling a recipe.

CONTRIVING CONNECTIONS

Teachers force contrived applications in order to bring in a content area. If students are asked to triple a recipe involving unusual fractions like sevenths, for example, they could reasonably question whether such a situation would ever really exist. Students asked to make an elaborate spreadsheet to represent basic cost and revenue data for a school function might rightly ask why they couldn't just do the obvious calculations with a calculator or a pencil and paper.

UNDERESTIMATING STUDENTS

Teachers use inappropriate content from a subject area, especially mathematics. Students make basic graphs beginning in early elementary school, yet one common way many teachers include mathematics in an interdisciplinary unit today is to ask students to graph the data. Asking students with several years of experience in making simple graphs to make yet another simple bar graph, without asking for more in-depth analysis appropriate to the grade level or a more complex way to represent the data, is condescending and trivializes the real mathematics relevant to the situation.

INTEGRATING EVERYTHING

Teachers may be expected to address all of the year's content for particular subject areas into integrated units. This is a particularly unrealistic expectation if the various subjects are to be developed well. Typically (although not always), in an integrated unit, one discipline takes the lead and others are relegated to supporting roles; often the supporting content comes from the disciplines that interest the teacher the least. The push for all of mathematics to be integrated with other subject areas means that important mathematics may not receive adequate attention, for example, when the focus of a unit is on a scientific idea or a social studies context. Some mathematical ideas, such as the meaning of multiplication, proportionality, or functional relationships, are central to the work of a grade level and to the mathematics that will follow in later grades; each of these topics needs to be the primary focus of attention, not a secondary tie-in.

What Can We Do?

There is nothing wrong with students using some basic applications of mathematics, even simple arithmetic or geometric shapes, as part of what they do in connecting with other subject areas. But we should not pretend that these glancing blows across content lines represent the richness of possible connections between mathematics and other subject areas, or across subject areas in general.

Let us applaud the successful efforts of talented and dedicated educators who continue to develop rich, motivational interdisciplinary projects involving extended planning and coordination. I especially commend those who structure whole years of instruction or even entire school programs around project-based learning of integrated content. For the rest of us, let us start by teaching good mathematics and incorporating as many relevant applications and problems as we can, especially those that might connect to other disciplines. Let us look for natural connections with mathematics that might occur as students engage in solving problems related to science, the arts, or the humanities. Let us develop the occasional well-integrated unit where we work closely with our colleagues over a fixed period of time to ensure that the connections we make are real, deep, and substantive. With enough of these experiences over the years, students will begin to realize that school is not just a set of isolated classes, but a place where they can apply what they learn to many different contexts.

Reflection and Discussion

FOR TEACHERS

- What issues or challenges does this message raise for you? In what ways do you agree with or disagree with the main points of the message?
- In what ways can you connect the mathematics you teach to other content areas, even if you don't develop entire integrated units with your colleagues?

- How might you work with your colleagues to develop a high-quality integrated unit involving one or more other disciplines?
- How can you reach out to colleagues who teach other subjects to help them incorporate meaningful applications of mathematics that might arise naturally in their instruction? If you yourself teach other disciplines besides mathematics, how can you incorporate into your own work meaningful applications of mathematics appropriate for your students' grade level?

FOR FAMILIES

- What questions or issues does this message raise for you to discuss with your son or daughter, the teacher, or school leaders?
- How can you help your daughter or son see how mathematics is used outside of school?
- How can you help your son or daughter make connections among mathematics and other disciplines outside of school?

FOR LEADERS AND POLICY MAKERS

- How does this message reinforce or challenge policies and decisions you have made or are considering?
- If your school is interested in moving toward integrated instruction, what kinds of professional learning opportunities and ongoing support can you provide for teachers?
- If your school is interested in a project-based approach to learning, either within classrooms or throughout the school, what steps can you take to increase the likelihood of success, and how can you involve teachers in the planning of such a significant shift?

RELATED MESSAGES

- Message 10, "It's Not Just About Math and Reading," builds a case for a well-balanced curriculum beyond reading and mathematics.
- Message 33, "Engaged in What?" discusses how to purposefully select the tasks we ask students to do.
- Message 13, "Seek First to Understand," reminds us of the power of working together across grades and disciplines to improve teaching and learning.

FURTHER READING

- *Understanding by Design* (Wiggins and McTighe 2005) is a recognized source about teaching students through the process of *backwards design*, emphasizing essential understandings and big ideas rather than covering lists of topics and skills.

- *Interdisciplinary Curriculum: Challenges to Implementation* (Wineburg and Grossman 2000) examines issues around integrated instruction and suggests that a successful interdisciplinary curriculum should draw on the strengths and methodologies of the various disciplines.

- *Project-Based Learning with Young Children* (Diffily and Sassman 2002) presents an overview of project-based learning that shows teachers how to structure classrooms around relevant student-centered projects.

- *Reinventing Project-Based Learning: Your Field Guide to Real-World Projects in the Digital Age* (Boss, Krauss, and Conery 2008) uses technology as the basis for creating a project-based, student-centered instructional program.

- *Integrating Differentiated Instruction and Understanding by Design (Connecting Content and Kids)* (Tomlinson and McTighe 2006) focuses on using principles of backwards design and differentiation to focus teaching on what students need.

22

We Don't Care About the Answer

YES, WE DO. LOOKING FOR BALANCE

One summer afternoon I came across a local television news story discussing an innovative summer math program in the school district where I live. I was pleased that a story on math would be on television, and I watched with interest as the interviewer spoke with the program's director. Based on the brief interview, it seemed to me that the program might be helpful for teaching students problem solving. Then the director made a statement that made me want to crawl under a table. I even uttered, "*Nooo!*" as I heard the director say, "We don't even care if students get the right answer. What we care about is how they approach the problem."

I understand what this educator meant. She meant that the *process* a student uses is as important as the answer a student gives. She meant that students could learn something from solving a problem, even if they initially stumble or come up with the wrong answer at first. She meant that mathematical processes are part of a student's developing set of mathematical tools.

But as mathematics educators, we must also care about whether students get a correct answer. In today's era of math reform, the notion that educators might not care about the answer is both false and dangerous. If parents or businesspeople think that today's mathematics teachers don't care about answers, they will appropriately become agitated over what is going on in school. After all, if students are not arriving at correct answers, or worse, if teachers don't care whether students' answers are right or wrong, most people would agree that something isn't working.

Caring About the Process

The educator in the interview above was right in her zeal to care about the process students use to solve a problem. She was reacting to the reality that some teachers don't care what process a student uses to arrive at an answer, as long as the answer is correct. Equally troublesome, some teachers prescribe only one method for arriving at an answer, leaving students who find a novel approach out of luck. Both of these philosophies deny students a critical element of their mathematical learning—developing efficient strategies for solving new problems.

The National Council of Teachers of Mathematics (NCTM) calls for a strong commitment to problem solving and mathematical processes like thinking, reasoning, and making connections (2000). This commitment is reflected in the kind of program the director was describing in the television interview. Specifically, students can benefit greatly from an opportunity to learn versatile and transferable processes for tackling complex problems. This means doing more than giving students word problems that call for them to use a procedure they just learned. Students need tasks that challenge them to have to figure out what operation(s) might be helpful and how they might connect different mathematical ideas, even if it means exploring a path or two that don't lead immediately to a solution. This is how mathematicians approach problems and it is an increasingly prevalent approach in the workplace. According to Thomas Friedman in *The World Is Flat* (2007), the twenty-first-century workplace demands workers with deep, transferable problem-solving and thinking skills. Friedman emphasizes that workers will need to be able to *versatilize*—transfer skills, generalize what has already been learned, and continue learning new skills for a job that might not have existed last year. Today's need for this kind of transferable critical thinking and complex problem solving is echoed by various business and policy groups such as the National Center on Education and the Economy and the Partnership for 21st Century Skills.

In order for students to learn problem solving well, instruction should start with rich problems calling for more than superficial application of procedures. Students need to work on the kinds of tasks that require them to put together more than one piece of mathematical knowledge, skill, or concept. Teachers need to ask questions that push students' thinking, not replace it. Questions like "If we multiply the answer by three, what do we have?" don't help students with this type of thinking. Instead, teachers can generate greater levels of student thinking by asking questions like: "Why do you think that's true?" "How might your thinking change if the numbers are larger?" Over time, students learn to both ask these kinds of probing questions of each other and also respond to questions that contribute to learning, whether other students or the teacher poses these questions.

Careful scaffolding with probing questions can help students address problems that may initially seem out of reach. But scaffolding loses its effectiveness if we tell students everything they need to know in advance of working on the problem; this takes all the challenge away. Effective scaffolding questions can help students develop increasing levels of independence and willingness to try harder problems than they might otherwise take on. But if overdone, questions intended to provide scaffolding actually can cut student thinking short.

Caring About the Answer

Regardless of the care we take to ensure that students learn to think on their own and develop sound approaches to solving problems, we cannot overlook the value of arriving at an answer that makes sense. It may not always be one answer; for some problems, one answer is sufficient, but for other problems, many possible answers can make sense. Regardless, students should be able to justify their answer and explain how they arrived at it. This kind of justification and explanation is a powerful part of learning and should not be overlooked. As a student talks through an explanation, he might recognize and even correct an error he made. And if the approach works, the student, simply by going through the steps again out loud, reinforces the strategy used. This reinforcement increases the likelihood that the student will be able to use the strategy (or one like it) for an appropriate problem in the future. In either case, explaining and justifying answers benefits the learning process, especially when guided by a teacher who is careful not to provide excessive direction. Equally important as the process, therefore, is a student's ability to arrive at an answer and verify that the answer makes sense while addressing all the necessary criteria in the original problem.

What Can We Do?

How we communicate what we do and why we do it is just as important as actually doing the right thing. One appropriate response the educator in the television interview might have offered is "We're teaching students that coming up with a way to solve a problem is equally important as coming up with a correct answer. We want our students to be such strong problem solvers that they can address all kinds of problems they will see outside of school, including those for which we don't know the answer in advance. We also want them to be able to justify the answer they find and verify that it makes sense for the problem." We care about the process a student uses. And we *do* care about the answer.

Reflection and Discussion

FOR TEACHERS

- What issues or challenges does this message raise for you? In what ways do you agree with or disagree with the main points of the message?
- How can you help your students develop effective problem-solving approaches that value both the process and the answer?
- How can you demonstrate to students the value of an incorrect answer as part of a learning process that eventually can lead to a correct answer?
- How can you communicate to the community the value of learning a process even when a student arrives at an incorrect answer?

FOR FAMILIES

- What questions or issues does this message raise for you to discuss with your son or daughter, the teacher, or school leaders?
- How can you support your daughter's or son's learning in ways that value both the process used to solve a problem and also the answer?

FOR LEADERS AND POLICY MAKERS

- How does this message reinforce or challenge policies and decisions you have made or are considering?
- How do you support teachers in helping students learn mathematical processes as well as arrive at answers?
- How can you communicate to the public the importance of mathematical processes as well as the value of arriving at a correct answer?

RELATED MESSAGES

- Message 14, "Balance Is Basic," considers the need for a program to include conceptual understanding, computational skills, and problem solving as well as mathematical thinking and reasoning.
- Message 16, "Hard Arithmetic Isn't Deep Mathematics," looks at the need for depth as well as breadth of mathematics.
- Message 36, "I Know What an 82 Means!" considers the challenges of comprehensively evaluating students' work, including considering the process used and the answer to a problem.

FURTHER READING

- *Good Questions for Math Teaching: Why Ask Them and What to Ask, K–6* (Sullivan and Lilburn 2002) and *Good Questions for Math Teaching: Why Ask Them And What to Ask, Grades 5–8* (Schuster and Anderson 2005) offer great examples of questions teachers can ask in support of both better solution strategies and better answers.

- *Mathematics Assessment: Myths, Models, Good Questions, and Practical Suggestions* (Stenmark 1991) is a great resource for teachers in designing and administering a variety of classroom assessments that address both the process used and the end result.

- *Tough Choices or Tough Times: The Report of the New Commission on the Skills of the American Workforce* (National Center on Education and the Economy 2008) is a comprehensive report by a group largely outside of education that advocates raising the bar on what we expect of students and shifting our view of what education should provide to prepare workers and citizens for the twenty-first-century workforce.

23

The Power of Patterns

DRAWING ON MATHEMATICAL PATTERNS
AS WE TEACH

I n his book *On the Shoulders of Giants*, Lynn Steen (1999) offers an elegant discussion of mathematics as the language and science of *patterns*. In addition to an opening discussion on patterns, the book presents a series of five essays by experts in their particular fields of mathematics. The essays look at mathematical content and ideas in ways different from those typically used to organize school mathematics. These five discussions on *dimension*, *quantity*, *uncertainty*, *shape*, and *change* give us insights into patterns that can help students develop a deeper and more robust knowledge of mathematics.

Describing What Students Learn

These organizing concepts are beginning to appear in a small but growing number of states' mathematics standards. It is now not unusual to find standards that include the developing threads *change* or *uncertainty* as part of, or instead of, traditional strands typically labeled *number*, *operations*, *algebra*, *geometry*, *measurement*, or *data*. The most notable idea in Steen's book is the treatment of patterns as a concept, tool, and mathematical topic. The study of algebra or algebraic thinking is now often found in curriculum documents titled *Patterns and Algebraic Thinking*.

The attention to patterns has become a nearly universal element within the development of algebraic thinking, from early childhood through high school and beyond. In my own experience with teaching mathematics in French in Burkina Faso, West Africa, from 1999 to 2001, I came to realize how much I have internalized the use of patterns in teaching mathematics. At the beginning of my teaching there, I struggled to find one or more words in French that would communicate the power of the word *pattern* as I wanted to use it. In conversations with French-speaking colleagues, I decided that the French translations they offered were too limiting (at least in part because French was not my first language). I chose to instead teach my French-speaking students the word *pattern* in English, and we collaboratively created a meaning for it that supported its importance in mathematics for my teaching. This helped me develop basic ideas of algebra as I wanted to do and as we often do in the United States. Patterns help students move from concrete, numerical examples to making generalizations that they can describe and represent with models, words, tables, graphs, and—eventually—algebraic symbols. As students describe the patterns they notice in different representations of relationships, they move toward generalizing relationships; their algebraic thinking deepens.

In my work as a teacher and educator, my observations about patterns in school mathematics have grown beyond considerations of how we develop algebraic thinking or specific mathematical topics. I am now interested in how patterns might be helpful in the broader study of mathematics as a discipline. For example, what can we notice about patterns that might support students' learning of mathematical algorithms and procedures? How do patterns contribute to our understanding of unifying themes and ideas that help establish connections in mathematics? How can patterns help us uncover and appreciate the beauty and form in mathematics? And what patterns can we find to help us make sense of the underlying structure and properties within the discipline of mathematics? How we see the bigger picture of mathematics and how we use patterns to build understanding and generalizations can make a big difference in how and what our students learn. Following are some thoughts and examples to stimulate your thinking and discussion.

Algorithms and Procedures

An algorithm lays out a step-by-step process for a particular type of situation, such as performing multidigit addition or constructing a figure congruent to another. As such, an algorithm reflects a fundamental generalization of a pattern. We want students to build a tool kit of useful procedures, understanding the underlying patterns so well that they recognize algorithms that help them solve problems. Ideally, for ultimate efficiency, students memorize the smallest number of procedures that will serve them for the greatest number of situations. For example, in finding perimeter, it may be efficient for a student to internalize the unique pattern(s) underlying the algorithm for the calculation of the perimeter of a rectangle, based on the characteristics of the rectangle itself. A student who has internalized such a pattern does not need to memorize the formula $P = 2l + 2w$, but can immediately recognize the need to double the length, double the width, and add the results, or perhaps to add the measures of two adjacent sides and double the sum. The power of patterns with respect to algorithms is that a pattern allows students to observe, make sense of, and generalize a relationship. Patterns help students selectively and automatically call on and use the most important algorithms they need when they need them. In this sense, patterns represent the very essence of algorithms and procedures. Accordingly, an effective teacher will tap into underlying patterns to help students build their procedural tool kit.

Themes and Ideas

One of the most exciting discoveries for me as a mathematics educator has been recognizing and identifying unifying themes and ideas that connect mathematical knowledge across grade levels and across mathematical topics. I think of these themes as big ideas or connecting threads. What they represent at their foundation are patterns that show up over and over again, often in many different contexts. The patterns that underlie key mathematical concepts such as equivalence or proportionality help students make sense of otherwise disconnected bits of knowledge. With an understanding of equivalence, the $=$ sign becomes less an indication to give an answer and more an indication of a fundamental mathematical relationship. When students internalize this relationship based on patterns they have noticed, they begin to categorize numbers and expressions as being equivalent or not equivalent. They might compare $6 + 2$ with $9 - 1$ using the $=$ sign, since both expressions name something the same; or they might recognize that $5(2 + 3)$ and $5 \cdot 2 + 3$ cannot be connected with the $=$ sign, because the two expressions don't represent what students have come to understand as the pattern of equivalence. Students can extend this understanding to other parts of mathematics, such as recognizing whether two particular geometric forms are equivalent or congruent. The ability to build on the unifying pattern of equivalence across topics and grade levels opens up many avenues for higher levels of learning about mathematics.

Likewise, if students understand the patterns inherent in proportional relationships, this understanding can connect their early work with multiplication (noticing how the row of multiples of three in a multiplication table grows in a particular pattern with respect to how the row of multiples of six grows); their later work with equivalent fractions (understanding the need for both the numerator and the denominator to grow proportionally); their study of scale drawings or similarity (looking at the scale factor); their work with percents (representing a consistent portion of every unit); and their study of linearity (seeing how two quantities might be related with a simple linear equation). In this way, patterns of proportionality can be a bridge to algebra and much of the mathematics that follows.

Most students are unlikely to build this bridge, or use it to access later mathematics, on their own. Rather, students rely on their teacher as the engineer, architect, and guide who will skillfully ensure that they use this conceptual bridge to understand and apply what they have learned and to travel on to pursue more complex patterns in higher-level mathematics.

Beauty and Form

Often mathematicians speak of the beauty and elegance of mathematics and sometimes teachers do. But rarely do students. As we think about patterns in mathematics, both within the discipline itself and in the world around us, we are apt to notice patterns of symmetry (or its partner, asymmetry). We see patterns in shape, form, and number in both the natural and human-made environment, from spiral patterns of seashells, to patterns in the numbers of petals of flowers, to complex three-dimensional geometric structures in architecture. We can also describe aberrations in terms of patterns they follow or do not follow. We can notice the order in the universe and in our lives, and we can even notice the patterns in disorder as we explore underlying patterns of chaos and experience the beauty of fractals. An insightful teacher's goal is to help students look around them and notice that the patterns they observe in mathematics don't only deal with numbers, but also help us understand geometry, algebra, and other mathematical ideas that contribute to making sense of the world.

Structure and Properties

One of the most powerful attributes of mathematics to those of us who love it is its underlying structure. The National Council of Teachers of Mathematics (NCTM) recognized the importance of understanding the structure of number systems when they included a separate standard at the high school level on the structure of the real number system in *Curriculum and Evaluation Standards for School Mathematics* (1989). As students look at patterns within the structure of the number system they use every day, they formalize intuitive ideas and many years of experience, uncovering the ground rules of the system. They articulate how and why they can rearrange the numbers in an addition or multiplication problem, but not in a subtraction or division problem. They study the relationship between addition and subtraction and between multiplication and division. They understand how to make reasoned arguments, starting with simple explanations of their thinking and progressing to complex problems, convincing justifications, or formal proofs. As part of this organized structure of mathematics, and because of the use of patterns across a range of situations, knowledgeable teachers can help students to access otherwise inaccessible mathematical notions starting with simple patterns of numbers, objects, and procedures. Over time, these simple patterns mature into more sophisticated ideas that unify important mathematical characteristics and properties.

What Can We Do?

Recognizing and describing patterns is important for particular types of mathematical development, especially algebraic thinking. But patterns are also an important teaching tool in mathematics, as we help students understand ideas, learn skills, and solve problems. Recognizing and describing patterns is helpful to teachers and other educators in identifying central themes and important aspects of mathematics when we design instruction and guide student learning. Gaining new insights about mathematics from the patterns we discover (or rediscover) can give any of us—students or adults—an *aha!* moment. We might realize for the first time (or remember again) what is beautiful, unifying, organized, predictable, and unpredictable about mathematics.

Reflection and Discussion

FOR TEACHERS

- What issues or challenges does this message raise for you? In what ways do you agree with or disagree with the main points of the message?
- What are some of the most interesting or useful types of patterns that you've observed and think that students should notice or appreciate in mathematics?
- In what ways do you use patterns to organize or enhance your mathematics teaching or your students' mathematics learning? How can you use patterns to help students access challenging mathematical concepts and skills?

FOR FAMILIES

- What questions or issues does this message raise for you to discuss with your son or daughter, the teacher, or school leaders?
- Where can you look for patterns with your daughter or son, whether you think the patterns are mathematical or not?
- How can you work with the teacher to connect the patterns you and your family see to important mathematical ideas the patterns represent or relate to?

FOR LEADERS AND POLICY MAKERS

- How does this message reinforce or challenge policies and decisions you have made or are considering?
- How does your curriculum reflect unifying themes and big ideas that connect important mathematical concepts and skills?
- What kinds of professional learning experiences can you offer teachers to help them see and use patterns to improve mathematics teaching and learning?

RELATED MESSAGES

- Message 3, "Making the Case for Creativity," discusses the need for helping students develop their creative abilities in exploring and learning mathematics.
- Message 24, "Do It in Your Head," reinforces the importance of helping students build on their observations of patterns to learn mental math facts and techniques.

FURTHER READING

- *On the Shoulders of Giants: New Approaches to Numeracy* (Steen 1999) is an elegant discussion of mathematics as the language and science of patterns, with illuminating essays on dimension, quantity, uncertainty, shape, and change.
- *Mathematics: The Science of Patterns: The Search for Order in Life, Mind, and the Universe* (Devlin 1997) looks at patterns within the world of mathematics.
- *Curriculum and Evaluation Standards for School Mathematics* (NCTM 1989) provides the first professional recommendations for what should be included in K–12 mathematics, including a high school standard on mathematical structure and systems.

24

Do It In Your Head

THE POWER OF MENTAL MATH

W hat does it mean to know mathematics? This is a complex question, but there is strong agreement that facility with numbers, understanding mathematical ideas, and skill in problem solving play important roles in knowing mathematics. *Principles and Standards for School Mathematics* (NCTM 2000) calls for students to be proficient with tools that include pencil and paper and technology, as well as mental techniques. I would like to make a case for raising the status of *mental math*—a critical component in students' tool kits of mathematical knowledge. Mental math is often associated with the ability to do computations quickly, but in its broadest sense, mental math also involves conceptual understanding and problem solving.

Mental Math Concepts

Understanding what numbers mean and what operations mean is the foundation for learning increasingly complex mathematics. Younger students should be able to recognize the number of objects represented in familiar patterns such as the five dots on the side of a die or eight objects arranged in two rows of four. For two- or even three-digit numbers, students might associate a numeral with a mental image of a base ten model that shows ones, tens, and hundreds; or students might devise other pictures based on patterns they notice as they work with the number. Carrying such mental pictures of the size and value of numbers prepares students for learning addition and multiplication facts and for solving simple problems involving computation. As students develop the mental ability to see numbers as being made up of other numbers (for example, seeing 125 as $100 + 20 + 5$ or as $100 + 25$ or as 12 tens and 5 ones), their understanding of the number system expands, along with their ability to use numbers.

Mental Computation

Ideally, students should have ready mental recall of single-digit addition and multiplication facts. Ready knowledge of such facts is an important component of mathematical knowledge and is helpful in solving problems. Beyond facts, students should also know how to multiply numbers mentally by ten, one hundred, or one thousand. Additionally, students should be able to come up with combinations that add up to ten or one hundred. Students should know the pairs of whole numbers that add up to ten, realizing that, for instance, both 6 + 4 and 4 + 6 represent the same thing, but also that these two expressions mean the same as 1 + 9. When presented with a two-digit number like thirty-seven, students should be able to think of its "hundred partner," in this case, sixty-three. There are many other quick tips and mental shortcuts that can help students perform calculations mentally or that can aid them as they perform paper-and-pencil calculations.

Mental Problem Solving

Problem solving continues to be a high priority in school mathematics. Some educators argue that it is the most important mathematical goal for our students. Mental math provides both tools for solving problems and filters for evaluating answers. When a student has strong mental math skills, she can quickly test different approaches to a problem and determine whether the resulting path will lead toward a viable solution. Estimation skills require both a sense of number and facility with mental computation. Using estimation skills, a student can generate a ballpark answer to a problem before attempting to solve it. Estimation also offers a comparison point by which to judge whether a result is reasonable for the given situation. Estimation is an important part of students' tool kits, whether they perform calculations with a pencil and paper or on a calculator.

Mental Math in the Big Picture

Mental math proficiency represents one important dimension of mathematical knowledge. Not all individuals will develop rapid mental number skills to the same degree. Some will find their strength in mathematics through other avenues, such as visual or graphic representations or creativity in solving problems. But mental math has a clear place in school mathematics. It is an area where many parents and families feel comfortable offering support and assistance to their children.

Mental math need not depend on rote memorization. In fact, the development of mental models for numbers and operations is greatly facilitated by students engaging in purposeful experiences with concrete objects and number patterns. Teachers play a vital role in making sure that these experiences are connected in meaningful ways to the mathematics we ask students to learn, both written and mental.

What Can We Do?

In today's world of standards and standardized tests, mental math seems to have taken a backseat to other aspects of mathematics. Perhaps this is because the development of mental techniques is not always explicitly identified in state standards, or perhaps it's because mental math is difficult to assess. Whatever the reason, the time has come to invest in helping students build mental math skills as part of their comprehensive mathematical understanding. The payoff for this investment can be tremendous, both in improving students' mathematical abilities and in sending a visible signal that we are committed to preparing students with the kind of mathematical proficiency that the public can readily see and appreciate.

Reflection and Discussion

FOR TEACHERS

- What issues or challenges does this message raise for you? In what ways do you agree with or disagree with the main points of the message?
- What are the most important mental math skills, tips, or shortcuts that students should know?
- What are some ways you can help students develop their facility with mental math?

FOR FAMILIES

- What questions or issues does this message raise for you to discuss with your son or daughter, the teacher, or school leaders?
- How can you help your daughter or son practice mental math skills at home? What guidance or help would you like to see the school or teacher provide to support efforts at home?

FOR LEADERS AND POLICY MAKERS

- How does this message reinforce or challenge policies and decisions you have made or are considering?
- How can you support the development of mental math?
- What kinds of professional learning experiences might help teachers strengthen students' mental math skills?

RELATED MESSAGES

- Message 14, "Balance Is Basic," looks at the characteristics of a balanced mathematics program.
- Message 27, "A Math Message to Families," makes recommendations for parents and family members on how to support students' mathematics learning, including mental math.
- Message 23, "The Power of Patterns," reminds us that patterns help students remember mathematical facts and build mental math skills.
- Message 18, "Faster Isn't Smarter," discusses the trap of timed tests, which can sometimes interfere with learning mental math.

FURTHER READING

- *About Teaching Mathematics: A K–8 Resource* (Burns 2007a) includes considerable attention to the role of mental math within a broader comprehensive discussion of school mathematics.
- "Marilyn Burns: Mental Math" (Burns 2007b) addresses the importance of including mental math in our school mathematics programs and discusses several aspects of helping students develop mental math skills.
- *Mental Math in the Primary Grades* (Hope, Leutzinger, Reys, and Reys 1988), *Mental Math in the Middle Grades* (Hope, Reys, and Reys 1987), and *Mental Math in Junior High, Grades 7–9* (Hope, Reys, and Reys 1988) all provide support for developing mental math skills through recognizing patterns and building an understanding of numbers and operations, supported by an array of classroom activities.

25 Pushing Algebra Down

IS SOONER BETTER?

W e expect more mathematics of our students in today's rapidly changing world than in years past. In response to these higher expectations, an increasing number of schools are choosing to offer, or require, a course in algebra for students in grade 8. Some schools are moving to teach Algebra 1 in even earlier grades.[1] The motivation for this move is admirable and appropriate; all students need to learn challenging high school mathematics that prepares them for postsecondary programs, and too many students have been excluded from studying such high-level courses. While this solution may help some students, it's not the solution that best serves all of our students.

How We Got Here

In contrast to the traditional United States secondary mathematics program, the curriculum that our colleagues in Canada, Mexico, and the rest of the world teach does not define Algebra 1 as a separate course (nor Geometry or Algebra 2), but rather integrates mathematics into a more continuous pre-K–12 program that includes content from various important mathematical areas of study, including algebra, geometry, trigonometry, and statistics. In the United States, we have struggled to bridge the gap between computational procedures at the elementary level and a secondary program anchored by a course called Algebra 1. In years past, we have used middle school to review and remediate

---

[1]Some schools organize high school mathematics with course names like Algebra 1, Geometry, and Algebra 2, but others call courses by different names or may offer integrated mathematics courses that include algebra, geometry, statistics and other topics. In this message, any reference to Algebra 1 can generally apply to the first year of high school–level mathematics.

students who have not mastered the arithmetic taught in elementary grades. Rather than bore the students who have mastered these skills, we have frequently followed the practice of accelerating them into Algebra 1 prior to grade 9. Thus we often created a cycle of inequity and untapped potential, where some students skipped over middle school (or junior high) mathematics and other students were destined to use those years to repeat what they had been taught before. Parents of students chosen for acceleration were proud that their sons and daughters were able to omit one or more years of middle school math, while we lowered our expectations for the rest of our students. In either case, we essentially gave up on middle school in terms of the possibility that students might gain something substantial in middle school mathematics itself.

Today, we recognize that this cycle of low expectations and missed opportunities for some students has resulted in a large number of students leaving secondary school ill-equipped for future options, particularly minority students and students living in poverty. One solution embraced by parents and policy makers has been to offer or require Algebra 1 or a high school integrated mathematics course earlier and for more, or all, students. Expecting all students to complete four years of high school mathematics that begins with this gatekeeper course is not only a good idea but also our moral and ethical responsibility. But moving in just a few years from a system that in the past limited many students to essentially no high school–level mathematics courses to a system that suddenly requires students to begin their study of high school mathematics in grade 7 or 8 may not achieve our desired goals. Worse, we may end up unintentionally disadvantaging the very students we claim to serve.

Going Further or Stopping Sooner?

One argument in favor of an early algebra course says that such a course makes it possible for more students to take five years of high school mathematics including Precalculus and Advanced Placement (AP) Calculus or AP Statistics. However, many communities are finding that students who start algebra early do not necessarily end up studying more mathematics. In fact, some students complete their mathematics requirement prior to grade 12 and choose not to enroll in any mathematics course for a year or more before they go on to postsecondary study or work. This is especially true if students have negative experiences in mathematics, and the result can have disastrous results after high school. Other students struggle in algebra classes, perhaps because of gaps in their background, because of inadequately prepared teachers, because of a lack of adequate support for students or their teachers, or simply because students are not prepared to deal with some of the abstraction of algebra. Many of these students repeat Algebra 1 over and over again.

Making Decisions About Early Algebra

Any system offering or requiring Algebra 1 in eighth grade or earlier should seriously consider at least two important questions. First, how can the system ensure that students develop the skills and thinking that constitute a rich, contemporary middle school program that leads into success in Algebra 1 (or its integrated mathematics equivalent)? Second, what lies ahead for students at the other end of their high school mathematics sequence?

In terms of the first question, many middle schools today offer all students the opportunity to explore a rich array of mathematical topics anchored in proportional reasoning that extends well beyond the unit I remember teaching on ratio, proportion, and percent when I started my career in the early 1970s. Students with a deep understanding of what it means when two quantities are proportionally related have an increased likelihood of success at Algebra 1 or the first year of an integrated high school program. As they study proportional relationships across mathematical topics, they connect critical notions of geometry, such as similarity and scaling, to ideas involving numbers and algebra. Ideally, middle school mathematics should continue to develop a strong thread of algebraic thinking begun in the elementary curriculum and should connect to important ideas in algebra and geometry. Students can use their increasing understanding of generalizations and relationships, as well as other more abstract notions, to deal with data and elementary statistics and to solve increasingly complex problems. If a middle school mathematics program does not offer this kind of powerful mathematics, balanced across all the threads of mathematics and focused on proportionality and algebraic thinking, then the school community should consider fixing the program, not accelerating students out of it. In some schools, students may be rushed to prepare for algebra as early as grade 6 or 7, narrowing their program even further to pre-algebra skills, or pre-pre-algebra skills, and missing even more of the mathematics curriculum.

The second point is equally important. There is little or no reason to accelerate a student into Algebra 1 unless the student intends to continue mathematics study through the equivalent of Geometry, Algebra 2, Precalculus (including Trigonometry), and a fifth year of secondary study in an academically appropriate course such as Calculus or Statistics. Furthermore, when students begin their high school study as early as grade 7, or when they are permitted to double up on mathematics courses via semester block scheduling, schools should ensure that even more options are available after the traditional high school mathematics sequence (such as an applied statistics course, discrete mathematics, or quantitative reasoning), so that students can study some mathematics every year they are in school. These options might be available as part of the high school's course offerings or offered in conjunction with a higher education institution. If a school does not make such courses available or does not encourage students to continue studying mathematics every year, there is little purpose to accelerating students into secondary mathematics prior to grade 9.

What Can We Do?

Whether students are in a good traditional program or a good integrated mathematics program, they should begin high school mathematics early only if they are motivated to do so, if they intend to study mathematics every year in school through at least the calculus or statistics level, if the system is structured to accommodate this advanced coursework, and if they also study proportionality and the most important components of a good middle school program prior to beginning high school study. Whenever students begin their study of algebra, what is most important is that they are taught a rich algebra program in a way that engages them in solving challenging problems and helps them learn powerful tools and mathematical habits of mind they can use long after they complete the course.

We must expect all of our students to learn mathematics well beyond what we previously expected. We need all students to be more proficient than in the past, and we need many more students to pursue careers based on mathematics and science. But we should move students into high school mathematics very carefully, not precipitously, and we should ensure that every student is supported well to succeed in a rich, relevant, rigorous mathematics experience every year they are in elementary and secondary school.

Reflection and Discussion

FOR TEACHERS

- What issues or challenges does this message raise for you? In what ways do you agree with or disagree with the main points of the message?
- How can we give students a stronger mathematics experience without necessarily starting them earlier?

(continued)

- How can we teach algebra at the elementary, middle, and high school levels in a manner that engages, challenges, and prepares all students for the mathematics they need for their future?

FOR FAMILIES

- What questions or issues does this message raise for you to discuss with your son or daughter, the teacher, or school leaders?
- What are the advantages and the challenges your daughter or son will face if accelerated into high school mathematics in grade 8 or earlier?
- Before making a decision about acceleration, what paths have you determined are possible through high school that include a mathematics course every year? Which path(s) might provide your son or daughter with the greatest likelihood of success and also the most options after high school?

FOR LEADERS AND POLICY MAKERS

- How does this message reinforce or challenge policies and decisions you have made or are considering?
- How is the development of algebra and algebraic thinking incorporated as a continuous part of your pre-K–12 curriculum, or how can it be incorporated?
- What provisions are in place for students when they complete Algebra 1, Geometry, and Algebra 2, or Integrated Mathematics 1, 2, and 3? Do you have adequate options for students every year in high school, regardless of whether students plan to pursue a mathematics-intensive major or proceed into other postsecondary study or workforce training programs?

RELATED MESSAGES

- Message 9, "Increasing Access or Ensuring Failure?," considers what needs to happen in a system as we raise graduation requirements.
- Message 2, "Untapped Potential," discusses the need for all students to have rigorous and relevant mathematics experiences.

FURTHER READING

- *Radical Equations: Civil Rights from Mississippi to the Algebra Project* (Moses and Cobb 2001) discusses the relationship of algebra to civil rights and presents a different and compelling perspective about students studying Algebra 1 in eighth grade, including a discussion of Moses's Algebra Project.

- *Thinking Mathematically: Integrating Arithmetic and Algebra in Elementary School* (Carpenter, Franke, and Levi 2003) looks at the development of algebraic thinking and its relationship to arithmetic in elementary grades.

- *College Knowledge: What It Really Takes for Students to Succeed and What We Can Do to Get Them Ready* (Conley 2008) discusses what it takes to succeed in college today beyond entrance requirements, including discussions of issues around the implementation of Advanced Placement courses and the discrepancies between what high schools and colleges expect of students.

- *Fostering Algebraic Thinking: A Guide for Teachers, Grades 6–10* (Driscoll 1999) describes how to incorporate meaningful experiences in algebraic thinking throughout middle school and high school so that students move smoothly from numerical skills to a powerful set of algebraic tools regardless of when they take a formal algebra class.

26 Beyond Pockets of Wonderfulness

WORKING ACROSS BOUNDARIES AND TRANSITIONS

A third-grade class is engaged in an innovative lesson on multiplication. An algebra teacher tries a new approach to teaching functions. A mathematician works with high school students on their geometry projects. What do these isolated events have in common? They all represent what I call "pockets of wonderfulness"— good ideas with great potential grounded in sound practice. Pockets of wonderfulness can appear in essentially any type of school setting. Students get excited, learn something new, and become motivated to pursue their study of mathematics. So what's the problem?

The problem is that when great events happen in isolation from the larger system within which they operate, we fall short of what might be possible otherwise. Educators generate tremendous power by talking to one another and working together. Articulation and collaboration are important tools for making lasting systemic change. When educators fail to take advantage of these tools, students are destined to restart, lose ground, and miss opportunities to connect mathematical ideas.

Articulation

When teachers communicate within and across grade levels, they can make joint decisions about when and how to develop important mathematical ideas. Teachers can work together to answer many kinds of questions, such as:

- At which grade level should teachers be responsible for developing multiplication as a concept?

- When should students spend the most time learning the meaning of fractions?

- If we teach length measurement in four consecutive grade levels, what should we teach differently each year and how can the work of each year build on the work of the previous year?

- To prepare for success in an algebra course, what kind of work in proportionality should students experience beforehand, and in what grades?

- How does the notion of equivalence develop across the grades?

- What key ideas should be the focus of the math curriculum at each grade level?

- Which elements of algebra contribute most to students' success in other mathematics or science courses?

Questions such as these create great opportunities for teachers to talk with one another about instructional decisions. Engaging in such discussions can liberate teachers from unspoken assumptions that can unnecessarily consume classroom time. When teachers agree on where they will focus their instructional time, students are able to spend more class time focusing on high-priority topics. By making curriculum decisions together, we can promote seamless articulation across the levels, enabling students to build a solid understanding of mathematical ideas that can be extended to deeper and higher-level mathematics. By discussing and planning instruction together, we can avoid unnecessary repetition and minimize the possibility of gaps in students' mathematical development. Even more important, by talking with each other, we can increase the likelihood that the wonderful thing that a teacher or a class does at one level will be used to students' advantage in following years.

Collaboration

Articulation across levels is one important arena for working with colleagues, whether done within a school system or across systems. Collaboration between and among teachers can also be a powerful aid to the success of teachers who are attempting to implement something new or different in their classrooms. Changing classroom practices often involves taking a risk—going outside the bounds of what is familiar to make improvements. It can be lonely for a teacher to innovate individually. But when we try something new with colleagues, we can rely on a ready-made support system of peers who are going through similar challenges or excitement together. As teachers commiserate together, think together, and tackle problems together, this collaboration greatly increases the probability that a new approach or program will succeed, with potentially greater gains for students. Looking at examples of student work provides a wonderful foundation for this kind of collaboration, as well as for informing articulation decisions such as those mentioned earlier. As they look closely at student work, teachers might discuss what is different about what they can expect at one grade level or another, or why students in one teacher's class seem to have a deeper understanding than students in another class. Anchoring collaboration and articulation discussions in what students are actually doing enriches the nature and outcomes of professional teacher interactions.

Building a Common Culture for Next Year

As for students, the most negative aspect of trying to succeed as they navigate a system made up of pockets of wonderfulness may be the time that a new practice or new expectations take to become established in the classroom. Teachers report that when they implement something new, such as a particular way of operating in small groups, it can take a few months before students become comfortable with it. This is especially true for comprehensive programs or dramatically different instructional techniques, such as interactive small-group instruction or a more student-centered classroom. Sometimes, just as students are getting comfortable with the new approach that this year's teacher uses, they move on to the next year's teacher. If that teacher has different expectations for how students are to ask or answer questions, organize their work, or participate in class, the students may take weeks (or longer) to adjust. Students can become frustrated and lose progress they made the previous year. If, on the other hand, teachers in a school work together to implement a new program or approach, students can build momentum, expanding their learning significantly each year. For some students, the ground they lose or steps they retrace each year can mask their true potential and hide from teachers what these students might be capable of achieving under a more aligned system.

What Can We Do?

Pockets of wonderfulness are, in a word, wonderful. Using great materials that engage and challenge students in rich mathematical tasks, or implementing an effective practice where students have to think and communicate mathematically, can have positive results for students. For teachers, learning about and trying out a student-centered classroom or placing more emphasis on understanding is part of healthy professional growth. But in today's rapidly changing world, these pockets of wonderfulness fall short of delivering to students the opportunity to learn all they can. Our challenge as educators is to work together and multiply the impact of the wonderful ideas that teachers have in classrooms, schools, districts, and states. When we do this, teaching becomes more coherent and students' learning becomes continuous and cumulative, resulting in year after year of wonderfulness.

Reflection and Discussion

FOR TEACHERS

- What issues or challenges does this message raise for you? In what ways do you agree with or disagree with the main points of the message?
- What challenges have you found in reaching out to other teachers to improve coordination and articulation within or across levels, and how can you address those challenges?
- What successes have you had in collaborating with others to understand and effectively use new practices or programs? How were those efforts initiated and supported?
- If you are the only math teacher in a school or at a grade level, in what ways does your situation make innovation harder or easier? How can you make up for this potential isolation by connecting with others?

FOR FAMILIES

- What questions or issues does this message raise for you to discuss with your son or daughter, the teacher, or school leaders?
- How can you help your daughter or son when expectations and classroom organization may change from year to year?
- If you see your son or daughter learning well and thriving in a particular type of classroom structure or program, how can you communicate to teachers and school officials the importance of continuing in this type of classroom?

FOR LEADERS AND POLICY MAKERS

- How does this message reinforce or challenge policies and decisions you have made or are considering?
- How can you sustain new programs over time so that teachers are not constantly changing the ground rules for students and so that students can build on what they know each year?
- What opportunities can you provide teachers so that they can work together across classroom, grade-level, and school lines toward a coherent program and consistent improvement?

RELATED MESSAGES

- Message 13, "Seek First to Understand," looks at the challenges of working across communities, both public and professional.
- Message 39, "Standing on the Shoulders . . . ," reminds us of the importance and value of learning from each other.
- Message 2, "Untapped Potential," discusses the need to raise expectations and support all students in meeting those expectations.

FURTHER READING

- *Leading the Way: Principals and Superintendents Look at Math Instruction* (Burns 1999) offers insights and suggestions from six leaders about their ongoing efforts to improve mathematics teaching and learning.
- *Failure Is Not an Option™: Six Principles That Guide Student Achievement in High-Performing Schools* (Blankstein 2004) provides inspiration and practical ideas on transforming schools systemically, including the importance of both collaboration and engagement of the broader community.
- *Learning By Doing: A Handbook for Professional Learning Communities at Work* (DuFour, DuFour, Eaker, and Many 2006) provides guidance for developing professional learning communities in support of the improvement of teaching and learning.
- *Whatever It Takes: How Professional Learning Communities Respond When Kids Don't Learn* (DuFour, Eaker, Harhanek, and DuFour 2004) describes the power of a professional community to work together in support of student learning.
- *Leading Every Day: One Hundred and Twenty-Four Actions for Effective Leadership* (Kaser, Mundry, Stiles, and Loucks-Horsley 2006) offers daily leadership activities organized around four themes that include leading professional learning communities and leading collaborative groups.

27 A Math Message to Families

HELPING STUDENTS PREPARE FOR THE FUTURE

The world is changing. Not too many years ago, perhaps when you were in school, all students were expected to study mathematics, generally focused on arithmetic procedures, through elementary and middle school. Much of school mathematics beyond middle school was viewed as optional, with only some students enrolling in Algebra 1 and more advanced courses. Those who showed promise in mathematics probably began high school Algebra 1 early so that they could take more mathematics to prepare for a mathematics-related field in college. But many other students only studied mathematics for a year or two, often stopping without ever studying algebra, geometry, or higher-level mathematics.

What's Wrong with Yesterday?

Today we acknowledge several things about yesterday's vision of school mathematics. First, within that past system, we failed to recognize the talents of many students. Many classrooms consisted solely of lectures—teachers tended to tell students the procedures they should learn and then assign exercises to practice those procedures. Students who "got it" were able to master those procedures and perhaps apply them to solve word problems. Excellent teachers—teachers who may have pushed all students to succeed—taught the most fortunate students. But many students' talents went unnoticed and undeveloped as they sat unengaged in math class. Perhaps these students didn't learn well as passive listeners; perhaps they missed a critical lesson and never caught up; perhaps they just required more time to learn what some students learned more quickly. For whatever reason, many students did not receive the benefit of a challenging, high-quality mathematics education. Perhaps you were someone who thrived in the system.

Or perhaps you were among those who never saw themselves as the math type and who never saw math in their future. Whatever your experiences as a student, your current perceptions and beliefs about mathematics can have a tremendous impact on your son's or daughter's experience with mathematics.

What Students Need Today

As Thomas L. Friedman describes in depth in *The World Is Flat* (2007) the rapidly changing global society we now face calls for a dramatically different vision of the worker of the future. Regardless of whether a student enrolls in college or chooses to enter the workforce directly after high school, he will need a much stronger educational background than previous generations did. The need for communication skills, the arts, and the social sciences is as great as ever, but now our young people face competition from well-educated workers around the world—workers especially strong in math and science skills. The workplace training programs and certification programs they might pursue for their future now demand more mathematics, science, and technology than ever before, and essentially all workers in jobs with a future need to be able to reason and think critically and creatively.

Even in life beyond the workplace, scientific issues dominate the nation's political and economic discussions and overflow into every dimension of our lives, calling for scientific literacy in issues ranging from health care to energy use in our homes to taking care of our planet. Today we need new mathematical skills to bring meaning and order to the flood of data and statistical information that hits us every day. Our definition of an educated person is now a much richer vision than in previous times, when reading, writing, and some basic arithmetic would suffice for day-to-day survival. Today's literacy also means quantitative literacy, scientific literacy, and high-level critical thinking and problem-solving skills.

What Can You Do?

So what can families do to support a student's education, especially in mathematics? Consider the following suggestions:

• Help students understand the value of education and the importance of math and science. Let them know that even though math may get difficult sometimes, it is critical for their future.

- Send positive messages about mathematics. Saying that you never were good at math or that you don't like it can have a lasting impact on a student. Even if you can't show your love of mathematics, you can communicate enthusiasm and support for your daughter's or son's work and interest in mathematics.

- Look for math around you. With young children, notice the shapes and numbers in nature, buildings, and so on; with older students, notice and discuss the numerical data, statistical information, and scientific news in the media.

- Help students learn to persevere, a talent uniquely lacking in the U.S. student population compared with students from other countries. Sticking with a challenging math problem to arrive at a solution is one of the most rewarding experiences a student can have and also one of the most important habits of mind a student can develop.

- Be comfortable with not knowing everything your son or daughter is studying. Look at the resources listed at the end of this message to provide support as you help with homework. Come up with a family math problem to work on together that involves mathematics you have never seen before.

- Volunteer to help at school, but be flexible, as not all schools are set up to make good use of volunteers, especially if volunteers come only occasionally or at unscheduled times. Understand that the biggest help you can provide, whether you volunteer in school or not, is to be supportive of your daughter's or son's mathematical development within your own family.

- Be open to a changing picture of school, of the mathematics being taught, and of the ways in which mathematics is taught, as society's needs change and as we continue to learn more about teaching and learning.

Ideally, this message and these recommendations will cause you to think of other ways in which you can support a rich and successful mathematics education for your son or daughter. Educating a student is far more effective when parents or caregivers work in partnership with the school. Each plays important roles that help students develop mathematical thinking, knowledge, and skills. Helping every student build a strong mathematical foundation opens the door to higher-level mathematics, science, and other disciplines that will enable students to tackle the critical problems facing the world today and build a strong future for themselves and their families.

Reflection and Discussion

FOR TEACHERS

- What issues or challenges does this message raise for you? In what ways do you agree with or disagree with the main points of the message?
- How might you choose to use this message or something like it to reach out to parents and caregivers in support of students' mathematics learning?

FOR FAMILIES

- What questions or issues does this message raise for you to discuss with your son or daughter, the teacher, or school leaders?
- Which recommendations from this message seem like steps you might choose to take in support of your daughter's or son's mathematics learning? Which ones do you question or think might be difficult to undertake?
- In what other ways might you support your son's or daughter's mathematics learning?

FOR LEADERS AND POLICY MAKERS

- How does this message reinforce or challenge policies and decisions you have made or are considering?
- How might you use the ideas from this message or other ideas to engage families in supporting students' mathematics learning?

RELATED MESSAGES

- Message 1, "Math for a Flattening World," makes a case for changing how schools prepare students for a rapidly changing twenty-first-century society.
- Message 18, "Faster Isn't Smarter," presents a changing view of timed tests on fact recall.
- Message 4, "Good Old Days," looks at swings of the pendulum over time with respect to changing our philosophy of teaching mathematics.
- Message 13, "Seek First to Understand," addresses the importance of involving families and other audiences in discussions and decisions involving school mathematics.

- The "For Families" discussion questions at the end of each message in this book can provide a starting place for involving families in the mathematics education of their children or teens.

FURTHER READING

- The Family Resources page of the National Council of Teachers of Mathematics (www.nctm.org/resources/families) provides resources and downloadable brochures for families, including tips for helping with homework and talking with your student's math teacher. It also includes links to other resources, such as NCTM's Figure This! website (www.figurethis.org/) that contains problems for families to work on together with their middle school students.

- *A Family's Guide: Fostering Your Child's Success in School Mathematics* (Mirra 2005) provides families and schools with ideas for how to involve families in their children's mathematics programs and how families can support their children's mathematics learning.

- *Family Math* (Stenmark, Thompson, and Cossey 1986) and the Family Math program at the University of California Lawrence Hall of Science (www.lawrencehallofscience.org/equals) provide activities (some in Spanish) that families can do together with elementary and middle school children. They also suggest ways for schools and communities to offer Family Math events.

- *Getting Your Math Message Out to Parents: A K–6 Resource* (Litton 1998) offers suggestions for educators in reaching out to families in support of students' mathematics learning, including ideas for newsletters, conferences, and how to involve family volunteers in schools.

www   This message is also available in printable format at
www.mathsolutions.com/fasterisntsmarter.

III

Real Students and Real Teachers

MATHEMATICS IN TODAY'S CLASSROOMS

28

So Now You're a Teacher

BEGINNING A PROFESSIONAL JOURNEY

When I began teaching more than three decades ago, I was full of idealism, energy, and optimism about what I could accomplish. I had learned my teaching skills in a fairly traditional teacher education program, and I knew my responsibility was to present lessons clearly, demonstrating the procedure or rule for the day and convincing students that it worked. My students may not always have followed what I was doing, but I hoped that experience would help me get better at this new craft. I naïvely gave myself three years to become an excellent teacher.

What I discovered after three years of teaching was that I was able to make it almost to spring break without having an emotional crisis over my effectiveness in the classroom. I was a better teacher three years into my career than when I started, but I still had a lot to learn. What I found myself doing in those early years, and what I have seen many teachers do as they begin their careers, was going through the motions— performing the mechanical act of teaching. Beginning teachers often fall into a pattern of mechanical teaching, doing what they think they're supposed to do, without making complex professional adjustments or pushing students too deeply. I filled out the lesson plan book, usually with a variation of the day or week before, gathered together whatever materials I needed, worked out the exercises ahead of time so I could anticipate questions, presented the lesson clearly, and tried to engage students by calling on them. I found interesting activities to spice things up from time to time, but I tended to use such tasks on a somewhat superficial level. Teachers from excellent teacher education programs today may enter teaching with a richer set of strategies, but I would argue that in their first year or two, these teachers still apply their strategies somewhat more mechanically than they eventually will as they become more experienced.

The Influence of the School Environment

The environment of a school clearly influences the attitudes and actions of a new teacher, even more than our teacher education experience. The school where I spent most of my early teaching years was an experimental junior high school with special funding to support shared decision making and innovative school organizational structures. We had a culture of open communication, we learned active listening skills, and we tried to operate in a cooperative environment. Because I was not yet experienced in how to do these things well, at the beginning I tended to fall back on the same set of questions to accompany each lesson and still relied heavily on my mostly traditional textbooks for each day's lesson. I realize now how fortunate I was to be in such a nurturing environment while I was going through this stage of my development as a teacher. Each year I came closer to the vision of teaching and learning our school embodied.

Not long ago I visited a school that was very different from the school where I started my teaching. Having spent time in the university teacher education program where most of the school's teachers were prepared, I was at first surprised by the relatively superficial level of teaching I saw in the school, compared to the progressive and engaging approach to teaching I saw at the university. But as I found out more about the school, I realized that the environment of the school was based on a very narrow view of teaching. The school culture and expectations clearly overrode what the new teachers had learned before starting to teach there. Instead of providing a nurturing environment where these early-career teachers might practice their tentative, fragile, and still developing skills to engage students in active discourse around mathematics, this school had implemented a system of regimented prescriptions for each day's mathematics teaching. School administrators had distributed notebooks containing daily objectives for each course, dissected from the state's mathematics standards. The materials essentially guided teachers and students through a list of accomplishments to check off on that day's notebook page. In such a restrictive environment focused on limiting and often low-level objectives, teachers might indefinitely remain stuck at a mechanical level of teaching.

The way in which a school system values, nurtures, and supports a new teacher can also make a tremendous difference in how successful the teacher will be. On a visit to a rural area of New England, I heard a story that dramatically communicated the importance of supporting new teachers. The teacher who was driving me to visit schools told me of a married couple, both first-year teachers. The wife was an English teacher and the husband was a mathematics teacher. In this rural area, teaching positions were scarce and they were not able to find teaching jobs in the same town. So they accepted jobs eighty miles apart and chose to live somewhere in between, each making a hefty commute.

They decided they would see how things went that year to determine whether they would stay in their respective schools for the future. During that first year, the English teacher, joining a staff of two or three other teachers, was assigned a full schedule of large classes, including the classes that more senior teachers did not want to teach. She was left on her own. Her husband, the mathematics teacher, was assigned a reduced schedule in a team-teaching structure so that he would have an opportunity to become grounded in teaching in his new school before assuming a full teaching load on his own the following year. The entire, albeit small, mathematics department saw it as their responsibility to support this new teacher as his mentors and colleagues. It is not surprising that after the first year, the wife decided not only to leave the school but also to leave teaching. The husband eagerly signed his contract to remain in the school where he now felt fairly confident about his future as a teacher, at least well enough to come back for the second year and continue to refine his teaching.

What Can We Do?

Looking at teaching in discrete stages presents an oversimplified and overgeneralized view of the complex act of teaching. But it is helpful to remind ourselves that new teachers, whether coming from teacher education programs or from other careers later in life, are in fact novices. We need to remember that as novices, we are not as effective now as we will be later in our careers. Our goal as early-career teachers should be to be the best teacher we can be now, focusing on developing competence, planning well, implementing what we plan, taking appropriate risks, paying attention to what is going on, and making adjustments when we need to. More than that, our goal should be to communicate to our students our passion about teaching and the value of the content we teach. We develop as teachers by committing to learning as much as we can about mathematics, about teaching, and about how students learn. We also develop by building on best teaching practices and the rapidly growing body of brain research and other research about learning. We become more accomplished teachers not only with experience but also by consciously stretching ourselves to try out what we learn and by collaborating with our colleagues, and even with our students, to constantly improve our students' learning experience. Getting beyond our first years of teaching requires not only this commitment from the teacher but also a commitment from those who support the teacher. This multifaceted commitment is essential if we are to value the investment already made in preparing the teacher and if we are to reduce the number of new teachers who leave the profession within their first few years. As teachers become more experienced and more effective, they can serve to mentor and support novice teachers entering the profession. We owe it to every new teacher to help them become the best teacher possible, and we owe students the opportunity to learn from a well-qualified and well-supported teaching force.

Reflection and Discussion

FOR TEACHERS

- What issues or challenges does this message raise for you? In what ways do you agree with or disagree with the main points of the message?
- Where are you in your development as a teacher? Are you still going through the motions at a mechanical level, or have you moved toward engaging students in deeper learning?
- What are your next steps in terms of your own professional learning to help you move toward more effective teaching?

FOR FAMILIES

- What questions or issues does this message raise for you to discuss with your son or daughter, the teacher, or school leaders?
- How can you work with and support new teachers in your school or community?

FOR LEADERS AND POLICY MAKERS

- How does this message reinforce or challenge policies and decisions you have made or are considering?
- How can you best support early-career teachers with an environment in which they can fine-tune their teaching and develop past the mechanical act of teaching toward more student engagement and, eventually, deeper learning?

RELATED MESSAGES

- Message 29, "The Evolution of a Mathematics Teacher," continues this discussion, considering the career-long development of a professional mathematics teacher.
- Message 26, "Beyond Pockets of Wonderfulness," reflects on the power of collaboration and articulation to improve teaching and learning.

FURTHER READING

- *Empowering the Beginning Teacher of Mathematics: Elementary School* (Chappell, Schielack, and Zagorski 2004), *Empowering the Beginning Teacher of Mathematics: Middle School* (Chappell and Pateracki 2004), and *Empowering the Beginning Teacher of Mathematics: High School* (Chappell, Choppin, and Salls 2004) discuss issues relevant to new teachers, with experienced educators and leaders providing advice and tips on every aspect of mathematics teaching.

- *Mentoring New Teachers Through Collaborative Coaching: Linking Teacher and Student Learning* and *Mentoring New Teachers Through Collaborative Coaching: Facilitation and Training Guide* (Dunne and Villani 2007b, 2007a) offer support for new teachers over their first one to three years.

- *So You Have to Teach Math? Sound Advice for K–6 Teachers* (Burns and Silbey 2000) and *So You Have to Teach Math? Sound Advice for Grades 6–8 Teachers* (Rectanus 2006) are useful question-and-answer resources for teachers, especially those beginning their journey as teachers of mathematics.

- *About Teaching Mathematics: A K–8 Resource* (Burns 2007a) addresses some of the most challenging issues of mathematics teaching and provides a wealth of classroom resources.

- *Math Matters: Understanding the Math You Teach, Grades K–8* (Chapin and Johnson 2006) helps teachers clarify their understanding of key topics in elementary and middle school mathematics.

29 The Evolution of a Mathematics Teacher

HOW WE DEVELOP AS PROFESSIONALS

In visiting classrooms over the years, I've had the opportunity to watch many teachers at various points in their careers. From coast to coast, teachers are accomplishing great things, sometimes in the face of tremendous adversity. Based on reflections over my own career in the mathematics classroom and patterns I have recognized in other teachers, I offer an arguably oversimplified, subjective progression of three stages in a mathematics teacher's career.

Stage 1: Teaching Mechanically

In the early years of teaching, we tend to go through the motions of doing what we think we're supposed to do, without necessarily making professional adjustments or pushing students too deeply. In Message 28, "So Now You're a Teacher," I share my own journey through this stage of teaching and reflect on how we can support a teacher during the early years. I observed in that message that in my first years of teaching I presented a fairly superficial treatment of mathematics. I taught in ways that were generally limited to whole-class lecture and discussions, with an occasional attempt at learning centers or group work.

Stage 2: Convincing and Engaging Students

After a couple of years, I got better at convincingly explaining rules and procedures and better at engaging students in interesting tasks. Supported by professional development, networking, and my commitment to learning from a variety of resources, I was able to help students see why a rule or procedure worked and what they might do with it. I used interesting tasks more often and implemented them more substantively. I had reached another level—that of being a good, conceptual explainer and engager. For the most part, my students followed what I was doing and they seemed to believe my explanations. I'm not sure they thought they could come up with solutions themselves unless they imitated what I had done, but they seemed stronger at doing mathematics than students I had taught earlier. I realize now that the change I began to observe was probably more about a change in my teaching than a change in students' inherent mathematical abilities.

Stage 2, then, is less mechanical (teachers are more comfortable with the steps they are going through) and more about learning to engage students in doing mathematics and thinking about mathematics. Several factors can help teachers advance to this stage of teaching, including opportunities to participate in innovative, research-based teacher-preparation programs, to use excellent instructional materials that engage students in challenging mathematics, and to experience high-quality professional learning experiences with colleagues.

Stage 3: Committing to Students Getting It

A third stage of teaching may be when we structure learning situations considerably less around the teacher and more around the student. We move through well-designed tasks that help students develop deep understanding and powerful mathematical thinking. At this stage, we help students *get* mathematics as we become more accomplished mathematics teachers.

When I describe the notion of *getting it*, I think of the 1962 movie *The Miracle Worker*, about Helen Keller. In a critical scene near the end of the movie, Helen, the blind, deaf, and mute young girl (portrayed by Patty Duke), finally gets what her teacher, Anne Sullivan (portrayed by Anne Bancroft), has been trying to teach her about words and language. Up until this point, Helen had been an excellent mimicker, copying back to her teacher the finger spelling of any word presented to her. But in this pivotal moment of the film, after months of conflict and frustration, Helen suddenly understands that the words she is making relate to the objects and the world around her. The look on her face is powerful; her expression communicates volumes as she gets what language is all about. Her excitement captivates the viewer as Helen runs around her yard, grabbing objects and people and having her teacher give her the words to *talk* about them.

Our goal as mathematics teachers is for students to *get* math. We want them to make the connection between what they are doing and the rest of their world within and outside of mathematics. We want to see the student's excitement so clearly that we know her life will not be the same afterward, in at least some small way. This can happen obviously and suddenly or subtly and over time. It happens when a student gets what fractions are so well that he can put them together, take them apart, and intuitively know how they relate to each other. It happens when a student gets what equivalence is all about and realizes the power of translating from one representation of a mathematical object or idea to another representation of the same object or idea. It happens when a student gets what it means for two quantities to be proportionally related.

What Can We Do?

It might be more appropriate to represent the evolution of a teacher as a continuum rather than a set of discrete stages. Whatever model is used, the underlying idea is that experience can help us improve how effectively we teach. But we can only improve if we are open to learning from that experience, and only if we commit to our career-long professional learning. The likelihood that a teacher will continue to grow and improve over time increases significantly if those who support the teacher are also committed to the teacher's growth in positive and constructive ways. As a teacher's expertise increases, the goal should be to learn more about how to focus teaching on what students do, what they learn, and how they learn. Most of all, the goal should be to help every student *get* mathematics.

Reflection and Discussion

FOR TEACHERS

- What issues or challenges does this message raise for you? In what ways do you agree with or disagree with the main points of the message?
- Where are you in your development as a teacher? Are you still going through the motions, or have you moved toward engaging students and helping them get mathematics?
- What are your next steps in terms of your own professional learning to help you move toward more effective teaching?
- What is one thing you can do to help one or more students get a particular mathematical concept, idea, or habit of mind?

FOR FAMILIES

- What questions or issues does this message raise for you to discuss with your son or daughter, the teacher, or school leaders?
- As you work with your son or daughter on mathematics, what topics or skills do you think he or she understands the most deeply? What topics and skills does he or she seem to have the most difficulty understanding?
- How can you help your daughter or son see beyond the surface of what she or he is learning to understand the underlying mathematics?

FOR LEADERS AND POLICY MAKERS

- How does this message reinforce or challenge policies and decisions you have made or are considering?
- What kinds of ongoing professional learning experiences and support can you provide to help teachers learn and grow according to their different needs as they move through their careers?
- How can you involve experienced and effective teachers in supporting novice teachers?

RELATED MESSAGES

- Message 28, "So Now You're a Teacher," discusses the beginning years of a teacher's career and how we can support that teacher.
- Message 38, "Ten Kinds of Wonderful," describes some of the many roles teachers take on as they help students become mathematical thinkers and problem solvers.
- Message 6, "'Teach Harder!' Isn't the Answer," considers what it takes to improve teaching and learning.
- Message 26, "Beyond Pockets of Wonderfulness," reflects on the power of collaboration and articulation to improve teaching and learning.

FURTHER READING

- *Putting It Together: Middle School Math in Transition* (Tsuruda 1994) tells the story of Gary Tsuruda's journey as a middle school teacher helping students become mathematical thinkers and problem solvers. It also offers ideas for teachers pursuing similar goals.
- *About Teaching Mathematics: A K–8 Resource* (Burns 2007a) addresses some of the most challenging issues of mathematics teaching and provides a wealth of classroom resources.

- *Math Matters: Understanding the Math You Teach, Grades K–8* (Chapin and Johnson 2006) helps teachers clarify their understanding of key topics in elementary and middle school mathematics.
- *Mathematics and Science for a Change: How to Design, Implement, and Sustain High-Quality Professional Development* (Weiss and Pasley 2009) offers guidance on designing and sustaining effective long-term programs of professional learning to improve mathematics and science teaching in support of student learning.

30

Crystal's Calculator

LEARNING FROM OUR STUDENTS

A fter twenty-five years as a mathematics educator, including many years of working directly with teachers, I decided to return to the classroom to teach one class of ninth-grade algebra for the year. I had been advocating for years what teachers should do in terms of raising expectations and implementing the National Council of Teachers of Mathematics (NCTM) standards (1989, 2000). I knew I was asking for a lot from teachers, and I thought I needed to get back into the classroom for a reality check. That teaching experience not only humbled me but also taught me many lessons. One lesson in particular has stayed with me, and it continues to influence my thinking about what needs to take place in today's mathematics classrooms. It involves a girl I call Crystal and her experience as a student of algebra and a student of arithmetic.

The Story of Crystal

My algebra class that year consisted of about twenty-five students. These students were allegedly the middle track of algebra students in a three-track system. As I got to know my students, it became clear that they covered a wide spectrum of potential and challenges.

Crystal had been placed in this algebra class because her eighth-grade math teacher believed that she could handle algebra. But when I gave out a short survey at the beginning of the school year, asking students to tell me what they were good at in math and how they saw themselves as math students, Crystal's response was, "Well, I'm okay at some things in math. But I can't do fractions. I can't add, subtract, multiply, or divide them. So please don't expect me to know fractions, because I don't." Crystal went on to say that she had noticed the "little blue calculators" at the back of the room (the TI Math Explorer™

calculators, which handled fractions). She said that if she could use one of those calculators, she thought she would be OK.

This was the first of what would be many tests for me regarding whether I could practice what I had been preaching. Would I allow a student to rely on a calculator, without too many restrictions, in order for her to study algebra? I decided to give it a try, and I checked out one of the calculators to her for the duration of the year.

After the first few months of school, we were well into the heart of algebra. Students were using algebra to represent situations, beginning to explore functions, solving equations, and so on. Crystal didn't seem to be having any significant difficulties, and I honestly didn't notice her achievement one way or the other. However, on one test in November, she did particularly well. As I returned the tests to the students, I said to her, "Crystal, you must have really studied hard for this test. You did a great job!"

Crystal responded, "I really didn't study all that hard. But, you know, I just kind of *get it*."

As the school year progressed, it turned out that Crystal did, indeed, *get it*. I came to see Crystal as one of the best algebraic thinkers I have ever known. She could represent essentially any word problem algebraically, from simple word problems to more complex problems calling for higher-level reasoning. And, provided she had her fraction calculator, she could solve the problem, represent the solution graphically, and interpret the graph and the solution in terms of the original problem. In short, she could do algebra in ways teachers hope and dream for all of our students—even though she couldn't do fractions. Wow.

The story could end right there and be a lesson to all of us: It is simply not the case that all students need to master all of the computation of arithmetic before they can tackle and succeed in algebra. Looking at the research (or lack of it) verifies my observation; there simply is no evidence that computational skill is the single path to success in algebra. But the story goes on. . . .

As the school year began to wind down, I was starting to get nervous. My students had accomplished a lot during our year of studying algebra. But Crystal wasn't the only one with lingering deficiencies in arithmetic. I knew that the following year my students would be entering the next math class (probably Geometry) and that other teachers would find out that some of my students couldn't do arithmetic. I worried about this a lot, and I tried to think of some way to address the problem. I wasn't willing to give up precious algebra class time.

Finally, I decided to tackle the arithmetic challenge head-on with student projects. My students had done a few outside projects during the year, where they had used algebra on more in-depth problems than class time allowed. But instead of assigning another algebra project during our last grading period, I decided to take on computation. I gave my students a short test of computational skills. I asked them to identify in writing a computational skill that they wished they could improve—something that was getting in their way in algebra. I told them that they could work with their brothers, sisters, parents, friends, or me, or that they could use any of the different books in the classroom. For those few students who were confident (and proficient) in their computational skills, there were other options.

When I asked students to indicate what skill they were going to work on, Crystal wrote that she was going to learn how to add, subtract, multiply, and divide fractions. She made two wonderful and insightful comments. First, she wrote, *The time has come!* Then she continued, *I'm wasting too much time using my calculator.* She told me that she was tired of being a two-calculator girl, having to use her fraction calculator for computation and then her graphing calculator for graphing and other algebraic applications. I thought her goal was ambitious, but I decided to see what would come of it.

A few weeks later, I began individual interviews with students. In these interviews students were responsible for convincing me absolutely and positively that they had learned what they had said they were going to learn. When it was Crystal's turn to meet with me, I said, "Now, before you show me what you have learned, I have to tell you something. You know I do a lot of talks for teachers, right?" She nodded. I continued, "I need to tell you that I've been talking about you. I call you Crystal, because I don't use your real name, and I tell people that even though Crystal doesn't do fractions, Crystal is one of the best algebraic thinkers I have ever known." She grinned and got a little embarrassed, and then she proceeded to convince me, absolutely and positively, that she had learned how to add, subtract, multiply, and divide fractions. Wow.

There's More to the Story

This story has several epilogues worth sharing. The first occurred on the last day of school that year. I gave my students a year-end survey, and I asked them what they liked about the class, what they didn't like, and what they thought I should tell teachers when I was giving presentations. As I read through the completed surveys, I smiled when I came across Crystal's survey. In response to my last question, she had written, *Tell them that Crystal can do fractions.* Wow.

I saw Crystal from time to time after that year ended. I often wondered whether her fraction learning lasted. I knew that she had learned these skills before, and I knew that the procedures had not stuck with her. But I was always reluctant to ask her; after all, it was a great story and I didn't want to lose it. Finally, about two years later, I decided I had to know. So when I saw her the next time, I asked her if she still knew how to do fractions. She responded, "Yeah! And it's coming in really handy in Algebra 2." It turned out that Crystal had gone on to study Geometry and Algebra 2, and the next year, she was headed for Precalculus. She went on to a state university, where she finished her degree in nutrition in four years. She later continued her education through graduate school. Wow.

The final epilogue I'd like to share happened a few months after I finished that year of teaching. In August of that year, I was invited to be the keynote speaker to kick off the new school year for a small urban district. The superintendent had decided that this would be the year of mathematics, and that everyone in the district should come to the presentation by the "math lady." *Everyone* meant that my audience included not only teachers and administrators but also bus drivers, cafeteria workers, custodians, and paraprofessionals, among others. I thought the best way to reach such a diverse audience was to tell some of my personal stories, including Crystal's story. The presentation was well received, and when I finished, a young woman came up to me in tears. She said she was an aide in an elementary classroom. Then she looked at me and said, "I know I was Crystal. And nobody ever found me." As she spoke, I couldn't hold back my own tears, and I hugged her. I think I apologized on behalf of the entire education system. On the long drive home after the presentation, I kept asking myself over and over how many Crystals I might have missed in my own teaching career.

What Can We Do?

Stories like Crystal's can help us make better classroom decisions. As we learn lessons from our students, we can choose to act in ways in the future that support higher-level learning for all students. The lessons from Crystal's story are numerous and perhaps obvious:

- Sometimes students can succeed at higher-level math, even without knowing everything we wish they knew about lower-level math. We owe it to all students to allow them to tackle the good stuff, and not reserve it just for some students.

- In the past, students without arithmetic proficiency would not have been able to deal with algebra. But in an age of calculators, we have a tool to allow all students to tackle algebra, regardless of computational gaps.

- Sometimes success at higher-level math—the good stuff—can motivate students to fill in their own deficiencies, to deal with the other stuff. Crystal finally learned fractions when she saw their usefulness in using algebra.

- Technology is neither good nor bad in and of itself. It depends on how students use it and how teachers guide that use. Different students may use technology in different ways within the same classroom with positive results for their learning.

- What we expect of students makes all the difference in the world, and we have a responsibility to help them achieve their fullest potential.

- We never fully know the impact that we have on our students and on others.

Over the years, I have told Crystal's story to hundreds of teachers and to diverse audiences. It always has a powerful effect. Some people even reconsider the limitations they place on students—limitations that seem to make sense at the time, but that may turn out to have unintended long-term negative consequences.

I ran into Crystal in a store not long ago. She was on her way to California for the next step in her life. I told her about the impact her story continues to have on so many others. She smiled at me and, with her usual sense of humor and acceptance of whatever life has to offer, said, "I do what I can."

Reflection and Discussion

FOR TEACHERS

- What issues or challenges does this message raise for you? In what ways do you agree with or disagree with the main points of the message?

- What assumptions have you made about what students need to know before they can access higher-level mathematics? How critical do you think those assumptions are?

- What is your philosophy and practice regarding the role of calculators for your grade level? How open are you to modifying that philosophy based on what you learn?

- How can you recognize and support the Crystals in your classroom, who have not mastered everything you wish they had mastered before they arrived at your class?

FOR FAMILIES

- What questions or issues does this message raise for you to discuss with your son or daughter, the teacher, or school leaders?

- How can you support your daughter's or son's progress into higher-level mathematics while helping with weaknesses in prior learning?

(continued)

- How open are you to the possibility that there may be ways to use a calculator in support of students learning rigorous and challenging mathematics?

FOR LEADERS AND POLICY MAKERS

- How does this message reinforce or challenge policies and decisions you have made or are considering?
- How can you help teachers raise their expectations of all students, including those with gaps in their computational background?
- What policies, if any, does your school or district have in place regarding calculator use in mathematics classrooms? How well do these policies support student learning?
- How do you handle equity issues with respect to who can afford a calculator? How does the school or district ensure that every student has access to appropriate technology, including its availability at home?
- How can you help teachers learn appropriate ways of incorporating calculator use in pursuit of high-level mathematics?

RELATED MESSAGES

- Message 31, "Do They Really Need It?," looks at the critical role of teacher expectations on students' mathematics learning.
- Message 20, "Putting Calculators in Their Place," considers the role of calculators when developing computational skills within a balanced math program.
- Message 34, "Forgetting Isn't Forever," challenges the vision of mathematics as a linearly organized discipline, where each new topic depends on mastery of the previous topic.

FURTHER READING

- The six principles underlying *Principles and Standards for School Mathematics* (NCTM 2000) present fundamental beliefs about equity, curriculum, teaching, learning, assessment, and technology. All six of these principles are relevant to Crystal's story, but the discussions of equity, teaching, and technology are particularly pertinent and helpful.
- *Fostering Algebraic Thinking: A Guide for Teachers, Grades 6–10* (Driscoll 1999) provides a comprehensive overview of how to help all students develop algebraic thinking and learn algebraic skills.

- *Algebra and Algebraic Thinking in School Mathematics: NCTM's Seventieth Yearbook* (Greenes and Rubenstein 2008) considers several issues related to the changing nature of algebra as an expectation for all students.
- "Technology and Equity in Mathematics" (Seeley 1995; www.utdanacenter.org/staff/cathy-seeley.php) discusses issues related to appropriate technology use in support of equity for all students learning challenging mathematics.
- *Algebra in a Technological World* (Addenda Series, Grades 9–12) (Heid, Choate, Sheets, and Zbiek 1996) discusses the changing nature of algebra in today's world, including ways to make algebra accessible to all students.

www   This message is also available in printable format at
       mathsolutions.com/fasterisntsmarter.

MESSAGE

31

Do They Really Need It?

A LESSON IN EXPECTATIONS FROM AFRICA

My most unique teaching experience took place from 1999 through 2001, when I taught middle school and high school mathematics as a Peace Corps volunteer in Burkina Faso, a small French-speaking country in West Africa. When I served there, the population was approximately twelve million. As many Peace Corps volunteers will tell you, volunteers often gain more from the experience than we can ever hope to contribute to our host country, and for me, the experience was full of life lessons and teaching *aha*/s. I had the good fortune to teach for two years at the Lycée Yamwaya in the town of Ouahigouya, the fourth-largest town in the country (population sixty-five thousand). Yamwaya is a large school; when I was there it had two-thousand students and a staff of fifty faculty. I was the only non-Burkinabè teacher in the group, and my colleagues came from several of the fifty ethnic/language groups in the country. As in other schools in Burkina Faso, we taught in the national language of French (a considerable challenge given that I learned my French language skills in high school many years before). I had one class of middle school–aged students (about thirteen to fifteen years old) and three classes of upper-level high school mathematics (about sixteen to nineteen years old). My classes averaged about seventy-five students.

One of the unique, surprising, and frustrating aspects of my educational experience in Burkina Faso was the number of disruptions and strikes that caused us to miss school days. The country is one of the most peaceful in Africa, and the people are inherently gentle, kind, and generous. But they exercise their right to protest over what they see as injustices. I would estimate that we missed more than one-fourth of the school year during each of my two years there. We missed school when teachers went on strike. We missed school when students went on strike. And—my favorite—we missed school when the government closed school so no one would strike. (This last case took place as the

166

anniversary of a politically sensitive event approached. Schools were seen as a possible gathering place for protests, so they were closed to avoid trouble.)

Accordingly, as the second year approached, I prepared an adjusted program of study for my classes. We had never actually finished the previous year, having missed the last week or two, as well as missing considerable time during the year, and we were starting the year late. So I focused on what I considered the most important topics to cover, given that we would have less time than in a normal year. I knew that I would have to deal with gaps from my previous year with the same classes of upper-level mathematics students, two of them on the mathematics and science track (*Première-C*), and one on the nonmathematics track (*Première-A*).

"You Have to Teach Delta!"

As a responsible Peace Corps volunteer, I presented my adjusted program of study to my Burkinabè colleague, Sylla. He would be teaching my students the year after I left, in their typically demanding final year of secondary school (the *Terminale* year). As I shared my proposed outline of topics to Sylla for the nonmath track, I explained that I did not have time to do everything considered part of the expected program for *Première-A*, so I would be omitting *delta* (the quadratic formula). Sylla looked at me seriously and said, "You have to teach delta."

I responded, "No, Sylla, I have to make some choices. There isn't enough time to do everything, so I'm not going to do delta."

Sylla looked at me again and said, "But, you have to teach delta."

I was beginning to get frustrated and passionately responded, "*Sylla!* You don't understand! They aren't going to like it. They aren't going to understand it. And, honestly, will they ever really *need* it?"

Sylla just looked at me and calmly but firmly said, "You *have* to teach delta."

Well, a good Peace Corps volunteer doesn't start an international incident, so I decided I was going to have to include delta in my program of study for *Première-A*. I was secretly hoping that strikes might prevent me from getting to the topic, but as luck would have it, I found myself preparing to teach delta in the spring of that school year. I used the same problem-solving approach I had used throughout the school year, posing problems as a stimulus for most of our lessons. I tried to find relevant applications of quadratic relationships that might be of interest, and I made a special effort to teach in ways that would engage every student.

Facing My Own Expectations

About two weeks into our work on quadratic functions, I gave my students a problem to work on in pairs at their desks. As I walked up and down the rows of desks, I suddenly realized that I was seeing and hearing students actively engaged in rich mathematical discourse—the kinds of thinking, interaction, and conversation that every mathematics teacher lives for. I watched as students tried different approaches to starting the problem. I heard students say things like, "Well, I think we could represent it with this kind of quadratic function," and "No, I think that would make the numbers get smaller, not bigger. Maybe we should try a negative number here." And so on. As I walked around the room watching students learning demanding mathematics, I found myself thinking, "What did I almost do to these students?" How could I have considered keeping them from this learning experience, not because of any limitations they might have had, but because of my own limited thinking?

To understand the power of this lesson for me, it is important to know that I have always thought of myself as the Queen of High Expectations. For decades, I have loudly called for teachers to raise expectations of all students, for schools to get rid of low-level options in mathematics, and for states to increase graduation requirements in mathematics. Yet when I found myself face-to-face with real students in a real classroom, it was so easy to be pulled back by my limited thinking and by old ideas, assuming that *these* students in the nonmath track might not understand the topic, might not like it, and probably wouldn't need it.

What right did I have to make such assumptions on the part of my students? What right did I have to withhold this learning opportunity from them? Thank goodness for Sylla and his insistence that I teach this topic in the program, even to these students who might not be pursuing mathematics in their future, and even if I had to choose to give up something else, perhaps something easier to teach.

I have wondered since this experience how many of those wonderful *Première-A* students have ever had occasion to use delta since our time together. Only 1 percent of young adults in Burkina Faso continue to the university; a small portion of that number chooses to pursue mathematics-related fields; and an even smaller portion of those students completes the university program. But whether or not any of my *Première-A* students will ever use delta again is far less important than the fact that they all had the opportunity to succeed at challenging mathematics. When the class completed our study of quadratic relationships, we celebrated. The students recognized that they had accomplished something significant.

What Can We Do?

How many of our students in the United States do we hold back, preventing them from experiencing this kind of success over challenging mathematics, not because of what they can or cannot do but because of our limited thinking and old habits? Most of the rest of the world recognizes that mathematics sometimes gets hard and that you may have to struggle and persevere to solve a good problem. Other countries also recognize that developing mathematical knowledge and mathematical thinking is so important that it's worth the work. Maybe it's time we gave our students the same opportunity as students around the world— the opportunity to work hard on challenging mathematics and to succeed. Every one of our students deserves this experience and this success. Those of us who teach mathematics need to challenge our own expectations so that we can provide that experience and ensure that success.

Reflection and Discussion

FOR TEACHERS

- What issues or challenges does this message raise for you? In what ways do you agree with or disagree with the main points of the message?

- What assumptions have you made in the past about what students could or couldn't do that you might make differently today?

- How can we allow all students to tackle challenging mathematics, even if they are not strong in prerequisite skills and even if they aren't headed for a mathematics-based job in the future?

- When you think about which students might be able to succeed at particular mathematics topics, what factors enter into your thinking?

FOR FAMILIES

- What questions or issues does this message raise for you to discuss with your son or daughter, the teacher, or school leaders?

- How can you communicate positive messages to your daughter or son that she or he can succeed at challenging mathematics?

(continued)

- In supporting your son's or daughter's homework and schoolwork, what kinds of help can you provide to support the development of confidence and persistence, rather than simply looking for a quick answer?
- If you think your daughter or son is not mathematically inclined, how sure are you that your observation is correct? How can you support your daughter or son in being as successful as possible in mathematics?

FOR LEADERS AND POLICY MAKERS

- How does this message reinforce or challenge policies and decisions you have made or are considering?
- How can you support teachers in learning to raise their expectations of all students?
- What structures do you have in place to ensure that every student has the opportunity to study challenging mathematics, whether at the elementary, middle school, or high school level?
- Have you eliminated (or can you consider eliminating) long-term tracking of students that automatically limits what we expect of them? What issues does this kind of move bring up, and how can you address those issues?

RELATED MESSAGES

- Message 16, "Hard Arithmetic Isn't Deep Mathematics," looks at what it means to study challenging mathematics.
- Message 2, "Untapped Potential," encourages us not to underestimate what every student might be able to accomplish in mathematics.
- Message 32, "Yes, but . . . ," examines some of the reasons we think students don't learn challenging mathematics.
- Message 17, "Constructive Struggling," makes a case for challenging all students with rigorous and complex mathematical tasks.
- Message 30, "Crystal's Calculator," tells the story of a successful ninth-grade algebra student who lacked the computational skills we often expect as a prerequisite to algebra.

FURTHER READING

- *Escalante: The Best Teacher in America* (Mathews 1989) tells the true story of Jaime Escalante's expectations for his students, who unexpectedly achieved the prestigious level of Advanced Placement calculus in East Los Angeles.

- *Stand and Deliver* (Warner Home Video 1988) is the movie of Jaime Escalante and his students' journey on their way to passing the Advanced Placement calculus test.

- *College Knowledge: What It Really Takes for Students to Succeed and What We Can Do to Get Them Ready* (Conley 2008) describes what it takes for students to succeed in college, beyond entrance requirements.

- *Generating Expectations for Student Achievement (GESA): An Equitable Approach to Educational Excellence (Facilitator Handbook* and *Teacher Handbook)* (Grayson and Martin 2001a, 2001b) provides an overview and guidelines on implementing a program that focuses on raising expectations for all students (based on its partner program, Teacher Expectations and Student Achievement (TESA).

- My website on Burkina Faso (http://csinburkinafaso.com) includes photos and stories about life and teaching during my Peace Corps assignment from 1999 through 2001.

32

Yes, but . . .

BELIEVING IN EVERY STUDENT

There are compelling reasons to change our mathematics teaching today. The rapidly evolving global workplace demands more quantitative and scientific knowledge and calls for workers who can think creatively, work together, and solve complex problems that don't yet exist. We also recognize the importance of providing students a well-balanced mathematics program so they can make sense of mathematics based on conceptual understanding, perform appropriate computational procedures, and solve a variety of challenging problems, often requiring them to use knowledge and skills that connect across topics.

A dramatic and challenging shift in what we expect of teachers today is the call to provide rigorous mathematics for all students at a level once reserved for only a fraction of our students—those who might be headed toward mathematics-intensive majors in higher education. Demands for de-tracking, heterogeneous grouping, differentiating instruction, and equity-based teaching practices can stretch many teachers beyond their comfort zone. In spite of good intentions and compassion for students, many teachers find themselves listening to the voice in their mind that says, "Yes, but . . ."

"Yes, but . . . some students don't do their homework."

"Yes, but . . . some students don't pay attention."

"Yes, but . . . some students don't have any support at home."

"Yes, but . . . some students hardly ever come to school."

"Yes, but . . . some students have learning disabilities."

"Yes, but . . . some students' first language isn't English."

"Yes, but . . . some students never learned what they were supposed to learn before they came to me."

"Yes, but . . . some students can go only so far."

Yes, many of our students face obstacles that make it difficult for them to learn. Some of these students are hard to teach, especially if teachers are expected to provide the same level of mathematics and the same tasks for these students as for other students. The research on tracking has been clear for some time that over all, students do not learn better when those who are behind are pulled out and taught apart from other students (Oakes 1987). And while a few extremely gifted students may benefit from additional opportunities to both accelerate and enrich their mathematics experience, the demand is strong for teachers to help all students achieve high levels of mathematics, whether we think these students are going to college or straight to the workforce. Yet dealing with students who have different gaps, face different barriers, and learn at different speeds and in different ways calls for teaching approaches most of us have never experienced, either as teachers or as learners. Nevertheless, there is no reason why committed, professional teachers can't learn new approaches to succeed with these students.

Why? And Why Not?

I often ask groups of teachers to list reasons why some students might not achieve the level of mathematics we would like them to. The list is usually long, and it often includes both student factors (lack of motivation, lack of effort, learning disabilities, language issues, gaps in knowledge) and teacher or school factors (not teaching conceptually, not engaging students in learning, not providing enough opportunities for students to learn high-level math, using limited teaching strategies). Sometimes even family or community factors are mentioned (the view that it's OK not to like math or not to be able to do it, the common perception that only a few people have math ability). Yet the answer to the second question I ask is telling; I ask teachers if any of these reasons mean that students *can't* learn mathematics. One after another, teachers shake their head "no." Maybe that's because they think that's how they are supposed to respond, or maybe it's because we know that for any one of these obstacles, we can always find an exception—a student who learned even though they faced an obstacle. Fortunately, there are teachers who refuse to accept a life sentence of low achievement for a student simply because no one has yet discovered what works for that student. These teachers do everything they can to find something to hook their "Yes, but . . ." students into mathematics and into school.

What worries me is that many of us do not seem to really believe that all of our students can learn meaningful or challenging mathematics. Too many teachers talk about students who "didn't learn it even though they were taught it." But teaching must be about learning, and surely it is our responsibility to continue to search for what we can do as teachers to help students learn, even those students who haven't yet or those who seem like they can't or won't.

What Can We Do?

I would argue that, just as we tell teachers that any student can learn high-level mathematics under the right circumstances, likewise we can expect any committed mathematics teacher to learn new strategies to help all students reach their full potential. We can learn how to select rich tasks or challenging problems to provide the starting point for some of our lessons. We can learn how to connect the mathematics students are learning to their lives. We can learn how to vary our strategies and engage students more fully in the learning process. We can learn to allow students to provide more of the mathematical conversation in the classroom than we provide. We can learn how to ask the questions that push students' thinking toward higher levels, without overly scaffolding or spoon-feeding them everything they need to solve a problem. We can learn how to pay attention to what students do and what they say so that we can provide course correction that helps them avoid lasting misconceptions.

We may not yet have found the key to helping many of our students reach their potential, and we may never find the key for every student. But learning how to improve our teaching so that we come closer to being able to help every student reach his potential is the career-long path that a caring, professional mathematics teacher willingly pursues.

Sometimes we read stories or watch videos about amazing accomplishments of students or teachers in challenging situations, and we are in awe. There's the story of a remedial high school mathematics class, where nearly every student had begun school without speaking English, and where many lived in homes where English still was not spoken. Almost all students in the class came from poverty, as evidenced by their qualification for a free or reduced lunch. All students had been placed in this class because they had essentially no chance of graduating from high school. And yet, at the end of the year, all twenty-five students passed the ambitious statewide end-of-course algebra test. When we hear about this class, we can marvel at what the teacher must have done and celebrate the accomplishments of the students. But it's also very easy to think about this class and say, "Yes, but . . . my students aren't like that," or "Yes, but . . . I couldn't do that."

You Can!

Yes, but . . . perhaps you can. Perhaps you can continue to grow and to learn how to teach in different ways that engage all students, regardless of their gaps and problems. Perhaps all of us can commit to not only saying that all students can learn but then also acting the way we say we believe. Perhaps we can set the bar high and then do whatever it takes to help every student reach that bar. Perhaps with hard work our actions, beliefs, and commitment can overrule the *Yes, buts* . . . in our mind.

Reflection and Discussion

FOR TEACHERS

- What issues or challenges does this message raise for you? In what ways do you agree with or disagree with the main points of the message?

- What are some of the "Yes, but . . ." messages you hear yourself saying about a student or a group of students? What would it take for you to fundamentally change your beliefs about how and whether your "Yes, but . . ." students can achieve?

- In your mathematics classroom, how do you provide for students with different gaps and backgrounds so that all students can have access to challenging mathematics?

- What are your next steps in terms of your own professional learning to help you move more effectively toward teaching all students?

FOR FAMILIES

- What questions or issues does this message raise for you to discuss with your son or daughter, the teacher, or school leaders?

- What are some of the "Yes, but . . ." messages you hear yourself saying about your daughter's or son's achievement in mathematics (or about your own learning of mathematics)?

- How can you help your son or daughter develop confidence so that he or she can accomplish high levels of achievement in mathematics?

FOR LEADERS AND POLICY MAKERS

- How does this message reinforce or challenge policies and decisions you have made or are considering?

- How have you eliminated low-level tracking in your school(s)?

- How can you support teachers in working with heterogeneous groups of students who have different backgrounds and needs?

- What kinds of ongoing professional learning experiences can you provide (or work with partners to provide) for your teachers to learn how to expect all students to reach high levels of achievement in mathematics and help all students to meet those expectations?

RELATED MESSAGES

- Message 2, "Untapped Potential," considers the assumptions we often make about who can and cannot do mathematics.
- Message 31, "Do They Really Need It?," examines an experience that challenged my own "Yes, but . . ." thoughts.
- Message 9, "Increasing Access or Ensuring Failure?" looks at the challenges of helping students meet rapidly increasing requirements.

FURTHER READING

- *The Shame of the Nation* (Kozol 2006) is a thought-provoking book that looks at lingering inequities in our schools as we enter the twenty-first century.
- *Whatever It Takes: How Professional Learning Communities Respond When Kids Don't Learn* (DuFour, Eaker, Harhanek, and DuFour 2004) describes how school communities can work together to ensure that all students learn, including those we might not expect to succeed.
- *Take It Up: Leading for Educational Equity* (Becerra and Weissglass 2004) provides professional development activities to address educational inequities in classrooms and schools.
- *Mathematics Success and Failure Among African-American Youth* (Martin 2000) provides insights from research and from conversations with students about what it takes for African American students to succeed in mathematics.
- *Whatever It Takes: Geoffrey Canada's Quest to Change Harlem and America* (Tough 2008) describes a controversial and comprehensive approach to transforming the system in which Harlem, New York students struggle to achieve, including their schools, their neighborhoods, and their families' priorities.
- *Unequal Childhoods: Class, Race, and Family Life* (Lareau 2003) investigates the different worlds of students living in opportunity and those living in inequality.
- *Good Morning Ms. Toliver* (The Futures Channel 1993) is a DVD that shows the award-winning teaching and remarkable learning in Kay Toliver's Harlem, New York middle school math classroom.
- *Work Hard. Be Nice.: How Two Inspired Teachers Created the Most Promising Schools in America* (Mathews 2009b) describes the journey of two former Teach for America teachers who started the Knowledge Is Power Program (KIPP), serving primarily urban children and demonstrating that students who had previously been unsuccessful can achieve.
- *Teaching Mathematics Meaningfully: Solutions for Reaching Struggling Learners* (Allsopp, Kyger, and Lovin 2007) presents a big-picture approach to teaching mathematics and provides suggestions on dealing with struggling students in grades K–12.

33

Engaged in What?

ACTIVITY ISN'T ALWAYS ENGAGEMENT

A principal accompanied a scientist who was visiting a few mathematics and science classrooms in the school district. As they left one particular science class, the principal said to them, "Wasn't that wonderful? Did you see how engaged those students were?"

The scientist paused, then responded, "Yes, but engaged in what?"

The students in the classroom were indeed busy. There was lots of activity and conversation, and students were actively using materials. But the scientist observed that all of this activity seemed to be going nowhere. It was not clear from talking with either the teacher or the students that the activity was involving the students in scientific thinking or learning. Rather, they were going through the motions of being hands-on and interactive without a well-designed path to a clear learning outcome.

Engaging Students in Their Learning

Student engagement, whether in mathematics, science, or other disciplines, involves more than having students talk to each other, work in groups, or handle some kind of materials. Student engagement involves switching on a student's brain so that she is interacting with mathematics in deep, thoughtful, and meaningful ways.

For teachers trying to learn how to engage students in either mathematics or science, it is easy at first to be fooled by appearances and notice the wrong things in videos of or visits to an effective classroom. Without deeply understanding both our content area and how students learn, we can sometimes be seduced by the mere sight of student activity and mistake it for effective instruction. Just because an excellent classroom we see involves students working in small groups or interacting with manipulative materials does not mean that any classroom where students work in small groups or interact with manipulative materials is excellent. Teaching well is a complex job. If teachers do not help students make the connection between an activity and the intended mathematical outcome(s) of the lesson (challenging students to think about the underlying mathematics), students are likely to miss the point of the activity and never learn what is intended. It should be no surprise that when a student's parent later asks what the student did in math class that day, the student replies, "We played with blocks."

The use of concrete materials, as part of a well-designed task in the hands of a skillful teacher, can be a tool that supports the development of conceptual understanding. Using concrete materials can also simply be an opportunity to play with blocks. Likewise, having students work together in groups can be a way to encourage rich student discussion about mathematics, but it can also be a time for students to get distracted or off task. Real student engagement depends significantly on the choices the teacher makes regarding the task students work on. How will it be organized? How can we structure the opportunities students will have for interactions involving the task—the mathematical discourse? Becoming adept at encouraging appropriate mathematical discourse and helping students internalize multiple potentially complex outcomes is part of the challenge of engaging students meaningfully in their mathematics learning.

What It Takes to Engage Students

Designing opportunities for discourse in the classroom starts with choosing a rich mathematical task that relates to students' lives. Then we need to structure the task so students interact with the activity, the teacher, and each other in productive ways. Students become engaged in mathematics when they are drawn in to what they are doing because it is interesting, or when something about the task intrigues them or stretches them to think. An engaging task may involve either using mathematics in an applied context that relates to something of interest to the student, or it may be a mathematically interesting problem with opportunities to think or figure something out. Students become engaged partly by the questions the teacher asks them ("What do you notice about the way Jorge and Sandra are dividing the marbles? Can you think of a more fair way to do it?") and partly by the connections they see between the task, what they already know, and what may be unknown but interesting.

Engagement in a mathematical task or activity can lead to new mathematical knowledge for the student when the teacher ensures that the engagement is connected to important mathematics. These connections can emerge naturally when a teacher values student thinking and helps students learn to talk with and question each other about the mathematical ideas, strategies, and solutions they have to offer. Students can engage in mathematics using a variety of communication tools. They can learn to represent ideas using many different forms, including words, pictures, materials, diagrams, graphs, and equations. Engagement involves students talking together, writing, and thinking about the task at hand and the mathematics that underlies that task.

What Can We Do?

The question for teachers is not only "Engaged in what?" but also "Engaged how?" or "How can I engage students in working with the important content I want them to learn?" In mathematics or science, engaging students involves more than making a classroom busy. It involves shifting our focus from what the teacher is saying to what the students are thinking, saying, and doing. It involves learning from the work students do to guide instructional decisions about what they should do next. In order for students to engage in meaningful learning, teachers must engage in meaningful teaching.

Reflection and Discussion

FOR TEACHERS

- What issues or challenges does this message raise for you? In what ways do you agree with or disagree with the main points of the message?
- How can you select tasks that provide opportunities for students to engage in mathematical thinking?
- What kinds of questions seem to keep students involved in a mathematical task or activity? What kinds of questions seem to shut down engagement?
- How can you respond in ways that cause students to think when they ask for help on a task or problem they don't know how to begin?
- What ways of engaging students in mathematics would you like to learn more about?

FOR FAMILIES

- What questions or issues does this message raise for you to discuss with your son or daughter, the teacher, or school leaders?
- How can you engage your daughter or son in conversation about the mathematics she or he is learning in school?

(continued)

- How can you help your son or daughter demonstrate engagement in mathematics by showing you what he or she is learning, drawing pictures or diagrams, describing connections between mathematical ideas and real-life situations, and so on?

FOR LEADERS AND POLICY MAKERS

- How does this message reinforce or challenge policies and decisions you have made or are considering?
- How can you support teachers in improving their teaching toward greater student engagement connected to learning important mathematics?
- How well do your teacher evaluation policies and practices address the quality of student engagement in a mathematics class?

RELATED MESSAGES

- Message 17, "Constructive Struggling," looks at the need for students to sometimes tackle challenging problems.
- Message 37, "Boring!," describes the consequences when students are disengaged from school and from mathematics.
- Message 21, "No More Pilgrim Pie," considers the challenges of integrating content areas for real-world relevance.

FURTHER READING

- *Professional Standards for Teaching Mathematics* (NCTM 1991) includes a rich description of how professional teachers design classrooms that encourage student discourse and engagement.
- *Good Questions for Math Teaching: Why Ask Them and What to Ask, K–6* (Sullivan and Lilburn 2002) and *Good Questions for Math Teaching: Why Ask Them and What to Ask, Grades 5–8* (Schuster and Anderson 2005) suggest questions to engage students in their learning.
- *Classroom Discussions: Using Math Talk to Help Students Learn, Grades K–6* (Chapin, O'Connor, and Anderson 2009) advocates the use of purposeful conversation as part of well-structured lessons to support students' mathematical understanding.
- The Teaching Student-Centered Mathematics Series *(Volume 1, Grades K–3; Volume 2, Grades 3–5; Volume 3, Grades 5–8)* (Van de Walle and Lovin 2005) includes popular topics and features from Van de Walle's classic textbook, *Elementary and Middle School Mathematics*, and additional material designed to help teachers shift the focus of their classrooms and engage students in meaningful mathematics.

34

Forgetting Isn't Forever

LETTING STUDENTS GET TO THE GOOD STUFF

Years ago, my daughter's second-grade teacher, Mr. Hill (one of the best teachers I have known), shared with parents at the beginning of the school year that his goal was for all of his students to learn their addition and subtraction facts so well that they would never forget them. As it turned out, in the process of working toward this goal throughout the year, he also taught my daughter the *good stuff*—a robust mathematics program that included geometry, measurement, and lots of opportunities to organize and interpret data and solve all kinds of rich problems.

Then summer arrived. Summer has a way of intruding on even the best accomplishments of the most effective teachers. Mr. Hill's students had a significant advantage that summer over many other students. His students had learned their facts based on a solid understanding of what addition and subtraction mean and how they are used in problems. Students in some of the other second-grade classrooms had learned their facts more superficially, practicing over and over, but never really understanding what they were doing or how those facts might be used. It seems likely that these other students could easily forget what they had learned in math class once they stopped using it over the summer months. But even some of Mr. Hill's students lost ground during the summer, especially those who didn't have opportunities to use what they had learned in some way at home, such as when practicing mental math or playing games with their family. Without any mathematical engagement over three months, it's understandable that students, regardless of the quality of teaching and learning they've experienced, can forget some of what they've learned, at least until they have a chance to remember what they know.

Forgetting isn't forever, however. When a student has learned something well, as in Mr. Hill's class, the next year's teacher need not start from the beginning all over again. Rather, students may be able to quickly regain what has slipped away by going on to new material that includes an opportunity to review and extend what they have learned. This is especially effective if Mr. Hill and the third-grade teacher have worked together and continue to talk with each other so that they both know what knowledge students are bringing to third grade.

Forgetting or Not Knowing?

There is a difference between a student who has never had experience with a mathematical topic or skill, a student who has a fragile and short-lived hold on the same knowledge based on superficial learning, a student with significant misconceptions or misunderstandings about that knowledge, and a student who has forgotten something for now (e.g., over the summer) and simply needs a refresher. Students with serious misconceptions or significant learning gaps need instruction that targets the areas where they need help. Yet what often happens is that when any student does not show that he knows the topic or skill on a test, especially at the start of the school year, he is treated as if he needs to learn it from the beginning. We may not distinguish between lack of knowledge, misconceptions, or simple forgetting. In too many cases, a student is sent back to re-learn material he may well remember as soon as he gets into it. Yet he is likely to waste precious instructional time going over it again anyway, often at the expense of getting to richer, more engaging mathematics.

If enough students do not show that they have mastered a topic or skill they have previously learned, the whole class is likely to be sentenced to extended review. When this happens, it is likely that the teacher won't have adequate time to develop new content—the *good stuff*—deeply and with long-term understanding. Instead, the teacher will be pushed to cover the rest of the mathematics program for that grade quickly and superficially. After all, the state test is coming in the spring. As students race through the program, the stage is set for next year's teacher to face a group of students who will likely not have learned the content of the previous grade with lasting understanding or proficiency, primarily due to a lack of time. Thus, the cycle of redundancy and endless review is entrenched for another year.

Getting to the Good Stuff

Not long ago a high school physics teacher told me that every year she was appalled at her students' lack of mastery of pencil-and-paper computational skills. She proudly stated that by the time those students left her class each year, they could all compute with whole numbers, fractions, and decimals. I asked her when her students had the opportunity to study physics. She looked at me like I hadn't heard her and restated that she willingly accepted the challenge to make sure her students could master (elementary school) computation before they left her (high school) physics class at the end of the year. I asked her again, "When do they get to do physics?" This teacher, like many other mathematics and nonmathematics teachers, had made the assumption that facility with computation (without a calculator) is necessary for success with anything that requires mathematical thinking. She had also made the assumption that not knowing computation after the summer meant needing to learn it all over again. In her focus on review (as if students were starting from scratch), she missed some wonderful opportunities to show students where mathematics is used and, thus, to potentially motivate students to review or remediate themselves. This teacher also fell victim to the belief that many of us hold that regardless of how many times a student has learned a mathematical fact or procedure before, *this time*, the student will learn it forever!

What Can We Do?

Let me offer three observations about what we can do (and not do) with respect to review.

REVIEW AS YOU GO

Not all students who don't remember something (especially after a long break from using it) need to start learning it all over again. A few students may need to start from the beginning or may need diagnostic intervention to correct misconceptions. But if students have learned something well the first time, most of them need to go on to higher-level content. Teachers can integrate short review exercises as they help students extend what they know with new, higher-level content.

START THE YEAR RIGHT

Putting a group of students through a multiweek period of review at the beginning of the school year wastes prime learning time. The start of the school year is when teachers set the tone for the year and when students are most excited about school and about learning. When the year starts with extended review, students see the same math they have seen before (sometimes several times), increasing the likelihood of boredom and robbing the teacher of precious time to teach new topics in depth.

GIVE ALL STUDENTS THE GOOD STUFF

No student should be sentenced only to practice low-level skills at the expense of getting to the good stuff. Sometimes the good stuff is what keeps the student engaged in mathematics and motivates him to do better on areas of weakness. All students need a balance of skills, conceptual understanding, and opportunities to solve engaging problems.

No matter how good a textbook is and how great the teaching is, not all students will arrive at school the next year knowing and remembering what the teacher wants them to know. Most students will forget something. We can aim at having all of our students learn what we teach them in a way that will last forever. We can create outstanding learning experiences. We can teach effectively to help our students learn to high levels and with deep understanding. But our students still may not always remember everything they have learned. The question is how we can help them remember what they may have forgotten without forever keeping them from getting to the good stuff.

Reflection and Discussion

FOR TEACHERS

- What issues or challenges does this message raise for you? In what ways do you agree with or disagree with the main points of the message?
- What assumptions do you make about topics or skills you think students absolutely must remember before they can do something else?
- How much time do you spend reviewing at the beginning of each year, and what other ways can you help students remember what they may have forgotten? How might you use the time at the beginning of the school year more effectively?

FOR FAMILIES

- What questions or issues does this message raise for you to discuss with your son or daughter, the teacher, or school leaders?
- How can you help your daughter or son remember what she or he has learned in mathematics, especially over long periods like the summer?
- How can you generate interest in and positive feelings about mathematics?
- How can you support your daughter or son's learning and remembering by using mathematics outside of school to play games, do mental math, and engage in other stimulating activities?

FOR LEADERS AND POLICY MAKERS

- How does this message reinforce or challenge policies and decisions you have made or are considering?

- How well do your state standards and assessments provide for in-depth learning that is not likely to lead to the need to reteach the following year? If the expectations seem too crowded for adequate attention to new and important content, how can you involve teachers in addressing this challenge?

- How can you help teachers learn to incorporate review in ways that don't take away valuable instructional time?

- How do you help teachers identify the most important mathematical priorities at each grade level and recognize which parts of the curriculum call for the most instructional time in the year?

RELATED MESSAGES

- Message 15, "Less Can Be More," examines the American preoccupation with intentional redundancy and review.

- Message 18, "Faster Isn't Smarter," considers the preoccupation we sometimes have with timed tests as a measure of long-term learning.

- Message 30, "Crystal's Calculator," challenges the view that mathematics has to be learned in a linear fashion with a story about a student whose success in algebra motivated her to finally learn the computational skills she lacked.

- Message 26, "Beyond Pockets of Wonderfulness," reminds us of the power of collaboration across levels to increase the efficiency of what we teach and remove unnecessary review and redundancy.

FURTHER READING

- *Accessible Mathematics: Ten Instructional Shifts That Raise Student Achievement* (Leinwand 2009) suggests how to shift classroom practice in ways that lead to deep and lasting student learning in mathematics.

- Every year in late spring, the National Council of Teachers of Mathematics (NCTM) generally posts on its website (http://nctm.org) ideas for helping students maintain their skills over the summer. Families of middle-school students can also refer to NCTM's Figure This! website (www.figurethis.org) for rich problems to work on as a family.

- *Making Sense: Teaching and Learning Mathematics with Understanding* (Carpenter et al. 1997) presents research-based recommendations and describes essential features for classrooms where students learn mathematics with understanding, including examples from several different programs.

- *Beyond Arithmetic: Changing Mathematics in the Elementary Classroom* (Mokros, Russell, and Economopoulos 1995) discusses how to expand our view of elementary mathematics based on lessons learned in classrooms during the development and field testing of TERC's Investigations in Number, Data, and Space program.

- *Elementary and Middle School Mathematics: Teaching Developmentally* (Van de Walle, Karp, and Bay-Williams 2009) is a widely recognized resource for elementary and middle school mathematics, especially for preparing teachers to teach mathematics with understanding and for long-term learning.

35

Putting Testing in Perspective

ASSESSMENT AS A PARTNER TO LEARNING

There is no question that large-scale accountability tests drive much of mathematics teaching today. Teachers, schools, school districts, and states face tremendous pressure to show high student test scores, sometimes with significant sanctions attached to those scores. The question for mathematics teachers is not whether testing should drive teaching, but rather the much more complex question of what the relationship should be between testing, teaching, and learning.

Preparing for the Test

When student performance on a large-scale standardized test becomes the primary goal of mathematics teaching, we should not be surprised to see many mathematics classrooms focused on preparing students for that test. Too often, this preparation includes students spending a disproportionate amount of time practicing items that look like those thought to be on the test or learning test-taking tricks and shortcuts. It takes a knowledgeable teacher to recognize that these types of superficial side trips can interfere with students learning substantive, deep mathematics. It takes a strong and confident teacher to resist the pressure to take students down this path, knowing that teaching challenging, rigorous mathematics to all students is the best road to lasting mathematics learning and, in the process, to positive test scores.

Testing and Teaching: Five Recommendations

Testing and effective teaching can coexist, and all teachers can learn how to use assessment in support of the mathematics learning of every student. I offer five suggestions toward this productive coexistence.

1. LEARN ABOUT ASSESSMENT

Nearly all teachers can learn more about assessment than they currently know. In particular, teachers need to understand what summative assessment (like the state accountability test) can tell us and how to use formative (day-to-day) assessment to inform our teaching and improve student learning. Most teacher education programs do not have enough time for courses devoted to the in-depth study of assessment, so this is a great topic for inservice professional learning or graduate work. A good beginning for learning about assessment is for teachers to work together around examples of student work. Teacher reflections and discussions can shed light on what students have learned. ("In looking at this student's explanation, I can see a misconception I didn't know she had.") Teachers can refine their assessment skills and also gain insights about how to improve their teaching as they consider differences that appear from student to student or from class to class. ("The answers your students are giving seem to give you better information than the answers my students are giving.") Ideally, as teachers grow in their knowledge of assessment, they also grow in their understanding of how to improve student learning.

2. UNDERSTAND YOUR STATE TEST

The summative tests used in most states tend to cover one or more years of learning and they rely primarily (often entirely) on multiple choice items. This is not surprising, since large-scale testing is expensive, and formats other than multiple choice are particularly costly. The quality of tests varies from state to state, and sometimes from year to year, and it may be hard to predict exactly what will be assessed on any year's test. From a practical standpoint, this type of summative assessment cannot address everything students are expected to learn in the year, so teachers must be knowledgeable about the standards and expectations that may not appear on the test. All teachers should be familiar with both their test specifications (which describe what will be tested and how it will be tested) and their state standards (which describe what students are expected to learn). Furthermore, it is important for teachers to recognize that the scores on this kind of test are neither diagnostic nor comprehensive; scores are but one of the pieces of information a teacher needs in order to inform instruction and improve student learning.

3. BE A SKEPTICAL CONSUMER OF TEST-PREPARATION MATERIALS

When schools feel pressure to perform on tests, it's not unusual for teachers, counselors, principals, and others to look for ways to improve performance. A little bit of test preparation, in terms of students working on a few items in a format similar to those on the test, helps students to become familiar with the way test items are posed. However, more is not necessarily better, and some quick-fix programs and test-prep tips can interfere with student learning in a number of ways. Such programs and tips can mislead students into thinking that all test items always follow predictable patterns (e.g., If three of the answer choices are similar and one is different, don't choose that one). While some of these strategies may work most of the time, they aren't a substitute for learning mathematics. Such materials and strategies too often distract students and take time away from the mathematics they should be learning. Looking for keywords or particular characteristics of numbers in test items not only is time-consuming and distracting but also fails as a test-taking strategy if an item happens to look different from what students have practiced. At least one state made a decision not to use any familiar keywords (*in all*, *fewer*, *successive*) in predictable ways on its test, so that students might learn to read each item and think about the mathematics involved, rather than try to remember what operation the word indicated.

Some test-preparation materials are mathematically sound and complement and support excellent mathematics instruction. But much of what is available has a greater likelihood to impede student learning than to help it. As skeptical consumers, teachers should look for materials that address excellent mathematics consistent with student expectations. Teachers should remember that a few minutes at a time, not necessarily every day or for weeks at a time, should be enough to help students learn how to show what they know on the test.

4. MAKE APPROPRIATE ASSESSMENT PART OF YOUR INSTRUCTION

The most important type of assessment for guiding instructional decisions and supporting student learning is formative assessment, or the day-to-day monitoring of what students are learning. Knowing how to assess student learning well should be a major goal of a teacher's own career-long professional growth. As in other aspects of improving teaching, focusing on analyzing student work provides an excellent foundation for a teacher or group of teachers to advance their understanding of learning and testing. Ideally, a skillful teacher will regularly analyze student work using a range of informal and formal tools to determine what students are learning and how they are developing as mathematical thinkers. From interviews and observations, to quizzes and tests, to project reports and class work, to portfolios, students can come to see assessment as part of their daily learning experience in mathematics. The breadth of information a teacher can gain from using different types of measures allows the teacher to determine when misconceptions might be starting and when a student has developed an unexpected, but productive, approach to solving a problem. As teachers incorporate increasingly sophisticated ways of monitoring and guiding student learning, it becomes indistinguishable whether tests are driving teaching or the other way around.

5. DON'T ALLOW A TEST TO SIDETRACK YOUR GOOD MATHEMATICS PROGRAM

No test should ever be allowed to interfere with a student's mathematics learning. Sometimes, what seems like a good way to raise scores this year can have far-reaching negative consequences two or three years later for one student or for an entire class of students. The best way to improve student test scores is to successfully teach every student challenging mathematics every year. An effective mathematics teacher will take a stand against any efforts to derail this goal so that every student has the opportunity to learn mathematics and develop his or her fullest potential year after year.

What Can We Do?

Assessment should support student learning. Period. It is the responsibility of professional mathematics teachers to seriously question the use of any test or assessment strategy that doesn't in some way support this goal for the short term or the long term. When used well, assessment can be a critical element of effective mathematics teaching. And when incorporated appropriately, not only can students learn good mathematics, they can also do well when test day arrives.

Reflection and Discussion

FOR TEACHERS

- What issues or challenges does this message raise for you? In what ways do you agree with or disagree with the main points of the message?
- How do you balance preparing for the state's accountability test and teaching the comprehensive mathematics program you know your students need?
- What types of tools or assessment procedures, either formal or informal, do you use for formative assessment to guide your teaching and monitor student progress?
- In terms of assessment, what are your greatest needs for professional learning, and where or how might you find opportunities to engage in this learning?

FOR FAMILIES

- What questions or issues does this message raise for you to discuss with your son or daughter, the teacher, or school leaders?

- How can you help your son or daughter do well on both large-scale and ongoing tests and other assessments in mathematics?

- How can you and your daughter or son interpret and make use of both the annual test score on the state's accountability test and the day-to-day test grades or evaluations done by the teacher?

FOR LEADERS AND POLICY MAKERS

- How does this message reinforce or challenge policies and decisions you have made or are considering?

- What kinds of test-preparation strategies or programs does your school or school district have in place, and how well do those strategies support improved student learning over the long term?

- How can you assist teachers in providing a comprehensive mathematics program for their students without spending too much time on test preparation?

- What kinds of ongoing professional learning experiences can you provide (or work with partners to provide) to help your teachers learn to effectively analyze student work and develop a range of assessment strategies to improve student learning?

RELATED MESSAGES

- Message 19, "Embracing Accountability," discusses issues related to accountability and large-scale assessment and describes how teachers can be involved in shaping these programs.

- Message 11, "Weighing Hens," discusses interim, or benchmark, testing within a larger context of assessment.

- Message 18, "Faster Isn't Smarter," addresses the downside of using timed tests for fact recall.

FURTHER READING

- *Mathematics Assessment: Myths, Models, Good Questions, and Practical Suggestions* (Stenmark 1991) is a great resource for designing and administering a wide variety of types of classroom assessments; it includes sample items and scoring rubrics.

- *This Is Only a Test: Teaching for Mathematical Understanding in an Age of Standardized Testing* (Litton and Wickett 2008) presents a discussion of how teaching for understanding can coexist with an environment of high-stakes accountability.

- *Mathematics Assessment Literacy: Concepts and Terms in Large-Scale Assessment* (Romagnano 2006) discusses assessment, with a focus on large-scale tests.

- *Uncovering Student Thinking in Mathematics: Twenty-Five Formative Assessment Probes* (Rose, Minton, and Arline 2006) and *Uncovering Student Thinking in Mathematics, Grades 6–12: Thirty Formative Assessment Probes for the Secondary Classroom* (Rose and Arline 2008) each present an overview of formative assessment and the use of probes and provide examples of probes for assessing mathematics learning.

- Four books in the National Council of Teachers of Mathematics' series Classroom Assessment for School Mathematics, K–12, *Mathematics Assessment: A Practical Handbook for Grades K–2* (Glanfield, Bush, and Stenmark 2003), *Grades 3–5* (Stenmark and Bush 2001), *Grades 6–8* (Bush and Leinwand 2000), and *Grades 9–12* (Bush and Greer 1999) provide a great background on a wide range of assessment issues specific to each grade band, including sample tasks, scoring rubrics, and more.

- Two more books in NCTM's series Classroom Assessment for School Mathematics, K–12, *Mathematics Assessment: Cases and Discussion Questions for Grades K–5* (Bush 2001) and *Grades 6–12* (Bush 2000) relate stories of teachers dealing with assessment as a tool for reflection and professional development.

36

I Know What an 82 Means!

GRADES AND GRADING IN THE 21ST CENTURY

In the early days of school reform in Texas, some of the discussion by state legislators involved making grading more consistent across the state. A select committee had identified many areas of attention for improving the schools, among them the notion that grades should be more consistent from school to school and from teacher to teacher. At one point, an unnamed state legislator was quoted as expressing his frustration over grades with a statement something like, "I don't know what all these Es and Ss and 'needs improvement' and happy faces are supposed to tell us. And teachers seem to all have different ideas about what a B is, or an A−, or a C+. But by golly, I know what an eighty-two means!"

This comment made me laugh and made me wonder. For policy makers, it was part of the passionate discussion that led to the imposition of a "uniform" numerical grading scale in the state. Yet how could anyone know exactly what an 82 represents, any more than any other rating given by a human being evaluating the work of another human being? The statement reminded me of the subjectivity and complexity in the issue of evaluating student work.

Why Grade?

Over the years, people have used grades for many purposes. We have assigned grades to provide feedback to students so that they know how they are doing; to recognize good work; to punish poor work; to determine who passes and who fails; to determine whether someone has met a goal for entering a program or the next grade level; to be accountable; or to get overall information about a program or a group of students. I would argue that the only reason to assign grades should be to improve student learning. Some of our many purposes may contribute to that goal, and others do not. But if the grading process doesn't contribute in some way to reaching this goal, why would we ask teachers to spend their valuable time on grading and ask students to suffer the consequences of grades to the degree that we do? If we accept the premise that grading should contribute to learning, then the next question becomes how to do it in meaningful ways that support this purpose.

Consistency in Grading

The legislator's comment, ". . . by golly, I know what an eighty-two means!" supports the idealized goal that grades can be consistent. However, consistency may be less about the grade itself than about the process by which that grade is determined.

My friend Vodene uses a piece of student work to demonstrate this point with teachers. She distributes copies of one student's completed (but ungraded) test that includes twenty noncontextual fraction computation exercises. The exercises are spread out on the page with room for student work. Vodene asks teachers to assign a grade to the student's test. The responses she has received from teachers have ranged from a grade of 25 to a grade of 85. How are such discrepancies possible on a straightforward test of numerical computation, with a nice number of problems that is a factor of 100? These differences are possible because this particular student included worked-out solutions for some of the items (but not for others), got some right answers and some wrong answers, showed some correct work and some incorrect work (not necessarily related to whether the associated answers were correct or incorrect), wrote somewhat illegibly, and did not answer one question. The teachers' grades varied greatly in how much partial credit they gave for any of these twenty test items and, therefore, the resulting numerical score they assigned varied greatly.

One point of this example is that no one really knows what an 82 means, even for the same set of exercises. Another is that every person has a different basis for judging work, especially if there are no clear criteria for what is expected or valued for individual items or for the test as a whole. Confounding the situation are differences in the difficulty level among tests developed by different teachers, differences in how well aligned tests are with what students are expected to learn, and differences in actual student performance, based not only on students knowledge, but also on students' learning styles or a range of factors that could influence performance on a test. Any illusions about the consistency of numerical grades simply do not survive close scrutiny.

Yet we can find ways to introduce a level of consistency to grading practices. Some states have mandated the length of grading periods and the frequency of reporting student grades or student progress. Some schools have organized professional learning opportunities around the analysis and comparison of student work. This can be a great way to increase teacher collaboration and also to increase common understanding of what certain grades represent. And some teachers have developed structured rubrics for evaluating open-ended problems, providing teachers and students with specific criteria to determine how many points or what grade will be awarded for different responses.

Dealing with the Problem

Over the years, I have known teachers and schools, especially before the current era of high-stakes accountability, who tried to find ways to avoid the issue of grading altogether. Some have chosen not to award grades at all, but just to write narrative comments about students' progress. Some have let students grade themselves or each other. Others have told students that they would all start with As until they did something negative that might reduce their grade. Still others have assigned grades solely based on class participation or on submitting assignments. Yet none of these practices has resulted in widespread use, and we still struggle over how to evaluate progress in support of helping students learn.

So we return to the original premise, that grading practices should contribute to improving student learning. Students need to know how they are doing. This can come in the form of a conversation with the teacher, written comments from the teacher, or a letter or numerical grade if that grade is based on observable, objective, specific criteria. Much of the knowledge we value today in mathematics goes far beyond a right-or-wrong, short-answer response to a straightforward question. Evaluating this kind of knowledge calls for a range of measures that include scoring rubrics that are provided to the student in advance. When students know the criteria against which their work will be evaluated, it can help them focus their learning. In this way, tests and grades can drive instruction and learning in very appropriate ways. Even for the simple fraction test mentioned earlier, if teachers agree that correct answers will be awarded a certain number of points and that correct procedures will be awarded a certain number of points, then grading the test becomes a more transparent and consistent process that should yield essentially the same results, no matter who evaluates it. And students should not be surprised by the grades they receive. But a teacher might want to consider whether such a test, even with clear scoring criteria, is the best way to determine what students know about computing with fractions. Perhaps the teacher could design a test that includes other types of problems beyond isolated computation exercises, such as problems calling for the student to apply reasoning skills and determine what operation is necessary, then follow through with computation to a reasonable answer. In some cases, an assessment can include a few rich problems that yield more information than a test of many superficial exercises. When a grade is awarded based on a comprehensive evaluation of the standards the student is expected to learn, the grade supports student learning and it becomes a meaningful indicator of what a student knows.

What Can We Do?

We know more today than ever before about how to assess and evaluate student work. We recognize the value of varied types of assessment measures, both formal and informal, and we know how to evaluate a student's performance on those measures. With well-designed assessments and with clear and specific grading criteria and rubrics, teachers can assign meaningful grades that let students know how they are progressing and where they need to focus their attention. This kind of communication should be one of our most important goals as teachers. A well-designed and professionally administered grading system also satisfies what many look for in terms of accountability to families and the broader public. We want every student to learn, and we want students, their families, and the community to see visible evidence of that learning.

Reflection and Discussion

FOR TEACHERS

- What issues or challenges does this message raise for you? In what ways do you agree with or disagree with the main points of the message?
- What observations or suggestions, if any, might you give to the teacher who designed the fraction test described in the message?
- How consistent is your grading system with that of your colleagues in your school? How do you know?
- What professional learning opportunities can you organize with colleagues around analyzing student work?
- How can you more effectively communicate to students and their families how students are progressing in their mathematics learning?

FOR FAMILIES

- What questions or issues does this message raise for you to discuss with your son or daughter, the teacher, or school leaders?

- How well do you understand the grading system used by your daughter's or son's mathematics teacher? How does it compare with how she or he has been graded in mathematics over the years?

- How can you find out more information about how your son or daughter is progressing in mathematics, including the identification of strengths and areas that need the most work and support at home?

FOR LEADERS AND POLICY MAKERS

- How does this message reinforce or challenge policies and decisions you have made or are considering?

- How much consistency in grading of mathematics work does your school or district provide from teacher to teacher and from school to school? How do you know?

- What kinds of ongoing professional learning experiences can you provide (or work with partners to provide) to help teachers improve their grading practices?

RELATED MESSAGES

- Message 35, "Putting Testing in Perspective," discusses some of the issues raised in this message with respect to assessment.

- Message 22, "We Don't Care About the Answer," recognizes the importance of considering both the answer and the process used to arrive at the answer.

- Message 18, "Faster Isn't Smarter," challenges some of our beliefs about how we can tell whether a student is a good math student based on timed tests of computation skills.

FURTHER READING

- *Mathematics Assessment: Myths, Models, Good Questions, and Practical Suggestions* (Stenmark 1991) is a great resource for teachers on how to design, administer, and evaluate student performance using a variety of classroom assessments; it provides sample items and rubrics for evaluating student work.

- "Teaching Students to Think, Leading to Change: Effective Grading Practices" (Reeves 2008) makes a case for reevaluating grading practices in schools.

- *Fair Isn't Always Equal: Assessing and Grading in the Differentiated Classroom* (Wormeli 2006) offers research and common-sense thinking for teachers and administrators on assessment and grading in differentiated classes.

- *How to Grade for Learning: Linking Grades to Standards, Grades K–12* (O'Connor 2002) includes eight updated models to assist teachers in designing and implementing grading practices that help students feel more in control of their academic success.

37

Boring!

IS KEEPING STUDENTS INTERESTED
A TEACHER'S JOB?

It was boring . . . the teacher just stood in front of the room and just talked and didn't really like involve you.

High school dropout, *The Silent Epidemic*
(Bridgeland, Dilulio, and Morison 2006)

Many students in the United States, especially high school students, are bored and unchallenged. This was the point made in a press release posted by the Gates Foundation in 2007 that summarized the results of a survey of young adults describing their educational experience. *The Silent Epidemic* and other reports relate the same situation as this study; namely, boredom and irrelevance are key factors in many students' dissatisfaction in school and in their decision to drop out of school before graduating. Several efforts are under way in both the private and the public sector to develop innovative school structures and to make the U.S. school curriculum more engaging and relevant for all students and the world they will face after high school. But these efforts are small in number and thus far limited in scope, and questions linger about whether addressing boredom should be a responsibility of schools or whether student boredom is simply a fact of life.

Does Boredom Matter?

Some students complain that they don't like school or don't like math because it's boring and because they can't see why they should learn it. Other students demonstrate their boredom by not coming to class or by not coming to school at all. Still others show their boredom through their behavior—by not participating in what is going on in class or by more blatantly misbehaving.

Boredom can affect students at any age, although students tend to verbalize the complaint more as they get older. But even elementary students can choose to disengage from what is going on in mathematics class if they are not actively involved in doing mathematics or if something outside of mathematics seems more interesting. Likewise, teachers often express a complaint about boredom's partner, motivation; they say that some students are not motivated to learn, that they won't participate and don't do their homework. In either case, if students do not participate in learning activities, they are not likely to learn much. I would argue that it's all about learning in discussions of school mathematics, so it follows that anything that interferes with student engagement demands our attention. In the bestselling book *Fires in the Bathroom* by educational journalist Kathleen Cushman, one student, identified as Montoya, noted, "When we don't pay attention because we're bored, we don't understand" (2005, 107). If boredom and motivation keep students from understanding what we want them to learn, then it's absolutely the case that boredom and motivation matter.

Is Overcoming Boredom the Teacher's Problem?

Some teachers suggest that students complain of boredom because they are lazy or simply want an excuse not to participate. A few teachers have said to me that it isn't their job to entertain students, that it's their students' responsibility to want to learn. There is merit in the argument that students have a role in whether they are bored or motivated. Certainly students need to accept responsibility for participating in classroom activities and for committing to their own learning. But is it possible to help students develop the interest, commitment, and responsibility teachers are looking for? And if so, is providing opportunities for this development something teachers should take on?

It may seem on the surface that boredom is an attribute of a student's character or that motivation to learn is a choice students make. On the other hand, there are those who suggest that it is what the teacher does or the mathematics task itself that motivates students. James Middleton and Photini Spanias, researchers who study motivation in the learning of mathematics, have observed that in order to improve student motivation, we must move beyond both of these limited views to a more sophisticated understanding of the interaction between the student, the task, the teacher, and even the social system within which mathematics takes place (2002).

In other words, students may not be interested in learning mathematics in general or in participating in a particular math activity. But perhaps we can choose activities or tasks that are more likely to engage these students than other tasks we might select. The way we structure the interactions in the classroom—the mathematical discourse—also can contribute to how well students participate. And if these efforts take place in a school where a culture of student participation in relevant learning experiences is well established, the likelihood of student participation is even greater.

Several years ago, I heard someone observe in a noneducational context that "action precedes motivation." This statement at first seemed backward until I took the time to reflect on it. Consider a task you may not feel motivated to undertake; for me, the example of getting my garage organized comes to mind. It's easy to dread the task and procrastinate getting started. But often, once we start in on the task, our progress toward our goal and the success we experience in small steps along the way help motivate us to complete it. As space is cleared in the garage, and we start seeing the possibility of knowing where things are, we build momentum and seem to be more motivated to keep going. As a friend suggested, "Starting is harder than doing." So perhaps our responsibility as teachers is to pull students into a math activity, however we can and whatever it takes. If we choose or design the task carefully, if we do our work well, and if we are lucky, once students become engaged in doing the task, they are likely to also become engaged in learning the mathematics that accompanies the task.

What Can We Do?

No one would argue that having fun without learning should be the primary goal of mathematics teaching. And learning with a sense of drudgery is next to useless, as it is not likely to last and can easily contribute to negative attitudes about mathematics. In between these two extremes, however, is a place where committed teachers willing to take risks can find ways of engaging students in tasks that are relevant or interesting or both, and where teachers make sure students know what mathematics they're learning. These teachers incorporate reasonable amounts of practice into their teaching without making practice the focus of every mathematics lesson. They allow students to go on to higher levels of mathematics without spending six weeks or more at the beginning of every year on review of what students have temporarily forgotten over the summer, and they build in appropriate review as students encounter new topics throughout the year. They help students learn to recognize when it may be appropriate to use a calculator and when to put it aside. They help students make connections among the mathematical ideas and skills they learn, and they show students a variety of contexts in which mathematics is useful. They invest in their students' learning, not just for the test next week or next month, but also for their students' future. Everything these teachers do works to prevent boredom from ever taking hold of reluctant students.

Boredom threatens to undermine student learning, but engagement in relevant mathematical activities can be the antidote to boredom. Instead of driving students away from education with irrelevant, low-level tasks, teachers have the opportunity to invite students into mathematics in challenging and interesting ways that can keep students interested, keep them in school, and help them learn the mathematics they need for their future.

Reflection and Discussion

FOR TEACHERS

- What issues or challenges does this message raise for you? In what ways do you agree with or disagree with the main points of the message?
- How do you know whether your students are bored? If they are bored, how do they express their boredom?
- How can you effectively engage students in learning mathematics and prevent boredom? How can you help students become motivated to learn?

FOR FAMILIES

- What questions or issues does this message raise for you to discuss with your son or daughter, the teacher, or school leaders?
- How do you know whether your daughter or son is bored? How does she or he express that boredom?
- How can you help prevent your son or daughter from being bored with the mathematics so that he or she is motivated to learn?

FOR LEADERS AND POLICY MAKERS

- How does this message reinforce or challenge policies and decisions you have made or are considering?
- What does it take to create a culture of engagement in your school(s)?
- What kinds of support can you provide teachers so that they are likely to teach in ways that minimize student disengagement?

RELATED MESSAGES

- Message 33, "Engaged in What?" takes a closer look at the nature of meaningful student engagement.
- Message 17, "Constructive Struggling," considers the value of challenging students with complex tasks as a way to engage them and support their learning.
- Message 34, "Forgetting Isn't Forever," recommends breaking the cycle of redundancy and endless review that can lead to student boredom and disengagement.
- Message 3, "Making the Case for Creativity," reminds us of the importance of helping students develop creativity, often a factor in engaging students and overcoming boredom.

FURTHER READING

- "Pedagogical Implications of the Research on Motivation in Mathematics Education" (Middleton and Spanias 2002) provides teachers with a research base for making instructional decisions to increase student motivation in mathematics.
- *Professional Standards for Teaching Mathematics* (National Council of Teachers of Mathematics 1991) offers a rich discussion of how to select tasks and orchestrate mathematical discourse to engage students in their learning.
- *The Silent Epidemic: Perspectives of High School Dropouts* (Bridgeland, Dilulio, and Morison 2006) contains revealing interviews with students who have dropped out of school.
- *Fires in the Bathroom: Advice for Teachers from High School Students* (Cushman 2005) presents high school students' descriptions of what they want and need from their teachers.
- *High School: A Report on Secondary Education in America* (Boyer 1983) offers an in-depth look at high schools in the 1980s and makes proposals for how to revamp schools; it is interesting today in terms of what has changed since then and what has not.

38 Ten Kinds of Wonderful

ROLES FOR TEACHERS IN THE 21ST CENTURY

Teachers face real challenges in implementing the numerous recommendations for teaching mathematics today, including the standards documents produced by the National Council of Teachers of Mathematics (NCTM). Many teachers recognize the possibilities for engaging students within a new vision of rigorous and relevant mathematics; at the same time they are bogged down by the overwhelming expectations for creating classrooms that model such a vision. Within the comprehensive description that NCTM's standards provide about what teachers should do and how they should act, ten metaphors emerge regarding teacher roles. Some of these roles may feel fairly comfortable, and other roles may remind us just how hard it is to live up to our own ideals.

Role 1: The Teacher as Architect

Architects create the environment in which we live and work—both the buildings and the feelings they evoke. Similarly, the teacher as architect creates the learning environment for students. From the arrangement of furniture that facilitates discussion, thoughts, and exploration to the feeling students experience when they walk into the classroom, the teacher establishes an atmosphere where mathematics and learning are important. Most of all, the teacher creates a place where students feel safe to take risks and are willing to share ideas while learning to value the opinions of each other.

Role 2: The Teacher as Composer

In the same way that a composer creates a musical score for performance by musicians, the teacher creates the tasks with which students will engage. Within the rich environment created by the teacher as architect, the teacher as composer designs or selects something for students to do that will engage their intellect, stretch their thinking, increase their mathematical understanding, and expand their toolkit of problem-solving strategies.

Role 3: The Teacher as Movie Director

Once a teacher creates the learning environment and develops the tasks on which students will spend their time, the teacher as movie director steps in to determine how the students, like actors, will relate to each other, their tasks, and their environment. Organizing a class for mathematical discourse includes considering questions like the following: How will students interact with each other as they go through an activity? What will the teacher do or say with students? What questions from the teacher can push a student's thinking just a little further? What kinds of communication can really help a student develop mathematical understanding? These elements of discourse provide a foundation for a student's reflection and communication that can lead to the power of making generalizations and reasoning mathematically.

These first three elements—*environment*, *task*, and *discourse*—form the foundation for mathematics teaching as described in NCTM's *Professional Standards for Teaching Mathematics* (1991).

Role 4: The Teacher as Stockbroker

Much as a stockbroker constantly analyzes the stock market, the teacher as stockbroker constantly analyzes the teaching and learning that occur within the classroom. What worked today and what didn't work? What will I do differently next time? What is worth the precious investment of my students' time tomorrow? As teachers reflect on and analyze what they do, they continue to refine their practice and improve their effectiveness.

Role 5: The Teacher as Ship Captain

When captains of large ships have set a course, they cannot afford to sit back and wait until the ship either arrives at its destination or crashes on the rocks. Ship captains must constantly be alert to shifts in weather, ship traffic, and coastlines, and they must be prepared for unexpected disasters. The teacher as ship captain deals with even more unpredictable factors than nature and commerce and must constantly be evaluating how and what students are learning. We cannot afford to wait until a student crashes on the rocks before noticing the student has veered off course. Rather, we must work closely enough with students so that we can provide ongoing course correction whenever misunderstandings begin. The teacher as ship captain may not always correct the student directly or immediately, but rather makes a decision about what kind of experience or guidance can help the student get back on course in a meaningful and timely way.

Role 6: The Teacher as Mayor

The mathematics classroom is sometimes described as a mathematical community, where students and the teacher are actively involved in creating their learning experience. This learning community needs the strength of a knowledgeable and compassionate leader who considers the needs and talents of the student citizens. An effective community leader can provide a vision of where the community is headed and support for getting there. Giving students responsibility for their own learning doesn't mean abdicating leadership, nor does it mean less work for the teacher. Rather, helping students develop responsibility means giving up some control while creating a new kind of classroom leadership that guides, encourages, and enlightens along the way.

Role 7: The Teacher as Bridge Builder

Bridges serve a critical role in helping us connect one thing to another, sometimes connecting short distances, sometimes connecting longer distances, and other times connecting two points of challenging terrain, often with complex on- and off-ramps. As a builder of many bridges, the teacher can help students construct the connections that enable them to make sense of what they are learning and what they already know. The teacher as bridge builder helps students experience the rich connections between the threads of mathematics like algebra, probability, measurement, numbers, and geometry. The teacher as bridge builder helps students see the links between mathematics and science, social studies, physical education, and the arts. And most of all, the teacher as bridge builder helps students make the vital connection between mathematics and the world outside of school.

Role 8: The Teacher as Student

Nowhere is a commitment to lifelong learning more important than in teaching. Even if every teacher today were completely knowledgeable about teaching mathematics effectively, using current technology, and understanding new fields of mathematics, within six months or a year or two years, there would be a need for new professional learning. Today's teacher cannot afford to remain static for more than a short time when the world is in a state of dynamic flux with almost daily changes in technology, mathematics, schools, students, and society. In this setting, the teacher as student makes a lifelong commitment to professional development, continually learning more about how to help students learn the mathematics they will need for the future.

Role 9: The Teacher as Recruiter

Mathematics teachers have traditionally done a good job of encouraging students to pursue mathematics-related fields, counseling them to become engineers, computer scientists, doctors, or statisticians, for example. Teachers have often been reluctant, however, to encourage their students to become mathematics teachers. We sometimes communicate to our students that teaching isn't as worthy a profession as other, more lucrative options. I would argue that if teaching isn't currently a career worthy of our future adults, then it is our responsibility as professional educators to transform it into something that is worthy of them. The responsibility of the teacher as recruiter is to communicate not only to students but also to the broader community how important and rewarding our profession can be.

The ideal of teacher as recruiter is reflected in an experience shared with me by Kathleen, a teacher who received the Presidential Award for Excellence in Science and Mathematics Teaching. As Kathleen stepped down from the platform after her statewide award ceremony, she felt a tap on her shoulder and turned to see her former high school mathematics teacher. Kathleen shared with her former teacher that she had been the inspiration for Kathleen choosing a career in teaching. As they were hugging, Kathleen felt a tap on her other shoulder. She turned to see a former student, who told Kathleen that Kathleen had been her inspiration for becoming a teacher. Let's hope that the torch will continue to be passed from generation to generation so that some of our finest minds can continue to prepare new generations of students to think and learn mathematically.

Role 10: The Teacher as Prospector

The role of prospector is the bottom line of teaching. Picture the scene: You're in a cave. It's dark, damp, musty, and cold, and you are surrounded by solid rock, with nothing but a dim bulb on your helmet and a pickax in your hand. But in the face of this bleakness, you keep chipping away, because you know that somewhere deep inside that solid rock are incredible uncut gems and well-disguised nuggets of high-grade ores. Those gems and nuggets are why you became a teacher. That's what keeps you teaching when pressures seem unbearable and new expectations seem unattainable.

And More . . .

It's clear that teaching is a complex profession; these ten roles represent a small sampling of the many roles teachers play throughout their careers. I consider this complex profession the most important job in the world. Education is the source of the solutions to the challenges confronting the nation and the world, and it provides the foundation for every person's future.

In today's high-stakes, rapid-change, accountability-focused educational environment, it's easy for teachers to become discouraged by the many pressures they face every day. But I would encourage all teachers to take heart and remember that there is a compelling reason why they chose teaching in the first place—when things seem the darkest, just remember the gems a good prospector can discover.

Reflection and Discussion

FOR TEACHERS

- What issues or challenges does this message raise for you? In what ways do you agree with or disagree with the main points of the message?
- Which roles do you feel most comfortable in, and which roles would you like to work on doing more effectively?
- What other roles do you see yourself playing as an effective and professional mathematics teacher?

FOR FAMILIES

- What questions or issues does this message raise for you to discuss with your son or daughter, the teacher, or school leaders?
- In what ways do you see your daughter's or son's teacher in light of the several roles the teacher plays? How can you support the teacher in succeeding at some of these roles?

FOR LEADERS AND POLICY MAKERS

- How does this message reinforce or challenge policies and decisions you have made or are considering?
- How can you help teachers recognize the many roles they play and learn to be more effective in these various roles?

RELATED MESSAGES

- Message 40, "Seven Steps Toward Being a Better Math Teacher," suggests steps teachers can take to grow professionally.
- Message 29, "The Evolution of a Mathematics Teacher," traces the path a teacher takes in becoming more accomplished.

FURTHER READING

- *Professional Standards for Teaching Mathematics* (NCTM 1991) is one of the best descriptions of what a professional teacher of mathematics does in the classroom and how other educators support that teacher. It includes a rich description of how professional teachers design classrooms that support mathematical discourse and student engagement.
- *About Teaching Mathematics: A K–8 Resource* (Burns 2007a) describes many aspects of what an effective teacher does within a broader comprehensive discussion of school mathematics.
- *Designing Professional Development for Teachers of Science and Mathematics* (Loucks-Horsley et al. 2003) presents a range of professional learning activities that can be used to structure professional development programs that help teachers expand their view of the job of mathematics (or science) teaching.
- *Teachers as Learners: Professional Development in Science and Mathematics* (Mundry and Dunne 2003) is a kit of materials, including a facilitator's guide and videos, that builds on the book *Designing Professional Development for Teachers of Science and Mathematics* (Loucks-Horsley et al. 2003). The resource provides relevant and lasting professional development for mathematics and science teachers.

39

Standing on the Shoulders . . .

LEARNING FROM EACH OTHER

If I have seen farther than others, it is because I have stood on the shoulders of giants.

Isaac Newton

In *On the Shoulders of Giants,* Lynn Steen (1999) helps us see mathematics in new ways. The title of the book comes from the above quote by Isaac Newton, who was honoring the work of such scientists as Galileo and Kepler as a foundation for his own considerable accomplishments in mathematics and science. In referencing Newton's quote, Steen acknowledges the contributions of earlier mathematicians as he describes a different way of looking at mathematics. Both men acknowledged what historians have long known: the most important advances in civilization have been built on work that has been done before by others.

In the same way that great thinkers in mathematics build on the work of others, teachers and leaders in school mathematics also build on the work of others every day, both those who are famous and those who are less well known. I could go on at length about the influence of the highly acclaimed educators and many other well-known giants I respect and in some cases have had the privilege to work with. But recently I have also reflected on the role of people who would not consider themselves giants—the colleagues next door who help us understand and appreciate great mathematics teaching.

Where We Find Inspiration

It can be daunting to be told to change our practice, to take risks, and to try something new. But when a colleague we know, whether next door or in another school far away, tries something different, it somehow becomes more concrete and, perhaps, achievable. Take, for instance, what I learned from Amy, a teacher in an Alabama middle school who confessed to me just before my visit to her sixth-grade class that she was about to try working with small groups of students for the first time. What I learned from Amy that day, aside from my considerable respect for her willingness to take a risk in front of a visitor, was that an effective and committed teacher can expand her teaching repertoire in ways that immediately make a positive difference for students, even if she hasn't yet worked out all the details that she will eventually refine. Or consider the lessons Maria taught me, without even realizing she was doing it. Maria is a teacher in rural Arizona whose Algebra 2 class was among the first to use graphing calculators in the late 1980s, in conjunction with teaching from an innovative mathematics textbook. My visit to Maria's class helped me understand the power of effectively incorporating these new tools. In her class, I listened to students use sophisticated mathematical language and interact around complex mathematical ideas in ways I never thought possible.

Perhaps we can become convinced of the need to ask good questions as part of an effective lesson, and perhaps we can even watch videos where experts skillfully elicit student responses and stimulate learning with their masterful use of questions. But we get better at asking good questions when we also rely on those colleagues who are more adept at this aspect of teaching. My friends and colleagues David and Bonnie helped me when I decided to return to the classroom. After working with teachers for several years, I volunteered to teach one ninth-grade algebra class for the year at a local high school. During that year, I found myself regularly on the phone with David and Bonnie, dusting off skills I had not used for quite some time. They helped me extend those skills and ask questions much more skillfully than I had done in my earlier years of teaching.

It's relatively easy to talk about high expectations. We may even think that we believe that all students can achieve high levels of challenging mathematics. But when we start to fall back into old habits and beliefs that unintentionally limit our students, it is our connections with the extraordinary teachers we know and work with every day that can pull us back and challenge us to stay true to those beliefs. When I taught in Burkina Faso, West Africa, my colleague Sylla helped me in just this way. He pushed me to teach a topic I was tempted to omit, to a group of students I thought would never need it and might not succeed with it, leading to a humble reawakening of my beliefs in the importance of high expectations.

Or perhaps we simply have a feeling that the lesson or unit we have planned seems a bit bland and unlikely to engage students. When we sit down with our colleagues, teammates, or best teaching buddies to talk about how we can jazz things up a bit, we can collectively learn from each other. We can brainstorm possibilities or borrow a good idea that we then turn into meaningful learning experiences for students.

What Can We Do?

We have a responsibility to continue to improve the mathematics experience of all students, and learning from each other is an important part of that responsibility. In my own career, I have been fortunate to have many wonderful opportunities—to teach, to serve, to lead. In every one of these roles, I have recognized that what each of us accomplishes would not be possible without what many others have accomplished before us. Equally important, we have a responsibility to build today's school mathematics on the best we know from the generations who preceded us. To do less is to disrespect the contributions, both exceptional and routine, of those who devoted their careers to improving our profession.

I also recognize that what we all accomplish today is likely to pale in comparison with what others will achieve tomorrow, both in teaching and in mathematics. Maybe some of those who will achieve such accomplishments are sitting in our elementary, middle school, high school, or university classrooms right now—future *giants* on whose shoulders other generations will stand to reach even greater heights than we can imagine.

Reflection and Discussion

FOR TEACHERS

- What issues or challenges does this message raise for you? In what ways do you agree with or disagree with the main points of the message?
- From whom have you learned important teaching lessons? How have those lessons shaped your teaching?
- In what ways can you learn from what others do to improve your own teaching practice?
- How can we help students understand the growing nature of human knowledge and the notion that people create new knowledge every day, building on what others have done in the past?

FOR FAMILIES

- What questions or issues does this message raise for you to discuss with your son or daughter, the teacher, or school leaders?
- How can you help your daughter or son come to understand that much of what we learn is based on work that others have done before us, that

much of mathematics remains to be discovered, and that each of us has the potential to build on what we learn?

FOR LEADERS AND POLICY MAKERS

- How does this message reinforce or challenge policies and decisions you have made or are considering?
- How can you provide more opportunities for teachers and leaders to learn from each other, either within your school or district or outside it?
- In what ways does your school or district build on current research, best practice, and professional guidance to advance what we know about teaching mathematics?

RELATED MESSAGES

- Message 41, "Thank you, Mr. Bender," celebrates teachers who make a positive difference in students' lives.
- Message 26, "Beyond Pockets of Wonderfulness," discusses the importance of collaboration and articulation among educators.
- Message 31, "Do They Really Need It?," recounts the episode described in this message about my teaching experience in Burkina Faso.
- Message 13, "Seek First to Understand," calls on all of us to work with and learn from those within and outside of our profession.

FURTHER READING

- *On the Shoulders of Giants* (Steen 1999) takes a fresh look at some long-standing ideas in mathematics.
- *Designing Professional Development for Teachers of Science and Mathematics* (Loucks-Horsley et al. 2003) is a comprehensive and highly acclaimed book that describes various types of professional learning activities, many of which involve working with colleagues or learning from each other.
- *Teachers as Learners: Professional Development in Science and Mathematics* (Mundry and Dunne 2003) is a kit of materials, including a facilitator's guide and videos, that builds on the book *Designing Professional Development for Teachers of Science and Mathematics* (Loucks-Horsley et al. 2003). The resource provides relevant and lasting professional development for mathematics and science teachers.
- My website on Burkina Faso (http://csinburkinafaso.com) includes photos and stories about life and teaching during my Peace Corps assignment from 1999 through 2001.

40

Seven Steps Toward Being a Better Math Teacher

A PATH OF LIFELONG IMPROVEMENT

What we ask of mathematics teachers today can be daunting, even for the most ambitious risk taker. In a 1994 opinion piece reflecting on the changes we were expecting of mathematics teachers, Steve Leinwand encouraged teachers to change 10 percent of what they do each year (preferably a different 10 percent each year). We could argue about whether that percentage is sufficient in today's rapidly changing global environment, but the concept holds—as part of a teacher's career-long path of improvement, some change each year is appropriate, and trying to change everything all at once is probably unreasonable and unproductive. In support of the notion of continual shifts toward improvement, I offer seven somewhat oversimplified steps targeting one thing at a time for a teacher's growth. Collectively, these steps cover more than most teachers would want to address during any school year. But committing to any of these steps can lead to positive change in the classroom for both the teacher and the students.

Step 1

OMIT ONE THING

Historically, in United States mathematics education, we have tried to address too many topics every year, leading to superficial coverage and little depth. New efforts in defining priorities and areas of focus, led by the National Council of Teachers of Mathematics' (NCTM) *Curriculum Focal Points* (2006), help educators recognize that not every topic needs to be addressed every year and that not every state mathematics standard carries the same priority at each grade level. Meanwhile, most mathematics textbooks still include all the topics necessary for many states, each of which has its own expectations and priorities. This leads to long and cumbersome textbooks that address the same topic in several grades, often with little growth from year to year. Yet some teachers are not willing to skip chapters in the textbook (even chapters they recognize as a review of what students already have studied) or give up lessons they have always taught (even if the lessons do not address appropriate topics for that grade level). My advice to teachers is to work with your colleagues to identify the priority topics and areas of concentration for each grade level. Then consider omitting one topic, unit, or lesson that you might otherwise have taught, if it does not support your identified priorities for the grade level or course. I once made this recommendation at a beginning-of-the-year presentation in a suburban school district in Georgia. The superintendent told me later that an early-career teacher sitting next to him in the audience had leaned over and said, "Am I allowed to do that?"

He told me he answered, "You bet you are!"

Step 2

PICK ONE MATHEMATICAL PROCESS FOR FOCUSED ATTENTION

As you narrow the list of priority topics in your curriculum, consider becoming more knowledgeable and more practiced about teaching one mathematical process, such as developing mathematical reasoning, communicating mathematically, making connections, using different forms of representation, or solving problems. These may sound familiar, as they are the five process standards from NCTM's *Principles and Standards for School Mathematics* (2000). Consider reading the corresponding sections of this comprehensive document, both the K–12 overview of a process standard and the grade-band description of that standard for your level. Work with a colleague to improve your teaching on this one process for the year, making a special effort to help students develop that process. This doesn't mean ignoring the other four processes; it just means targeting one you think might benefit from extra attention on your part during the year.

Step 3

FOCUS ON ONE MATHEMATICAL CONTENT AREA OR FOCAL POINT

Likewise, consider targeting one particular mathematical content area, such as algebra and algebraic thinking, number and operations, geometry, measurement, or data analysis and probability (NCTM's five content standards [2000]) for extra attention on during the year. Alternatively, consider targeting one of NCTM's curriculum focal points (2006) for one grade at the elementary or middle school level, presenting a somewhat more integrated approach to priority mathematics topics for the grade. Seek out workshops, articles, and learning opportunities related to the content area you select, particularly at conferences with a menu of offerings, and work on teaching that content in richer, more engaging ways than in the past.

Step 4

USE TECHNOLOGY IN AT LEAST ONE POWERFUL NEW WAY

The applications and potential of technology change every year. Because calculators are probably the most readily available technology resource that can be used by every student at the same time, consider learning a new and worthwhile use of a calculator that supports the mathematics learning you expect of students at your grade level. If there is a teacher in your school or in another district who is using technology effectively, ask to visit her or his classroom and schedule time to talk about what you might be able to do in your classroom, with a focus on the mathematics topics or skills you want students to learn. It's also critical to talk with colleagues and school leaders about your school's policies to ensure that all students, regardless of their economic situation, have access to appropriate technology, both in and outside of school.

Step 5

READ AT LEAST ONE CHALLENGING BOOK TOWARD IMPROVING YOUR MATHEMATICS TEACHING

Consider taking time during the year or over the summer to read a book that will push your thinking or challenge your beliefs about mathematics teaching. *Faster Isn't Smarter* is intended to be this kind of book. One other good option is the NCTM publication *Professional Standards for Teaching Mathematics* (1991), which offers a rich description of the role of the teacher in selecting worthwhile tasks, managing a conducive learning environment, and structuring opportunities for mathematical discourse. Additional possibilities include *The Schools Our Children Deserve* (Kohn 2000), *Making Sense: Teaching and Learning Math with Understanding* (Carpenter et al. 1997), or *How Students Learn: Mathematics in the Classroom* (Bransford and Donovan 2005). Any book that causes you to reflect about your practice and think about and discuss important issues can help you improve your teaching. Consider organizing a discussion group with colleagues or progressing through a book as part of a continuing class or study group. Be sure to reflect, discuss, keep a journal, and note what you might do differently in your teaching as a result of what you learn.

Step 6

SHIFT THE FOCUS OF AT LEAST ONE TEST

Consider shifting the focus of one test or assessment you administer to include a better evaluation of the big ideas and connections you want students to learn. Look at the balance of content you assess and the way(s) in which you assess that content to determine whether you are addressing all the aspects of mathematical understanding, proficiency, and mathematical processes you expect your students to learn. Notice whether you are asking students to connect ideas and look for common threads in their learning, as well as whether you are asking students to stretch and apply their learning to new, but related, areas.

Step 7

HELP ONE STUDENT ACCOMPLISH SOMETHING YOU DIDN'T THINK SHE OR HE COULD DO

Perhaps the most important thing you can do to improve your teaching is to pay attention to your own beliefs and preconceptions about what individual students or groups of students can accomplish. Consider looking at one student (or possibly a group of students if you're ambitious and well supported by colleagues) for whom you have lower expectations than for other students. Try setting a challenge that is somewhat beyond the student's reach. Talk with the student about your belief that he is capable of accomplishing more challenging mathematics than he has done before. Ask the student to make a collaborative commitment between the two of you that you will both do whatever it takes for him to reach the goal you set. My guess is that with a strong commitment and lots of work, you both will be able to accomplish far more than you thought you could. The result may extend beyond this one new accomplishment to a lasting shift in the underlying beliefs you both hold about what it takes to be smart in mathematics.

What Can We Do?

I offer these suggestions as positive steps that a teacher might reasonably tackle over a period of time, recognizing that any of them, in their own right, can present challenges and rewards. Today's teaching calls for traveling a path of constant refocusing and rethinking how we can help students learn important mathematics. Taking one step after another is the way to follow this path if we are to survive the journey and help all students fulfill their greatest potential—as well as our own.

Reflection and Discussion

FOR TEACHERS

- What issues or challenges does this message raise for you? In what ways do you agree with or disagree with the main points of the message?
- How reasonable are these seven suggestions for growth and improvement? What might you modify about these recommendations in terms of your own goals?
- What are your top three goals for professional improvement for this (or the next) school year?

FOR FAMILIES

- What questions or issues does this message raise for you to discuss with your son or daughter, the teacher, or school leaders?
- How can you let the teacher know that you support her or his continued efforts to improve teaching in support of student learning?

FOR LEADERS AND POLICY MAKERS

- How does this message reinforce or challenge policies and decisions you have made or are considering?
- What opportunities can you create for teachers to implement reasonable change in their classroom practice or professional knowledge?
- How can you support teachers as they attempt to make significant changes in their mathematics teaching?
- How might you adapt these seven steps to the needs of your particular mathematics teachers?
- How can you use NCTM's resources, including *Principles and Standards for School Mathematics* (2000) and the NCTM Professional Development Focus of the Year (that alternates from year to year among principles, process standards, and content standards), to help your teachers undertake the seven steps or a variation of those steps you can determine together?

RELATED MESSAGES

- Message 6, "'Teach Harder!' Isn't the Answer," considers what we ask of teachers and how teachers can transform their teaching.
- Message 20, "Putting Calculators in Their Place," addresses appropriate uses of calculators with respect to the teaching of computation.

- Message 38, "Ten Kinds of Wonderful," presents ten metaphors for teacher roles in helping students learn mathematics.
- Message 12, "Beyond Band-Aids and Bandwagons," looks at educational fads we sometimes impose on teachers and discusses how we can focus on substantive change instead.

FURTHER READING

- "Four Teacher-Friendly Postulates for Thriving in a Sea of Change" (Leinwand 1994) challenges teachers to change ten percent of what they do every year.
- Every year since 2004, NCTM has identified a Professional Development Focus of the Year addressing one of the principles or standards from *Principles and Standards for School Mathematics*, for which they provide a list of targeted resources. A list of resources for each year is available at the NCTM website under Professional Development (www.nctm.org/profdev). For any current year's focus, in-person and online learning experiences are also available.
- *Leading in a Culture of Change* (Fullan 2007a) offers insights about how change happens in schools and other institutions.
- *The Schools Our Children Deserve: Moving Beyond Traditional Classrooms and "Tougher Standards"* (Kohn 2000) challenges us to consider an alternative scenario to the back-to-basics, high-stakes testing environment sweeping the nation's schools.
- *Making Sense: Teaching and Learning Mathematics with Understanding* (Carpenter et al. 1997) presents research-based recommendations and describes essential features for classrooms where students learn mathematics with understanding, including examples from several different programs.
- *How Students Learn: Mathematics in the Classroom* (Bransford and Donovan 2005) builds on research about learning to provide teachers with suggestions for helping all students achieve in mathematics.
- *The Intended Mathematics Curriculum as Represented in State-Level Curriculum Standards: Consensus or Confusion?* (Reys 2006) surveys state standards to look at various features of the standards, including the number of student expectations called for in various states (current as of the date of the surveys).

41 Thank You, Mr. Bender

CELEBRATING TEACHERS WHO MAKE A DIFFERENCE

I would like to take this opportunity to thank my seventh-grade math teacher, Mr. Bender. I'm not sure I realized it at the time, but Mr. Bender's mathematics class changed my life. Throughout my elementary school experience, I was a mediocre student in arithmetic. That's what elementary school math consisted of back then. I didn't like memorizing facts and doing all those calculations, so I didn't learn 9×6 until long after I was supposed to, and my scores on the Iowa Test of Basic Skills were predictably lackluster.

But in seventh grade, I entered Mr. Bender's math class. The textbooks we used that year were red paperback books. I found out later that this was the era of new math, but at the time, I just thought the books were different and kind of cool. What I remember most about that year is not the books, but Mr. Bender introducing me to the world of mathematics. He showed me that mathematics is much more than arithmetic. He helped me discover the beauty of geometry and see mathematics all around me. He helped me solve different kinds of math problems, not just one- or two-sentence word problems. He pushed me to think about mathematics by using parts of my brain I didn't know I had. He challenged me, he motivated me, he inspired me, and he planted a seed that would grow into a decision to pursue a mathematical path for my future.

After Mr. Bender, I had the good fortune to experience other great mathematics teachers. Wilhelmina Bell helped me see geometry when I was in high school. She required all of us to carry index cards and toothpicks so that we could model three-dimensional relationships. She seemed to know everything there was to know about mathematics. She expected us to study and work hard. Her bulletin board always displayed newspaper and magazine articles about mathematics and always included clippings about women doing math.

Rebecca Crittenden was a tremendously influential role model for me. She was a young, smart, and creative mathematics professor at a predominantly male engineering university. Her tests pushed me harder than I had ever been pushed before. She tolerated my youthful arrogance while helping me develop the confidence to learn abstract concepts that might have seemed beyond my grasp.

Over the years, I have had the opportunity to know many wonderful math teachers, either as their student or as their colleague. I have known teachers whose knowledge and love of mathematics were so infectious that their students could not sit in their classrooms without growing to like the subject. I have known teachers who made up songs to communicate mathematics to students who didn't think they wanted to sing or do math. I have known teachers who could think up problems on the spot related to whatever was going on in the world or in their students' lives. I have known teachers who were tough but fair, challenging their students to learn far more than those students ever expected of themselves. I have known teachers whose eyes filled with tears when they described students who were so full of discouragement that learning mathematics seemed impossible to them. I have known teachers who lived every day to see the light of learning in their students' eyes. I have known teachers who developed lessons that engaged even the most reticent students. I have known teachers who knew exactly the right question to ask to push their students' thinking just a bit more. I have known teachers who were so committed to their own lifelong learning that they were still learning about mathematics as they entered retirement. I have known wonderful math teachers, each of them unique in his or her talents. Some were outgoing, creative, and vivacious. Others were quiet, thoughtful, and patient. The bottom line was that they all knew mathematics, wanted to keep learning more, and were committed to doing whatever it took to help their students learn.

As I reflect on my life as a learner and a teacher, I send out my gratitude to the Mr. Benders, the Wilhelmina Bells, and the Rebecca Crittendens of the world. Thanks for what you've given me. And thanks for what you've given and continue to give students like me. Thanks not only for the mathematics but also for believing in and encouraging us. I know that I couldn't have done it without teachers like you.

Reflection and Discussion

FOR TEACHERS

- What issues or challenges does this message raise for you? In what ways do you agree with or disagree with the main points of the message?
- If you've known a teacher who made a positive difference in your life, what characteristics did that teacher have? What made him or her remarkable? How did he or she help you as a student of mathematics? What lessons can you learn for your own teaching?

FOR FAMILIES

- What questions or issues does this message raise for you to discuss with your son or daughter, the teacher, or school leaders?
- If you've known a teacher who made a positive difference in your life, what characteristics did that teacher have? What made her or him remarkable? How did she or he help you as a student of mathematics?

FOR LEADERS AND POLICY MAKERS

- How does this message reinforce or challenge policies and decisions you have made or are considering?
- If you've known a teacher who made a positive difference in your life, what characteristics did that teacher have? What made him or her remarkable? How did he or she help you as a student of mathematics?

RELATED MESSAGES

- Message 39, "Standing on the Shoulders . . . ," describes the power of learning from each other.
- Message 40, "Seven Steps Toward Being a Better Math Teacher," suggests a path for continuing improvement as a teacher.
- Message 26, "Beyond Pockets of Wonderfulness," reminds us of the power of working collaboratively within and across schools.

FURTHER READING

- *The Courage to Teach: Exploring the Inner Landscape of a Teacher's Life* (Palmer 2007) provides insights into teaching and the life of a teacher and offers hope for teachers to find (or re-find) their purpose in teaching.

- *Putting It Together: Middle School Math in Transition* (Tsuruda 1994) tells the story of Gary Tsuruda's journey as a middle school teacher helping students become mathematical thinkers and problem solvers and offers ideas for teachers pursuing similar goals.

- *Good Morning Ms. Toliver* (The Futures Channel 1993) is a DVD that shows the award-winning teaching and remarkable learning in Kay Toliver's Harlem, New York middle school math classroom.

- *On Their Side: Helping Children Take Charge of Their Learning* (Strachota 1996) describes Bob Strachota's journey as a teacher helping students assume responsibility for their learning and includes his personal reflections.

Afterword

The Sum of the Parts Is Greater Than Some of the Parts: *Lessons from Geese*

So many challenges confront schools and communities today that there was no shortage of topics I could have chosen to include in this book. Plenty of topics remain for another book. But I hope this book is as much about opportunities as it is about challenges. The many individuals and groups interested in improving mathematics teaching and learning have great potential to accomplish that goal, provided we work together.

In Message 13, "Seek First to Understand," I reminded all of us how much we can learn from each other as we strive to improve mathematics teaching and learning. In Message 26, "Beyond Pockets of Wonderfulness," and other messages in the book, I suggested that students would benefit if their teachers and other adults worked together to coordinate their learning experience. In the same way, we can address the broader challenges facing education today and solve many serious problems if we work together with our students' benefit in mind. A single individual can make a significant difference with a student or a group of students. But in order to fundamentally change the system for the benefit of *all* students, including those in school today and those who will follow in years to come, that individual needs to join forces with others.

Studies tell us that geese intuitively know the power of working together to fly farther than they could alone. They cover tremendous distances in their familiar V-formation. Geese understand the importance of utilizing teamwork and shared leadership to get where they want to go. Each plays its part, takes its turns with the hardest tasks, and supports the others; the community shifts leadership from one to another as needed. Surely we can learn lessons from geese.

Alone we can accomplish good things, and we should celebrate every one of these accomplishments. But together, with creativity, wisdom, energy, and, most of all, commitment, there is no end to what we might do. We can build active coalitions, including the best thinking of those with different perspectives, different demographics, and different areas of expertise. We can engage in conversations that cross racial, ethnic, language, cultural, and socioeconomic lines, and we can invite conversations among teachers, administrators, families, mathematicians, teacher educators, students, business and community leaders, and others. We can learn to listen to each other, respect diversity in opinions, and recognize our common goals to prepare a generation of well-educated young people who can reason, think, and use a strong base of knowledge to tackle tomorrow's problems. Building on our collective strengths, we can turn ideas and collaboration into actions and accomplishments.

So please take the ideas you generate from reading these messages and combine them with additional ideas, joining together with others to turn your best thinking into real actions throughout a school, across a school system, or within your community. Advocate for visionary, ambitious, systemic thinking and positive, connected, supported actions beyond your community to take on some of our nation's greatest challenges in school mathematics and in education in general. Most of all, let us come together with an unprecedented local and national commitment to do whatever it takes to once and for all create a uniquely American, world-class education system where all students reach their full potential. Individually we can dream it; collectively we can make it our children's reality.

Acknowledgments

To adequately acknowledge the many people who have influenced my thinking over the years and helped me shape this book would require many pages. I will try to be as concise as I know how.

I must begin with a heartfelt "thank you" to the National Council of Teachers of Mathematics (NCTM). Not only did the Council and all of its members honor me with the best job I've ever had, but the NCTM staff also provided tremendous personal and professional support both during my presidency and in the writing of this book. In particular, they allowed me to include updates of several of my original eighteen President's Messages, including "Math for a Flattening World," "Untapped Potential," "Technology is a Tool," "'Try Harder!' Isn't the Answer" ("'Teach Harder!' Isn't the Answer"), "Seek First to Understand," "Hard Arithmetic Isn't Deep Mathematics," "Embracing Accountability," "Do the Math in Your Head" ("Do It in Your Head"), "Pushing Algebra Down," "Pockets of Wonderfulness," and "Thank You, Mr. Bender," as well as incorporate portions of "Coming Home" in the book's introduction.

I have to especially thank Jodi Flood, my NCTM editor, for devoting her days to bringing my thoughts and words into coherent form month after month, always finding a way to squeeze the most pertinent of my ideas clearly and concisely onto that one page. So many other NCTM staff members have provided support and encouragement that I must thank them as a group for fear of omitting someone. Aside from their daily work, they surprised me by submitting two of my President's Messages for EXCEL Awards from the Society of National Association Publications, resulting in a gold and a silver award.

I sincerely appreciate my colleagues at the Charles A. Dana Center, with whom I work every day. They continue to support my passion, challenge my thinking, contribute different perspectives, and teach me from their individual and collective wisdom on a regular basis.

I am deeply indebted to the Math Solutions staff. Toby Gordon and, later, Doris Hirschhorn shepherded me through the early stages of this project, then Jamie Cross jumped in to commit everything she had to move this book forward on an accelerated time line. Jamie continually found ways to enhance the end result, while encouraging me at every step along the way. She has moved me from being a writer to becoming an author. Joan Carlson has been invaluable as a friend and colleague in a role somewhere between sounding board and editorial advisor. Her insights and suggestions ring true as a voice from the classroom and beyond. And Carolyn Felux continues to be my brilliant, insightful, supportive friend, offering critical input at key points in the process.

Numerous professional friends and colleagues have helped me grow as a teacher and as a leader over many years. Some of these individuals are named or mentioned anonymously in various messages and others have contributed to what I know and think without attribution. If you recognize something in one of the messages that sounds like your thoughts or advice, it probably is. If you wonder about something you read in a message that describes a less than positive attitude, event, or situation, I'm sure it's from or about someone else.

And of course, I must thank the thousands of students, teachers, and other educators and leaders with whom I have interacted during my career, in and outside of the classroom, across the nation, and around the globe. Over and over, I see teachers who strive passionately to do their job the best way they can. I salute those who are willing to venture outside of their comfort zone as they try new approaches and constantly work to improve their craft so that all of their students might reach their full potential. The policy makers and community members I have encountered care deeply that all of their students learn. Many of them take hard stands in visionary directions and make incredible commitments in the face of significant challenges, just because it's the right thing for students, even while others push for policies that may have unintended consequences interfering with that goal. Then there are the students. Whether mine or yours, they continue to inspire me with how much they can accomplish—many in spite of significant barriers. They sometimes soar and sometimes falter, always reminding us of their tremendous potential to reach great heights if we just do our part on their behalf.

I have been blessed on many levels by the people and circumstances in my life. Most especially, I thank my family for their continued support as I have pursued the rich and often divergent paths that life continues to present. To my daughters, my sisters, and my parents, I appreciate your patience and understanding over these years, and I am grateful every day for your love and support.

Readings and References

Italicized numbers found at the end of selected entries refer to the message number in which the reference is listed as a Further Reading.

Achieve. American Diploma Project (ADP) Network. Washington, DC: Achieve. http://achieve.org. *8*

ACT. 2006. *Ready for College and Ready for Work: Same or Different?* Iowa City: ACT. www.act.org/research/policymakers/reports/workready.html. *8, 9*

Adams, Karlyn. 2006. Sources of Innovation and Creativity: A Summary of the Research. Paper commissioned by the National Center on Education and the Economy. Washington, DC: National Center on Education and the Economy. www.skillscommission.org/pdf/commissioned_papers. *3*

AeA, Business-Higher Education Forum, Business Roundtable, Council on Competitiveness, Information Technology Association of America, Information Technology Industry Council, Minority Business RoundTable, National Association of Manufacturers, National Defense Industrial Association, Semiconductor Industry Association, Software and Information Industry Association, TechNet, Technology CEO Council, Telecommunications Industry Association, and U.S. Chamber of Commerce. 2005. *Tapping America's Potential: The Education for Innovation Initiative.* Washington, DC: Business Roundtable.

Allsopp, David H., Maggie M. Kyger, and Lou Ann Lovin. 2007. *Teaching Mathematics Meaningfully: Solutions for Reaching Struggling Learners.* Baltimore, MD: Paul H. Brookes. *32*

Anderson, Lorin W., David R. Krathwohl, Peter W. Airasian, Kathleen A. Cruikshank, Richard E. Mayer, Paul R. Pintrich, James Raths, and Merlin C. Wittrock. 2001. *A Taxonomy for Learning, Teaching, and Assessing: A Revision of Bloom's Taxonomy of Educational Objectives, Abridged Edition.* Boston: Allyn & Bacon.

Becerra, Ana M., and Julian Weissglass. 2004. *Take It Up: Leading for Educational Equity.* Santa Barbara: National Coalition for Equity in Education, University of California. Based on the work of educators in projects affiliated with *The National Coalition for Equity in Education,* http://ncee.education.ucsb.edu. *2, 32*

Blankstein, Alan M. 2004. *Failure Is Not an Option™: Six Principles That Guide Student Achievement in High-Performing Schools.* Thousand Oaks, CA: Corwin Press. *13, 26*

Boaler, Jo. 2008. *What's Math Got to Do with It? Helping Children Learn to Love Their Least Favorite Subject—and Why It's Important for America.* New York: Viking. *6*

Boss, Suzie, Jane Krauss, and Leslie Conery. 2008. *Reinventing Project-Based Learning: Your Field Guide to Real-World Projects in the Digital Age.* Washington, DC: International Society for Technology in Education. *21*

Boyer, Ernest L. 1983. *High School: A Report on Secondary Education in America*. New York: Joanna Cotler Books. *37*

Bransford, John D., and M. Suzanne Donovan, eds. 2005. *How Students Learn: Mathematics in the Classroom*. Washington, DC: National Research Council; National Academies Press. *40*

Bridgeland, John M., John J. Dilulio, Jr., and Karen Burke Morison. 2006. *The Silent Epidemic: Perspectives of High School Dropouts*. Washington, DC: Civic Enterprises. www.civicenterprises.net. *8, 37*

Brodesky, Amy R., Fred E. Gross, Anna S. McTigue, and Cornelia C. Tierney. 2004. "Planning Strategies for Students with Special Needs: A Professional Development Activity." *Teaching Children Mathematics* 11 (3): 9.

Burns, Marilyn. 1989. "Timed Tests." *Math Solutions Newsletter* Spring (7).

———. 1999. *Leading the Way: Principals and Superintendents Look at Math Instruction*. Sausalito, CA: Math Solutions. *6, 26*

———. 2007a. *About Teaching Mathematics: A K–8 Resource*. 3d ed. Sausalito, CA: Math Solutions. *18, 24, 28, 29, 38*

———. 2007b. "Marilyn Burns: Mental Math." *Instructor* 116 (6): 51–54. *24*

Burns, Marilyn, and Robyn Silbey. 2000. *So You Have to Teach Math? Sound Advice for K–6 Teachers*. Sausalito, CA: Math Solutions. *28*

Bush, William S., ed. 2000. *Mathematics Assessment: Cases and Discussion Questions for Grades 6–12*. Classroom Assessment for School Mathematics, K–12 Series. Reston, VA: National Council of Teachers of Mathematics. *35*

———. 2001. *Mathematics Assessment: Cases and Discussion Questions for Grades K–5*. Classroom Assessment for School Mathematics, K–12 Series. Reston, VA: National Council of Teachers of Mathematics. *35*

Bush, William H., and Anja S. Greer, eds. 1999. *Mathematics Assessment: A Practical Handbook for Grades 9–12*. Classroom Assessment for School Mathematics, K–12 Series. Reston, VA: National Council of Teachers of Mathematics. *35*

Bush, William H., and Steven Leinwand, eds. 2000. *Mathematics Assessment: A Practical Handbook for Grades 6–8*. Classroom Assessment for School Mathematics, K–12 Series. Reston, VA: National Council of Teachers of Mathematics. *35*

Carpenter, Thomas P., Megan Loef Franke, and Linda Levi. 2003. *Thinking Mathematically: Integrating Arithmetic and Algebra in Elementary School*. Portsmouth, NH: Heinemann. *25*

Carpenter, Thomas P., James Hiebert, Elizabeth Fennema, Karen C. Fuson, Diana Wearne, and Hanlie Murray. 1997. *Making Sense: Teaching and Learning Mathematics with Understanding*. Portsmouth, NH: Heinemann. *34, 40*

Chapin, Suzanne H., and Art Johnson. 2006. *Math Matters: Understanding the Math You Teach Grades K–8*. 2d ed. Sausalito, CA: Math Solutions. *28, 29*

Chapin, Suzanne H., Catherine O'Connor, and Nancy Canavan Anderson. 2009. *Classroom Discussions: Using Math Talk to Help Students Learn Grades K–6*. 2d ed. Sausalito, CA: Math Solutions. *33*

Chappell, Michaele F., and Tina Pateracki, eds. 2004. *Empowering the Beginning Teacher of Mathematics: Middle School*. Reston, VA: National Council of Teachers of Mathematics. *28*

Chappell, Michaele F., Jeffrey Choppin, and Jenny Salls, eds. 2004. *Empowering the Beginning Teacher of Mathematics: High School*. Reston, VA: National Council of Teachers of Mathematics. *28*

Chappell, Michaele F., Janie Schielack, and Sharon Zagorski, eds. 2004. *Empowering the Beginning Teacher of Mathematics: Elementary School*. Reston, VA: National Council of Teachers of Mathematics. *28*

Charles A. Dana Center at the University of Texas at Austin and Achieve. 2008. Fourth-Year Capstone Courses. Charles A. Dana Center and Achieve, Inc. www.utdanacenter.org/k12mathbenchmarks/resources/capstone.php. *7*

Chval, Kathryn B., and Sarah J. Hicks. 2009. "Contemporary Curriculum Issues: Calculators in K–5 Textbooks." *Teaching Children Mathematics* 15 (7): 430–37. *20*

Coggins, Debra, Drew Kravin, Grace Dávila Coates, and Maria Dreux Carroll. 2007. *English Language Learners in the Mathematics Classroom*. Thousand Oaks, CA: Corwin Press. *2*

Committee on Prospering in the Global Economy of the Twenty-First Century: An Agenda for American Science and Technology; Committee on Science, Engineering, and Public Policy; National Academy of Sciences, National Academy of Engineering, and Institute of Medicine of the National Academies. 2007. *Rising Above the Gathering Storm: Energizing and Employing America for a Brighter Economic Future*. Washington, DC: National Academies Press. www.nap.edu/catalog.php?record_id=11463.

Conley, David. 2008. *College Knowledge: What It Really Takes for Students to Succeed and What We Can Do to Get Them Ready*. San Francisco, CA: Jossey-Bass. *25, 31*

Covey, Stephen R. 2004. *The 7 Habits of Highly Effective People: Powerful Lessons in Personal Change*. Rev. ed. New York: Free Press. *13*

Cushman, Kathleen. 2005. *Fires in the Bathroom: Advice for Teachers from High School Students*. New York: New Press. *8, 37*

Dacey, Linda, and Rebeka Eston Salemi. 2007. *Math for All: Differentiating Instruction, Grades K–2*. Sausalito, CA: Math Solutions. *16*

Dacey, Linda, and Jayne Bamford Lynch. 2007. *Math for All: Differentiating Instruction, Grades 3–5*. Sausalito, CA: Math Solutions. *16*

Dacey, Linda, and Karen Gartland. 2009. *Math for All: Differentiating Instruction, Grades 6–8*. Sausalito, CA: Math Solutions. *16*

Devlin, Keith. 1997. *Mathematics: The Science of Patterns: The Search for Order in Life, Mind, and the Universe*. New York: Henry Holt/Scientific American Library. *23*

Diffily, Deborah, and Charlotte Sassman. 2002. *Project-Based Learning with Young Children*. Portsmouth, NH: Heinemann. *21*

Driscoll, Mark. 1999. *Fostering Algebraic Thinking: A Guide for Teachers, Grades 6–10*. Portsmouth, NH: Heinemann. *25, 30*

DuFour, Rebecca, Robert Eaker, Gayle Harhanek, and Richard DuFour. 2004. *Whatever It Takes: How Professional Learning Communities Respond When Kids Don't Learn*. Bloomington, IN: Solution Tree. *26, 32*

DuFour, Richard, Rebecca DuFour, Robert Eaker, and Thomas Many. 2006. *Learning By Doing: A Handbook for Professional Learning Communities at Work*. Bloomington, IN: Solution Tree. *26*

Dunne, Kathy, and Susan Villani. 2007a. *Mentoring New Teachers Through Collaborative Coaching: Facilitation and Training Guide*. San Francisco, CA: WestEd. *28*

———. 2007b. *Mentoring New Teachers Through Collaborative Coaching: Linking Teacher and Student Learning*. San Francisco, CA: WestEd. *28*

Education Development Center. 2003–2009. *Addressing Accessibility in Mathematics*. Newton, MA: Education Development Center. www2.edc.org/accessmath.

———. 2007a. "Guiding Questions for Planning Accessibility Strategies." *Addressing Accessibility in Mathematics*. Newton, MA: Education Development Center. www2.edc.org/accessmath/resources/strategies.asp.

———. 2007b. "Instructional Strategies to Increase Accessibility." *Addressing Accessibility in Mathematics*. Newton, MA: Education Development Center. www2.edc.org/accessmath/resources/strategies.asp.

The Education Trust. Washington, DC. www2.edtrust.org/edtrust. *2*

Elementary and Secondary Education Act of 2001 [No Child Left Behind], Public Law 107-110, 107th Congress, 1st session (January 8, 2002).

Exemplars: Standards-Based Assessment and Instruction. Underhill, VT. www.exemplars.com. *17*

Findell, Brad, and Jane Swafford, eds. 2002. *Helping Children Learn Mathematics*. Washington, DC: National Academy Press. *14*

Findell, Carol. 1996. "Mathematics Education Then and Now: The Need for Reform." *Journal of Education* 178 (2): 3–13. *4*

Finn, Chester E. Jr., and Dianne Ravitch. 2007a. *Beyond the Basics: Achieving a Liberal Education for All Children*. Washington, DC: Thomas B. Fordham Institute. *10*

———. 2007b. "Not By Geeks Alone." *Wall Street Journal*, August 8, 2007, A13. http://online.wsj.com/article/SB118653759532491305.html?mod= googlenews_wsj. *10*

Friedman, Thomas L. 2007. *The World Is Flat: A Brief History of the Twenty-First Century*. 3d ed. New York: Picador. *1, 7*

———. 2008. *Hot, Flat, and Crowded: Why We Need a Green Revolution—and How It Can Renew America*. New York: Farrar, Straus and Giroux. *1, 10*

Fullan, Michael. 2007a. *Leading in a Culture of Change*. San Francisco, CA: Jossey-Bass. *40*

———. 2007b. *The New Meaning of Educational Change*. 4th ed. New York: Teachers College Press. *12*

The Futures Channel. 1993. *Good Morning Ms. Toliver*. DVD. Burbank, CA: The Futures Channel. *32, 41*

Gilliland, Kay. 2001. "The Need for Speed in Mathematics." *Mathematics Teaching in the Middle School 7* (4): 216. *18*

Glanfield, Florence, William S. Bush, and Jean Kerr Stenmark, eds. 2003. *Mathematics Assessment: A Practical Handbook for Grades K–2*. Classroom Assessment for

School Mathematics, K–12 Series. Reston, VA: National Council of Teachers of Mathematics. *35*

Goldberg, Kenneth P. 2006. *Using Technology and Problem Solving in Middle and High School Mathematics: Investigations Using Scientific and Graphing Calculators, Spreadsheets, and The Geometer's Sketchpad.* Upper Saddle River, NJ: Prentice Hall. *5*

Gould, Stephen J. 1996. *The Mismeasure of Man.* Updated ed. New York: W. W. Norton. *11*

Grayson, Dolores A., and Mary D. Martin. 2001a. *Generating Expectations for Student Achievement (GESA): An Equitable Approach to Educational Excellence: Facilitator Handbook.* Tehachapi, CA: Gray Mill. *31*

———. 2001b. *Generating Expectations for Student Achievement (GESA): An Equitable Approach to Educational Excellence: Teacher Handbook.* Tehachapi, CA: Gray Mill. *31*

Greenes, Carole E., and Rheta Rubenstein, eds. 2008. *Algebra and Algebraic Thinking in School Mathematics: NCTM's Seventieth Yearbook.* Reston, VA: National Council of Teachers of Mathematics. *30*

Groves, Susie, and Kaye Stacey. 1998. "Calculators in Primary Mathematics: Exploring Number before Teaching Algorithms." In *The Teaching and Learning of Algorithms in School Mathematics.* 1998 Yearbook. Reston, VA: National Council of Teachers of Mathematics.

Hall, Gene E., and Shirley M. Hord. 2005. *Implementing Change: Patterns, Principles, and Potholes.* 2d ed. Boston, MA: Allyn & Bacon. *12*

Heid, M. Kathleen, Jonathan Choate, Charlene Sheets, and Rose Mary Zbiek. 1996. *Algebra in a Technological World.* Addenda Series, Grades 9–12. Reston, VA: National Council of Teachers of Mathematics. *30*

Hope, Jack, Barbara Reys, and Robert Reys. 1987. *Mental Math in the Middle Grades.* Lebanon, IN: Dale Seymour. *24*

———. 1988. *Mental Math in Junior High: Grades 7–9.* Lebanon, IN: Dale Seymour. *24*

Hope, Jack, Larry Leutzinger, Barbara Reys, and Robert Reys. 1988. *Mental Math in the Primary Grades.* Lebanon, IN: Dale Seymour. *24*

Hyde, Arthur. 2006. *Comprehending Math: Adapting Reading Strategies to Teach Mathematics, K–6.* Portsmouth, NH: Heinemann. *10*

Jimerson, Shane R. 2001. "Meta-Analysis of Grade Retention Research: Implications for Practice in the Twenty-First Century." *School Psychology Review* 30 (3): 420–37. http://education.ucsb.edu/jimerson/retention/SPR_MetaAnalysis2001.pdf.

Kaser, Joyce S., Susan E. Mundry, Katherine E. Stiles, and Susan Loucks-Horsley. 2006. *Leading Every Day: One Hundred and Twenty-Four Actions for Effective Leadership.* 2d ed. Thousand Oaks, CA: Corwin Press. *26*

Kennedy, Mary. 2006. *Inside Teaching: How Classroom Life Undermines Reform.* Cambridge, MA: Harvard University Press. *6*

Kilpatrick, Jeremy, Gary Martin, and Deborah Schifter, eds. 2003. *A Research Companion to Principles and Standards for School Mathematics.* Reston, VA: National Council of Teachers of Mathematics. *14*

Kilpatrick, Jeremy, Jane Swafford, and Brad Findell, eds. 2001. *Adding It Up: Helping Children Learn Mathematics*. Washington, DC: National Academy Press. *12, 14*

Kohn, Alfie. 2000. *The Schools Our Children Deserve: Moving Beyond Traditional Classrooms and "Tougher Standards."* New York: Mariner Books/Houghton Mifflin Harcourt. *16, 40*

Kozol, Jonathan. 2006. *The Shame of the Nation: The Restoration of Apartheid Schooling in America*. New York: Three Rivers Press. *2, 32*

Lareau, Annette. 2003. *Unequal Childhoods: Class, Race, and Family Life*. Berkeley: University of California Press. *32*

Lawrence Hall of Science (EQUALS). *Family Math*. Equals Series. Berkeley: University of California, Lawrence Hall of Science. http://lawrencehallofscience.org/equals. *27*

Leinwand, Steven. 1994. "Four Teacher-Friendly Postulates for Thriving in a Sea of Change." *Mathematics Teacher* 87 (6): 392–93. *40*

———. 2000. *Sensible Mathematics: A Guide for School Leaders*. Portsmouth, NH: Heinemann. *4, 14*

———. 2009. *Accessible Mathematics: Ten Instructional Shifts That Raise Student Achievement*. Portsmouth, NH: Heinemann. *16, 34*

Levine, Mel. 2003. *A Mind at a Time: America's Top Learning Expert Shows How Every Child Can Succeed*. New York: Simon and Schuster. *2*

Litton, Nancy. 1998. *Getting Your Math Message Out to Parents: A K–6 Resource*. Sausalito, CA: Math Solutions. *27*

Litton, Nancy, and Maryann Wickett. 2008. *This Is Only a Test: Teaching for Mathematical Understanding in an Age of Standardized Testing*. Sausalito, CA: Math Solutions. *35*

Loucks-Horsley, Susan, Nancy Love, Katherine E. Stiles, Susan Mundry, and Peter W. Hewson. 2003. *Designing Professional Development for Teachers of Science and Mathematics*. 2d ed. Thousand Oaks, CA: Corwin Press. *38, 39*

Martin, Danny Bernard. 2000. *Mathematics Success and Failure Among African-American Youth: The Roles of Sociohistorical Context, Community Forces, School Influence, and Individual Agency*. Mahwah, NJ: Lawrence Erlbaum. *2, 32*

Math Is More. 2009. www.mathismore.net. *7*

Mathematical Sciences Education Board and National Research Council. 1989. *Everybody Counts: A Report to the Nation on the Future of Mathematics Education*. Washington, DC: National Academies Press. *4, 7*

Mathews, Jay. 1989. *Escalante: The Best Teacher in America*. New York: Henry Holt & Company. *31*

———. 2009a. "The Latest Doomed Pedagogical Fad: Twenty-First-Century Skills." *Washington Post*, January 5, 2009, B02. www.washingtonpost.com/wp-dyn/content/article/2009/01/04/AR2009010401532.html. *1*

———. 2009b. *Work Hard. Be Nice.: How Two Inspired Teachers Created the Most Promising Schools in America*. Chapel Hill, NC: Algonquin Books. *32*

Merseth, Katherine K. 2003a. *Windows on Teaching Math: Cases of Middle and Secondary Classrooms*. New York: Teachers College Press. *7, 9*

————. 2003b. *Windows on Teaching Math: Cases of Middle and Secondary Classrooms: Facilitator's Guide.* New York: Teachers College Press.   *7, 9*

Middleton, James A., and Photini A. Spanias. 2002. "Pedagogical Implications of the Research on Motivation in Mathematics Education." In *Lessons Learned from Research*, ed. J. Sowder and B. Schappelle, 9–15. Reston, VA: National Council of Teachers of Mathematics.   *37*

Mirra, Amy, ed. 2005. *A Family's Guide: Fostering Your Child's Success in School Mathematics.* Reston, VA: National Council of Teachers of Mathematics.   *27*

Mokros, Jan, Susan Jo Russell, and Karen Economopoulos. 1995. *Beyond Arithmetic: Changing Mathematics in the Elementary Classroom.* Lebanon, IN: Dale Seymour.   *16, 34*

Moses, Robert P., and Charles E. Cobb, Jr. 2001. *Radical Equations: Civil Rights from Mississippi to the Algebra Project.* Boston, MA: Beacon Press.   *25*

Mundry, Susan, and Kathy Dunne. 2003. *Teachers as Learners: Professional Development in Science and Mathematics.* Thousand Oaks, CA: Corwin Press.   *38, 39*

National Center on Education and the Economy. 2008. *Tough Choices or Tough Times: The Report of the New Commission on the Skills of the American Workforce.* San Francisco, CA: Jossey-Bass.   *9, 22*

National Commission on Excellence in Education. 1984. *A Nation at Risk: The Full Account.* 2d ed. Portland, OR: USA Research.

National Commission on Mathematics and Science Teaching for the Twenty-First Century. 2001. *Before It's Too Late: A Report to the Nation from the National Commission on Mathematics and Science Teaching for the Twenty-First Century.* Washington, DC: Glenn Commission. www.ed.gov/inits/Math/glenn/index.html.

National Council of Supervisors of Mathematics. 1977. *Basic Mathematical Skills.* Denver, CO: National Council of Supervisors of Mathematics. http://ncsmonline.org/NCSMPublications/position.html.

National Council of Teachers of Mathematics. 1980. *An Agenda for Action.* Reston, VA: National Council of Teachers of Mathematics. www.nctm.org/standards.

————. 1989. *Curriculum and Evaluation Standards for School Mathematics.* Reston, VA: National Council of Teachers of Mathematics.   *4, 23*

————. 1991. *Professional Standards for Teaching Mathematics.* Reston, VA: National Council of Teachers of Mathematics.   *17, 33, 37, 38*

————. 2000. *Principles and Standards for School Mathematics.* Reston, VA: National Council of Teachers of Mathematics.   *4, 14, 30*

————. 2005. Computation, Calculators, and Common Sense. Position Statement. Reston, VA: National Council of Teachers of Mathematics. www.nctm.org/about/content.aspx?id=6358.   *20*

————. 2006a. *Curriculum Focal Points for Prekindergarten Through Grade 8 Mathematics: A Quest for Coherence.* Reston, VA: National Council of Teachers of Mathematics.   *16*

————. 2006b. "Math Homework Is Due Tomorrow—How Can I Help?" Reston, VA: National Council of Teachers of Mathematics. www.nctm.org/resources/content.aspx?id=2147483782.   *14*

————. Family Resources. http://nctm.org/resources/families.aspx. *14, 18, 20, 27*

————. Figure This! Math Challenges for Families. www.figurethis.org/. *27, 34*

————. Illuminations. http://illuminations.nctm.org/. *17*

————. Large-Scale Assessment Tool: A Framework to Evaluate Large-Scale Assessments of Mathematics. www.nctm.org/resources/content.aspx? id=10796. *19*

————. Professional Development Focus of the Year. www.nctm.org/profdev. *40*

November, Alan. 2008. "Students as Contributors: The Digital Learning Farm." http://novemberlearning.com/resources/archive-of-articles/digital-learning-farm/. *5*

O'Connor, Ken. 2002. *How to Grade for Learning: Linking Grades to Standards, Grades K–12*. Thousand Oaks, CA: Corwin Press. *36*

Oakes, Jeannie. 1987. "Tracking in Secondary Schools: A Contextual Perspective." *Educational Psychologist* 22 (2): 129–53.

Olson, Mel, Janie Schielack, and Judy Olson. 2002. *Explorations: Integrating Handheld Technology into the Elementary Mathematics Classroom*. Dallas: Texas Instruments. *5, 20*

Palmer, Parker J. 2007. *The Courage to Teach: Exploring the Inner Landscape of a Teacher's Life*. San Francisco, CA: Jossey-Bass. *6, 41*

Partnership for 21st Century Skills. 2008. www.21stcenturyskills.org. *1, 10*

Perie, Marianne, Scott Marion, Brian Gong, and Judy Wurtzel. 2007. The Role of Interim Assessments in a Comprehensive Assessment System: A Policy Brief. Washington, DC: Aspen Institute; Achieve, Inc.; National Center for the Improvement of Educational Assessment, Inc. www.achieve.org/files/TheRoleofInterim%20Assessments12-13-07.pdf. *11*

Pink, Daniel. 2006. *A Whole New Mind*. New York: Riverhead Trade. *3*

Pollock, Jeffrey. 2007. One Hundred Seventy-Five New Schools Open as Part of a National Movement to Address Dissatisfaction with High School. Bill and Melinda Gates Foundation Press Releases, August 27. www.gatesfoundation.org/press-releases/Pages/transforming-high-schools070827.aspx.

Polya, George. 1945, 2004. *How to Solve It: A New Aspect of Mathematical Method*. Princeton, NJ: Princeton University Press.

Rectanus, Cheryl. 2006. *So You Have to Teach Math? Sound Advice for Grades 6–8 Teachers*. Sausalito, CA: Math Solutions. *28*

Reeves, Douglas B. 2008. "Teaching Students to Think, Leading to Change: Effective Grading Practices." *Educational Leadership* 65 (5): 85–87. *36*

Reys, Barbara, ed. 2006. *The Intended Mathematics Curriculum as Represented in State-Level Curriculum Standards: Consensus or Confusion?* Charlotte, NC: Information Age. *15, 40*

Robinson, Ken. 2001. *Out of Our Minds: Learning to Be Creative*. Mankato, MN: Capstone. *3*

Romagnano, Lew. 2006. *Mathematics Assessment Literacy: Concepts and Terms in Large-Scale Assessment*. Reston, VA: National Council of Teachers of Mathematics. *19, 35*

Root-Bernstein, Michele M., and Robert S. Root-Bernstein. 2001. *Sparks of Genius: The Thirteen Thinking Tools of the World's Most Creative People*. New York: Mariner Books. *3*

Rose, Cheryl M., and Carolyn B. Arline. 2008. *Uncovering Student Thinking in Mathematics, Grades 6–12: Thirty Formative Assessment Probes for the Secondary Classroom*. Thousand Oaks, CA: Corwin Press. *35*

Rose, Cheryl M., Leslie Minton, and Carolyn B. Arline. 2006. *Uncovering Student Thinking in Mathematics: Twenty-Five Formative Assessment Probes*. Thousand Oaks, CA: Corwin Press. *35*

Schmidt, William H., Curtis C. McKnight, and Senta A. Raizen. 1997. *A Splintered Vision: An Investigation of U.S. Science and Mathematics Education*. Norwell, MA: Kluwer Academic. *15*

Schuster, Lainie, and Nancy Canavan Anderson. 2005. *Good Questions for Math Teaching: Why Ask Them and What to Ask, Grades 5–8*. Sausalito, CA: Math Solutions. *22, 33*

Seeley, Cathy. 1995. "Technology and Equity in Mathematics." Austin: Charles A. Dana Center, The University of Texas at Austin. www.utdanacenter.org/staff/cathy-seeley.php. *30*

———. 2009. *Cathy Seeley, PCV in Burkina Faso*. http://csinburkinafaso.com. *17, 31, 39*

Senge, Peter M. 2006. *The Fifth Discipline: The Art and Practice of the Learning Organization*. New York: Doubleday Business. *12*

Sparrow, Len, and Paul Swan. 2001. *Learning Math with Calculators: Activities for Grades 3–8*. Sausalito, CA: Math Solutions. *20*

Steen, Lynn Arthur, ed. 1999. *On the Shoulders of Giants: New Approaches to Numeracy*. Washington, DC: National Academies Press. *23, 39*

———. 2007. "Facing Facts: Achieving Balance in High School Mathematics." *Mathematics Teacher* 100 (Special Issue): 86–95. *4, 7*

Stenmark, Jean Kerr, ed. 1991. *Mathematics Assessment: Myths, Models, Good Questions, and Practical Suggestions*. Reston, VA: National Council of Teachers of Mathematics. *11, 22, 35, 36*

Stenmark, Jean Kerr, and William S. Bush, eds. 2001. *Mathematics Assessment: A Practical Handbook for Grades 3–5*. Classroom Assessment for School Mathematics, K–12 Series. Reston, VA: National Council of Teachers of Mathematics. *35*

Stenmark, Jean, Virginia Thompson, and Ruth Cossey. 1986. *Family Math*. Equals Series. Berkeley: University of California Lawrence Hall of Science. *27*

Stigler, James W., and James Hiebert. 1999. *The Teaching Gap: Best Ideas from the World's Teachers for Improving Education in the Classroom*. New York: Free Press. *17*

Strachota, Bob. 1996. *On Their Side: Helping Children Take Charge of Their Learning*. Portland, ME: Stenhouse. *41*

Sullivan, Peter, and Pat Lilburn. 2002. *Good Questions for Math Teaching: Why Ask Them and What to Ask, K–6*. Sausalito, CA: Math Solutions. *22, 23*

TERC. Investigations in Number, Data, and Space. Cambridge, MA: TERC. http://investigations.terc.edu/index.cfm.

TIMSS International Study Center. 1995–2001. *The Third International Mathematics and Science Study (TIMSS)—1995*. Chestnut Hill, MA: TIMSS International Study Center, Boston College. http://timss.bc.edu/timss1995.html.

TIMSS and PIRLS International Study Center. Chestnut Hill, MA: Trends in International Mathematics and Science Study and Progress in International Reading Literacy Study International Study Center, Lynch School of Education, Boston College. http://timss.bc.edu/.

Tobias, Sheila. 1995. *Overcoming Math Anxiety*. Rev. ed. New York: W. W. Norton. *18*

Tomlinson, Carol Ann, and Jay McTighe. 2006. *Integrating Differentiated Instruction and Understanding by Design (Connecting Content and Kids)*. Alexandria, VA: Association for Supervision and Curriculum Development. *21*

Toppo, Greg. 2009. "What to Learn: 'Core Knowledge' or 'Twenty-First-Century Skills'?" *USA Today*, March 4. www.usatoday.com/news/education/2009-03-04-core-knowledge_N.htm. *1, 10*

Tough, Paul. 2008. *Whatever It Takes: Geoffrey Canada's Quest to Change Harlem and America*. New York: Houghton Mifflin Harcourt. *32*

Tsuruda, Gary. 1994. *Putting It Together: Middle School Math in Transition*. Portsmouth, NH: Heinemann. *29, 41*

University of Arizona Institute for Mathematics and Education. 2008. High School Fourth Year Mathematics Courses. Tucson: University of Arizona. http://ime.math.arizona.edu/2007-08/1013_fourthyear.html. *7*

Van de Walle, John, and Lou Ann Lovin. 2005a. *Teaching Student-Centered Mathematics: Grades K–3*. Vol. 1. Teaching Student-Centered Mathematics Series. Boston, MA: Allyn & Bacon. *33*

———. 2005b. *Teaching Student-Centered Mathematics: Grades 3–5*. Vol. 2. Teaching Student-Centered Mathematics Series. Boston, MA: Allyn & Bacon. *33*

———. 2005c. *Teaching Student-Centered Mathematics: Grades 5–8*. Vol. 3. Teaching Student-Centered Mathematics Series. Boston, MA: Allyn & Bacon. *33*

Van de Walle, John, Karen Karp, and Jennifer M. Bay-Williams. 2009. *Elementary and Middle School Mathematics: Teaching Developmentally*. 7th ed. Boston, MA: Allyn & Bacon. *14, 33, 34*

Vermont Mathematics Initiative. Burlington, VT. www.uvm.edu/~vmi. *13*

Wagner, Tony. 2008. *The Global Achievement Gap: Why Even Our Best Schools Don't Teach the New Survival Skills Our Children Need—And What We Can Do About It*. New York: Basic Books. *1, 2, 3*

Warner Home Video. 1988. *Stand and Deliver*. DVD. Burbank, CA: Warner Home Video. *31*

Weiss, Iris R., and Joan D. Pasley. 2009. *Mathematics and Science for a Change: How to Design, Implement, and Sustain High-Quality Professional Development*. Portsmouth, NH: Heinemann. *12, 29*

Wesson, Kenneth. 2008. "The Neuroscience of Learning." Symposium, meeting of SMARTT: Science and Mathematics: Assessment, Research and Technology Together with a T^3 Conference Within a Conference. Overland Park: Kansas Association of Teachers of Science (KATS) and Kansas Association of Teachers of Mathematics (KATM). http://allensylv.googlepages.com/home.

Wiggins, Grant, and Jay McTighe. 2005. *Understanding by Design*. Expanded 2d ed. Upper Saddle River, NJ: Prentice Hall.   *21*

Wineburg, Samuel S., and Pamela L. Grossman, eds. 2000. *Interdisciplinary Curriculum: Challenges to Implementation*. New York: Teachers College Press.   *21*

Wormeli, Rick. 2006. *Fair Isn't Always Equal: Assessing and Grading in the Differentiated Classroom*. Portland, ME: Stenhouse.   *36*

Index

About the Author

For more than thirty-five years, **Cathy Seeley** has been a mathematics educator and change facilitator at the local, state, and national levels. She is deeply committed to a high-quality mathematics education for every student. Among her experiences in K–12 education, she has worked as a mathematics teacher, district mathematics coordinator, and state K–12 mathematics director. After her return in late 2001 from teaching mathematics (in French) as a Peace Corps volunteer in Burkina Faso, Cathy was elected to serve a two-year term as President of the National Council of Teachers of Mathematics. In that role, she was awarded an EXCEL Gold Award from the Society of National Association Publications (SNAP) for one of her President's Messages, "Embracing Accountability." Cathy has given presentations in forty-nine states, Mexico, Canada, Portugal, France, Germany, South Africa, and China. She has appeared on television and radio and authored or coauthored various publications, including mathematics textbooks. Currently, Cathy is affiliated as a Senior Fellow with the Charles A. Dana Center at the University of Texas, working on state and national policy and improvement efforts in mathematics education, with a focus on grades pre-K–12. For more information, see Cathy's website at www.cathyseeley.com.